D1549516

Mysteries of Prediction

Great Mysteries

Mysteries of Prediction

by Angus Hall
and Francis King

Aldus Books London

New enlarged edition
SBN: 490 004296

Printed and bound in Yugoslavia by
Mladinska Knjiga, Ljubljana

Introduction

For most people, most of the time, the future is a closed book, only available to us a page at a time, as tomorrow inevitably passes into today. But for some, the future appears to be curiously accessible. Some see the unfolding of events yet to come in dreams, some predict them from the chance arrangement of cards, some study complex charts of the stars. This strange ability to see the future in the present has led some men to speculate about the nature of time itself—do we exist on a long strip of time, present following past, and future always lying ahead, or do we perhaps live on a series of levels in which past, present, and future exist simultaneously? Whatever the ultimate answer may be, our curiosity about our own personal futures has encouraged the development of immensely varied methods of prediction. Palmistry, crystal gazing, the Tarot deck, and the queen of sciences, astrology, have all been eagerly consulted and all have impressive stories of amazingly precise prophecies that were fulfilled. How do these methods work? Is it truly possible to look from today into the mysteries of tomorrow?

Contents

Chapter 1
The Future is Now!

Is it possible to know ahead of time what the future will bring? Many world-famous disasters have been foretold, by fortune telling, astrology, dreams, or even just by an eerie presentiment of something about to happen. If the future can be foreseen, can it be changed? Pondering these questions, philosophers have argued about the nature of time itself, whether it exists as an absolute outside of us, or simply in our minds. Does the future perhaps run concurrently with the present, but on a separate track? Here is a look at some of the evidence, fascinating in its ambiguity.

On a cold April night in 1898 the *S.S. Titan*—the largest, most luxurious, and above all, the safest ocean liner in the world—set out on her maiden voyage. She was plowing the Atlantic between the English port of Southampton and New York when the unthinkable happened: she struck an iceberg, foundered, and sank. Most of her 2500 passengers were lost. This was not too surprising when it was realized that the 70,000-ton ship had only 24 lifeboats, capable of holding less than half those aboard. Even so, this tragedy of giant proportions went unnoticed by the public in 1898. Why? Because the sinking occurred in a novel entitled *The Wreck of the Titan*, a story made up by a struggling and little-known English writer named Morgan Robertson. The book caused only a ripple at the time it was published.

Fourteen years later, however, Robertson's novel was belatedly hailed as a sensation, and described as "the most astounding instance of prophecy" of the 19th or 20th century. For, on the chilly night of April 14, 1912, the real 66,000-ton liner *Titanic* hit an iceberg and sank, with a calamitous loss of life. Like the fictional ship with such a similar name, the *Titanic* was on her maiden voyage across the Atlantic. Also like her fictional predecessor, she was a triple-screw vessel capable of a top speed of 25 knots. Both ships had a large number of passengers and crew, and far too few lifeboats for them—only 20 on the real one. Finally, both vessels were said to be unsinkable. One of the *Titan* deck hands in the book told a passenger

Opposite: the biggest ship in the world of its day, the new *Titanic* sank with great loss of life on its maiden voyage in 1912. Fourteen years before this tragic event, a novel uncannily foretold the occurrence.

Warnings of Impending Doom

that "God Himself could not sink the ship." With her 16 watertight compartments, the real ship *Titanic* was considered by her owners to take "first place among the big steamers of the world," and to be absolutely safe.

Almost as the *Titanic* went down, her survivors were already starting to talk of how the ship had been "doomed," and how they had felt all along that "something terrible" was going to happen. No one had forecast the catastrophe of the *Titanic* as accurately and vividly as the author Robertson had done in 1898, but there were some who later provided evidence of foretelling the tragic fate of the ship. Two seers who had been consulted by one of the passengers—the British journalist W. T. Stead—both said they had warned him against traveling on water in advance of his fatal journey. One of the fortune tellers had told Stead he would sail to America within a year or two from the time of the consultation. "I see more than a thousand people—yourself among them— struggling desperately in the water," he told Stead. "They are screaming for help, and fighting for their lives. But it does none of them any good—yourself included."

Stead himself had forewarnings of the ship's—and his own—unhappy end. Some years earlier, while editor of a London newspaper, he had published a fictitious account of the sinking of a huge ocean liner, supposedly written by a survivor. Stead added a prophetic editor's note to the story saying: "This is exactly what might take place, and what will take place, if liners are sent to sea short of boats." A few years after this, Stead wrote a magazine article in which he described the catastrophe of a liner colliding with an iceberg. Only one passenger in Stead's fictional article escaped with his life. Incredible as it seems, Stead also had a dream in which he saw himself standing on the deck of the sinking *Titanic*—without a life belt, and with the last lifeboat pulling away into the night.

Stead ignored all signs and omens of things to come, and lost his life on the *Titanic*. The case was different for a countryman of his, J. Connon Middleton. In a letter published in the journal of the Society of Psychical Research in London, Middleton recounted an "uncomfortable" dream which made him "most depressed and even despondent." He had booked passage on the *Titanic* to attend a business conference in New York, he said. Ten days before the sailing date, he dreamed of the vessel "floating on the sea, keel upward, and her passengers and crew swimming around her." He had the same dream the following night, but this time, he told his wife, he seemed to be "floating in the air just above the wreck." Two days afterward, he received a cable that the conference had been postponed, and lost no time in canceling his booking. It was a lucky cancellation.

Colin Macdonald, a 34-year-old marine engineer, might also have died on the *Titanic*. However, he had a strong feeling of bad things to come for the big new ship. Three times he refused to sign on as the *Titanic*'s second engineer. In 1964 Macdonald's daughter was interviewed by a leading American psychical researcher and psychiatrist. She told him that her father had a "strong impression" that something was "going to happen" to

Below: the 66,000-ton *Titanic* is here shown being towed out of port on the morning of April 10, 1912.

These two drawings of the big liner's end were based on eye-witness accounts given at the time.
Left: the great ship went down by the head. "She turned right on end," the third officer related.

Below: a heroic act ended the career of the *Titanic's* captain, who lost his own life while saving a tiny baby passenger. One witness overheard the captain saying that he would follow after his ship.

Left: a contemporary photograph shows one of the *Titanic's* lifeboats nearing rescue and safety.

Does Time Exist?

the *Titanic*, and that there were also other times when he foresaw the future. The second engineer who took the *Titanic* job Macdonald turned down was drowned.

At the time of the *Titanic* disaster, 20th-century man was just beginning to question the prevailing materialistic philosophy that denied the unexplained. Precognition—that is, knowledge of future events by means outside the five senses—was viewed as freakishness or trickery. This was so whether the foreknowledge came through dreams, palmistry, astrology, or simply a feeling that something—usually threatening—was about to happen. One scholar, cited by James Laver in his book *Nostradamus*, put it like this: "As the 19th century drew to its

close, the rationalist and the materialist seemed to have established a permanent empire over thought. . . . [But] in times when the air is heavy with the sense of impending disaster . . . men find their rationalism shaken, and turn once more to the old superstitions which perhaps, after all, are not quite so completely superstitious as 'advanced' people used to think."

The big debate was on the question of time. Ordinarily we use it as a measurement. In the simplest physical sense of the concept of time, we use it exactly like length, width, or volume. In this sense time does not exist independently. It is linear and ongoing, just as clocks and calendars are linear. But this concept of time does not take into account our intimate

Below: does time exist, or is it all in the mind? Do past, present, and future occur at the same moment, or are they strictly separate in experience? Such debates on time occupy the minds of philosophers as well as believers in the occult. As though to illustrate the debate, this painting by an unknown Elizabethan artist around 1596 shows the past, present, and future at one time in the form of Sir Henry Unton's life from his birth to his death.

Different Ways of Viewing Time

psychic relations with time past and time future, and ignores another time that we all experience—dream time. Taking these into account, it is possible to conceive of time as an entity in its own right—a psychic entity perhaps, but nonetheless real. If this was so, what was time's nature? Did time exist outwardly, or was it only in people's minds? Was it stationary or mobile? Was it strictly contained in separate capsules of past, present, and future, or did all three exist side by side at the same moment? This last notion was most passionately argued. There were those who believe that the future already exists, and that we approach coming events the same way as passengers on a train arrive at stations lying ahead of them along the line. Short of suicide, there was no way of intentionally avoiding these stations—and, it was argued, suicide itself could be the name of one of the stops ahead. In his book *What is Time?*, G. J. Whitrow relates how a Cambridge University philosopher used the death of the British queen in 1714 to give an example of the view that the future exists now. "At the last moment of time—if time has a last moment—it will still be the death of a Queen," the university professor stated. "And in every respect but one, it is equally devoid of change. But in one respect it does change. It was once an event in the far future. It became every moment an event in the nearer future. At last it was present. Then it became past, and will always remain past." This view agrees with what the American psychologist and philosopher William James called the "block universe," in which the future is like a strip of film whose pictures are revealed to us as the film unfolds.

A contrary view holds that people can affect their future by acting on warnings of things to come. This belief that man is not

Below right: whether simple or learned, people have always been concerned with time and telling time. This 16th-century German woodcut shows an untutored farmer reading the time from the shadow cast on his hand by a stick held under his thumb.

Below: wooden "fan" calendars like the one shown here were used in medieval England. The 12 sides of the six strips corresponded to the months of the year, and holy days were clearly marked by pictures.

just a pawn to be maneuvered about and then finally sacrificed on the chessboard of the future, was restated in the late 1950s by the American novelist Jack Kerouac. He had one of his characters say: "Mankind will someday realize that we are actually in contact with the dead and with the other world—right now we could predict, if we only exerted enough mental will, what is going to happen within the next hundred years, and be able to take steps to avoid all kinds of catastrophes."

Strangely enough, it was neither philosopher or scientist who did most to analyze dreams, time, and visions of the future, and put them into a system. It was an aircraft designer, John William Dunne. His system was complicated and controversial, but not implausible. Dunne, who designed and built the first British military airplane, first became fascinated by "nighttime revelations of the future" in 1889 when he had an otherwise ordinary dream that foresaw the success of a Cape Town-to-Cairo expedition. From then on, he made a habit of writing down his dreams immediately on waking—or at whatever time of day he recalled them—and then waiting for some element in the dreams to come true. His dreams were not at all unusual until 1916, when he had a "night vision" of an explosion in a London bomb factory. Such an explosion occurred in January 1917, with 73 workers killed, and more than a thousand injured.

Right: this pillar, erected by the Mayans in 497, is like an almanac that covers five years. Predictions of future events are included.
Below: mechanical clocks came into being around the early 14th century. These handsome antique lantern clocks were made in England.

Dunne's Theory of Immortality

Below: John William Dunne, one of the best-known time theorists, was not a man given to fancies. An aeronautics engineer who designed the first British military plane, he became interested in theories of time when he started to have clearly predictive dreams.

Left: in one of his books, Dunne used this drawing to illustrate his theory of "the infinite regress." In it, an artist tries to paint a picture of the universe. Having started with the landscape before him, he realizes that he is missing from it. So he moves his easel back and paints himself in. Then he realizes that, to be right, the picture should have him painting himself. So he moves his easel back again—and goes on painting himself into the scene endlessly.

By then, Dunne had come to the conclusion that he was "suffering, seemingly, from some extraordinary fault in my relation to reality, something so uniquely wrong that it compelled me to perceive . . . large blocks of . . . experience displaced from their proper position in Time." That realization, and the persistence of other clairvoyant dreams, led him to write his best-selling book, *An Experiment with Time*. He described the book as "the first scientific argument for human immortality." On its publication, he was flooded with letters from readers claiming to have had similar extrasensory experiences. This led him to note in the book's second edition: "It has been rather surprising to discover how many persons there are who, while willing to concede that we habitually observe events before they occur, suppose that such prevision may be treated as a minor logical difficulty, to be met by some trifling readjustment in one or another of our sciences or by the addition of a dash of transcendentalism to our metaphysics. It may well be emphasized that no tinkering or doctoring of that kind could avail in the smallest degree. If prevision be a fact, it is a fact which destroys absolutely the entire basis of all our past opinions of the universe."

In his book *Man and Time* J. B. Priestley devotes a whole chapter to Dunne. Although Priestley himself is best known as a novelist and playwright, he is also recognized as one of Dunne's chief interpreters. "Those of us who are Time-haunted owe him [Dunne] an enormous debt . . ." Priestley starts out.

It is to Dunne's work on dreams that Priestley gives greatest importance. Dunne, he said, established that ordinary dreams contain "a definite element of prevision of precognition." Following from this, Dunne effectively showed that the dreaming self cannot be entirely contained within time as we usually think of it. According to Dunne's time theory, we live in the flow of time as Observer 1 in Time 1. To the side of us is another self, Observer 2 in Time 2. From this, Priestley explains how Dunne's theory applies to seeing the future in dreams.

"What [Observer 2] observes are what Dunne calls 'the brain states' of Observer 1 (his experience in Time 1)—'the sensory phenomena, memory phenomena, and trains of associative thinking' belonging to ordinary waking life. Now when Observer 1 is awake, 2 is attending to what Observer 1 is discovering in Time 1, using the three-dimensional focus with which we are all familiar." [By this is meant the concept of ordinary time as flowing from the past through the present into the future.] Priestley goes on:

"But Observer 2 in Time 2 has a four-dimensional outlook. This means that the 'future' brain states of Observer 1 may be as open to Observer 2's inspection as 1's past brain states. But it also means that when Observer 1 is asleep, his three-dimensional focus can no longer act as guide or 'traveling concentration mark' for Observer 2. The latter is now left with his four-dimensional focus, which has a wide Time 1 range—much of it 'future' to Observer 1.

"But Observer 2 cannot attend and concentrate properly. Now and then he may succeed, as he must do in a clear precognitive dream. Usually, however, unguided by the inactive

From Inventor to Theorist on Time

John William Dunne was a British airplane designer who developed a new theory about time. The son of General Sir John Hart Dunne, he served in the Boer War and World War I, and designed Britain's first military plane in 1906–7. From about 1889 Dunne became interested in dreams, and started writing down his own experiences. His dreams were not very unusual until in 1916 he had a "night vision" of an explosion in a London bomb factory. In January 1917 such an explosion occurred, with 73 workers killed and more than 1000 injured. To explain the apparent prophetic nature of some dreams, Dunne worked out a philosophical theory that he explained in *Experiment with Time* (1927), *The Serial Universe* (1934), and *The New Immortality* (1938). After publication of the first book, Dunne was flooded with letters from readers who claimed to have had similar clairvoyant dreams. Dunne's basic theory was that human beings experience time on several different levels. On one of these levels the individual can observe the past and the future as clearly as he can the present. In this way, the individual human being might well have clear prophetic visions. Dunne was convinced that humans are immortal, and he called *An Experiment with Time* "the first scientific argument for human immortality." His theories of time have influenced writers such as J. B. Priestley and W. Somerset Maugham.

Above: J. B. Priestley owes his fame to his novels and plays, but he is also well known as a disciple of time theorist John William Dunne. On a British television program in 1963, an appeal was made to viewers to write to him about any unusual time experiences they may have had. He is pictured here as he looks over the many hundreds of letters he received.

sleeping Observer 1, Observer 2 with his four-dimensional focus is all at sea. . . .

"This relation between Time 1 and Time 2, between Observer 1 and Observer 2, enables Dunne to explain why we find most of our dreams so bewildering."

Priestley gives some examples of dreams that support Dunne's ideas of prevision. One of the most interesting is that of Dr. Louisa E. Rhine, who wrote about it herself in the American *Journal of Parapsychology*. She felt that the dream had helped her save the life of her one-year-old son. In her article she wrote: ". . . I had a dream early one morning. I thought the children and I had gone camping with some friends. We were camped in such a pretty little glade on the shores of the sound between two hills. It was wooded, and our tents were under the trees; I looked around and thought what a lovely spot it was." In the dream she decided to wash the baby's clothes and carried him with her down to the stream. She put him on the ground, went back to the tent to get the soap she had forgotten, and returned to find her son—who had been throwing pebbles into the water—lying face down in the stream, drowned.

She woke up "sobbing and crying," worried over the dream for a few days, and then forgot about it. It did not return to her until later that summer, when she and a group of friends went camping in a spot just like the one in her dream. She went to the stream to wash the baby's clothes, settled her son on the bank, and walked back for the missing soap. As she did so the infant picked up a handful of pebbles and began to toss them into the water. "Instantly," she stated, "my dream flashed into my mind. It was like a moving picture. He stood just as he had in my dream—white dress, yellow curls, shining sun. For a moment I almost collapsed. Then I caught him up and went back to the beach with my friends. When I composed myself, I told them about it. They just laughed and said I had imagined it. That is such a simple answer when one cannot give a good explanation. I am not given to imagining wild things." Such "displacement of time" can happen to anyone any night during sleep, and its frequent occurrence reinforced Priestley's faith in Dunne.

In the last part of his *Man and Time* chapter on Dunne, Priestley cites Dunne's strong belief that we are immortal. He interprets this part of Dunne's theory as follows:

"It is true that we 'die' in Time 1 when our Observer 1 reaches the end of his journey along the fourth dimension. And then all possibility of intervention and action in Time 1 comes to an end. This limits Observer 2's experience (through Observer 1's brain states) of Time 1, but it does not involve the death of Observer 2, who exists in Time 2. No longer having any Time 1 experience to attend to . . . Observer 2 now experiences Time 2 as Observer 1 did Time 1: that is, it is for him ordinary successive time as we know it. He has to begin learning all over again as his four-dimensional focus moves along the fifth dimension of Time 3. People and things will be the same and yet not the same. We catch glimpses, though confused and distorted, of this afterdeath mode of existence in our dreams.

"He [Dunne] suggests that in our Time 2 'afterlife,' once we

The Premonition of a Navy Officer

have understood how to live it, we shall be able to blend, combine, build, with all the elements of our Time 1 existence, using them more or less as a composer does his notes, an artist his paints."

Priestley himself collected many stories about premonitions and other unusual time experiences. Among them was one reported to him by Sir Stephen King-Hall, a writer who was a naval officer for many years. Sir Stephen's story was as follows:

While on duty as officer of the watch on the *Southampton* in the war years of 1916, Sir Stephen had an overriding premonition that a man would fall overboard when the ship got to a small island off the coast of Scotland. His feeling grew stronger the nearer the convoy his ship led came to the island. With only his premonition to go on, Sir Stephen gave orders to the crew to get ready to save a man overboard. Of course, his orders were challenged by his superior officer.

". . . The Commodore said, 'What the hell do you think you are doing?" Sir Stephen recounted. "We were abreast the island. I had no answer. We were steaming at 20 knots and we passed the little island in a few seconds. Nothing happened!

"As I was struggling to say something, the cry went up 'man overboard' from the *Nottingham* (the next ship in the line, 100 yards behind us) then level with the island. Thirty seconds later 'man overboard' from the *Birmingham* (the third ship in the line, and then abreast the island). We went full speed astern; our sea boat was in the water almost at once and we picked up both men. I was then able to explain to a startled bridge why I had behaved as I had done."

In the 1930s, Air Marshal Sir Victor Goddard had a precognitive experience that seemed made to order for time theorists such as Dunne and Priestley.

While flying over Scotland during a storm, Sir Victor decided to descend in the area of the abandoned Drem airfield to get his bearings. He flew lower. When he was about a quarter of a mile away from Drem, something extraordinary happened: he found himself in both the present and the future.

"Suddenly the area was bathed in an ethereal light as though the sun were shining on a midsummer day," he said. The field was astir with activity as mechanics worked on biplanes in newly repaired hangars. Although Sir Victor was only 50 feet above the hangars, his plane went entirely unnoticed. He flew back into the storm and continued on his way.

What Sir Victor had seen came to pass four years later when Drem was rebuilt and reopened as a flying training school. "And then I knew that I had to sort out my ideas about free will and fate and determinism," Sir Victor declared.

In deciding this, Sir Victor was only one of the many divination converts who had gone before, and of the many more who were to come.

A Flight into the Future

Air Marshal Sir Victor Goddard was lost. Flying over Scotland in a Hawker Hart biplane, he was caught in a heavy storm. He needed a familiar landmark to get his bearings, and so flew lower to see if he could sight Drem, an abandoned airfield whose location he knew. He did sight it—but instead of the deserted and dark scene he expected, he saw a busy scene in bright sunlight (as shown by an artist's impression on opposite page). Mechanics in blue overalls were hard at work on a group of yellow planes. He wondered that no one paid any attention to his low-flying plane, but, wondering, headed up into the clouds once more and went on toward his final destination.

That was in 1934 when Drem was indeed nothing but a ruin. In 1938, however, the airfield was reopened as an RAF flying school in the face of the war threat. Between these two dates, the color of British training planes was changed from silver to yellow—a fact that Sir Victor could not have known at the time of his strange experience. Thus, in 1938, anyone flying over Drem would have seen exactly what Sir Victor had seen four years before the event!

N-A

Chapter 2 Shamans and Other Soothsayers

Are there some who have developed power to look into the future? Tribes around the world have believed that there were individuals with magical gifts who could discover and pass on to the community what their likely fate would be—predicting the weather, the abundance of the harvests, or where the most profitable hunting would be. How did these shamans discover their powers? Methods of divination are various and intriguing: Is it possible to see the future in leaping flames? Do sand pictures indicate events to come? Can the dominoes predict a happy marriage, or can tragedy show itself foreshadowed in the pattern of tea leaves in an empty cup?

The young man had been behaving strangely for some days. First he had withdrawn into himself, shunning his friends and relatives and wandering off into the woods near his village. Then he had begun to sing, talk animatedly in his sleep, and experience visions that frightened those near him. Worse, however, was to come. After losing consciousness several times a day, he suddenly turned violent, and bodily threatened anyone who approached him. It was clear—especially to himself—that he could no longer remain in the community. Shouting abuse, he fled to the forest. There he remained, eating tree bark for food and drinking any water he could find. Occasionally he threw himself suicidally into a stream, wounded himself with his knife, or set fire to a branch and deliberately burned himself. He also caught and gnawed animals, and generally behaved wildly. A week passed in this manner. Then—bloodstained, filthy, and smelly—he returned to his home. There he was welcomed as a hero by his fellow villagers. They crowded around him, waiting to hear his words of wisdom and prophecies for the future. For the young man had passed his initiation tests, and was now a *shaman*—a magician-priest-doctor.

It took two more weeks before the new shaman was able to speak of his experiences, and to tell the people of his primitive central Asian village exactly what would befall them—whether they would prosper or fail, survive or go under in the years immediately ahead. Meanwhile, he continued to have periodic

Opposite: this drawing from a book published around 1810 shows the decorative ceremonial dress of a Tungus shaman from Siberia.

The Ancient Art of Shamanism

Above: a Lapp shaman lies in a trance in preparation for his fortune telling activities. His vital magic drum remains on his back.

Below: a shaman of the Siberian tribe Karagass is robed in ornate dress trimmed with fur, feathers, and appliqués, and carries a drum.

bouts of strange behavior and trances, during which it was believed he left his body and went to the realm of the dead to converse with the spirits there. From the spirits he learned what the likely fate of the community would be—which winters would be harsh and which mild, whether the herds of cattle would increase or perish, and, perhaps most significant of all, who the next shaman (or shamans) might be.

Shamans are good magicians as opposed to sorcerers, who are only interested in power and self-aggrandizement. They have been in existence for some 25,000 years, and are still to be found today in the Arctic and in Asia, particularly Siberia. To become a shaman involves more than just a cruel and self-harmful initiation. Before reaching this point, the candidate must have shown that he is worthy to undergo the tests. It is preferable if his nomination is hereditary, because everyone then expects him to behave as if possessed one day. However, there are various other ways someone can show that he is one of the chosen—one of those whose magical powers make them the most important and revered men in their tribe. It can be by an accident, such as falling from a tree or being touched by lightning; by feeling the call, much as a member of the Christian clergy gives himself to God; or by the simple expedient of a bold announcement that he is a shaman, and that he will prove it by bizarre and masochistic behavior.

In Lapland and Siberia, shamans would beat on their multi-colored and many-imaged drums when calling up visions or seeking news of the future. The images—painted in reindeer blood or alder juice—represented the various gods of the wind, sun, and moon, as well as the spirits of humans and animals of the underworld. The shamans took their drums from special skin containers, and placed small brass rings on them. Then, tapping the drums with hammers, the shamans could see the future as the rings vibrated on the images. Ordinary Laplanders also used a drum as a fortune-telling device until the 18th century. No home was without its magic drum. The head of the household—wearing his best and newest clothes—consulted it on important domestic matters. However, when it came to issues that affected the whole community, it was left to the shamans to go into a self-induced trance, and to interpret the message of the drums.

There have been many debunkers of shamans. Some say that all of them are no more than deranged exhibitionists and frauds, and that their gifts of prophecy are restricted to finding lost or strayed dogs, cattle, or sheep. Others protest that the shaman's great powers of healing are no more potent than a quack doctor's, and that they fool themselves and their fellow tribesmen when they claim both to visit the dead and to guide the souls of the newly deceased to the other world.

One writer on Arctic shamans, agreeing with the view that they were disturbed personalities, stated: "The excessive cold, the long nights, the desert solitudes, shortage of vitamins, etc., took their toll of the nervous constitution of the Arctic populations, producing either mental illnesses . . . or the shamanic trance. The only difference between a shaman and an epileptic was that the latter could not bring about a trance at will."

Madmen or not, humbugs or otherwise, shamans are recognized as masters in transporting themselves and their followers into a state of ecstasy. It is true, too, that shamans have a far more extensive vocabulary than their co-villagers and, like the priests in the Middle Ages, use their superior knowledge to gain sway over the general group. As far as divination is concerned, their greater knowledge may enable them to convince their communities that they can see the future.

Another authority on shamans, who studied their role as prophets and healers among the tribes of the Sudan, believed that they were as balanced and normal as the rest of their tribesmen. "No shaman," he states, "is, in everyday life, an 'abnormal' individual, a neurotic, or a paranoiac; if he were, he would be classed as a lunatic, not respected as a priest . . . I recorded no case of a shaman whose professional hysteria deteriorated into serious mental disorders."

The controversy still surrounding the shamans is an indication of how fascinated mankind is with fortune tellers. Of course, there are many ways of foretelling the future besides shamanism. Some have long and colorful histories, which are still being added to by those who practice the prophesying arts today.

One of the oldest methods of soothsaying is the reading of sand, and, to several North American Indian tribes, this practice has a clearly magical quality. The Navahos in particular use colored sand in certain of their rites. Painting mystic pictures with colored sand is an ancient custom of theirs, and they believe that the legendary chief, Thunderbird, was sent down from the sky especially to instruct them in the making and interpretation of sand pictures. By trickling sand through their fingers, the tribal wise men made patterns on the ground. These patterns revealed how someone should act in a given situation, whether or not a sick person would get well, and how to solve difficult and worrying problems. The pictures—which only the medicine men could correctly interpret—had to be erased before the sun sank. If they were left for anyone to see after that, it was believed that they not only would lose their magic, but also that evil men could study them, and perhaps learn Thunderbird's secrets of the sand to put to evil use.

Sand paintings are essential to the Navaho healing ceremonies, which are done today in the traditional way of long ago. The medicine man creates one or more paintings with colored sand on the ground. He may set others to help work on the designs because their complexity often requires many hours of labor. The sand pictures, properly called "dry paintings," are often elaborate and always symbolic. The patient must sit within the main sand painting during the long ceremony, which in some cases can last for several days. At the very beginning of the ritual cure, some of the sand from the painting is rubbed on the sick person's body. This is done to draw the spirits' attention directly to the patient and his or her illness.

Today, reading sand pictures can be a party game that adds a little spice of magic to the fun. Whoever is chosen to act as seer is blindfolded, and given both a tray containing fine dry sand and a pencil. The *querant*—that is, the person seeking

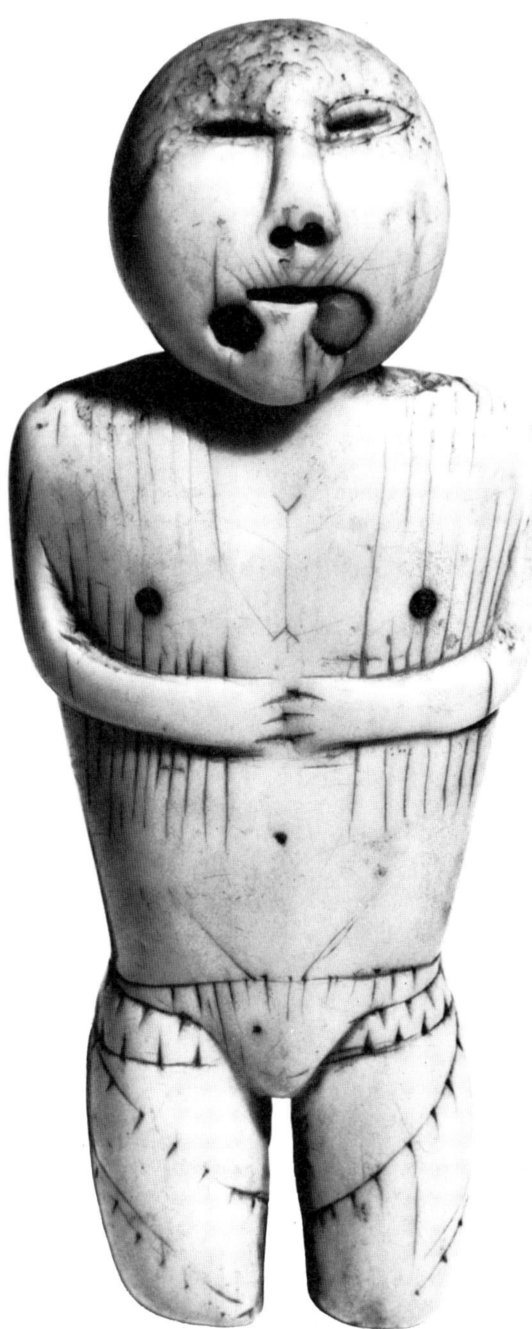

Above: this small ivory doll was worn as a charm by Eskimo shamans during communication with spirits.

Magic Ritual for a Successful Hunt

The hunt was all-important to the Cro-Magnon community of more than 12,000 years ago. Failure meant hunger, and, perhaps, death. The hunters were skilled and had weapons—but even brave ones quailed at the thought of the danger. However, the hunters got magical aid from the shaman, their magician-priest, who performed a ritual for a successful hunt. He might burn clay models of animals to represent their killing, for example, but whatever he did, he enacted man's mastery as a way of making it come true.

European cave paintings of the period 28,000–10,000 B.C. often depict a creature part man and part animal, as below. Many scholars think these are shamans in dress of skins and headpieces.

Above: around the finished sand painting are prayer sticks, rattles, and the colorings used.
Above right: the Navaho medicine man, like other shamans, is a healer as well as a fortune teller. He begins a ritual cure by painting a greatly symbolic design on sand.

information—sits quietly near the sand diviner, concentrating on the question he or she has asked. The seer holds a pencil in his hand, with his wrist resting on the rim of the tray. By the time three to five minutes have passed, and provided that both the querant and the fortune teller have cleared their minds of everything but the question, the pencil should move as of its own accord. Initials, if not words, will appear in the sand. A "y" will stand for yes, an "n" for no, an "m" for maybe, and a "p" for perhaps. Instead of letters or words, lines may be formed—a long deep one tells of a journey, and a short deep one announces an unexpected visitor, for example. In still another way, shapes may be drawn on the sand. A triangle stands for a successful career; a small circle for a coming marriage; a large circle for misfortune near at hand; a cross for a hazard to face or obstacle to overcome; an X, or "kiss" cross, for a love affair—happy if the cross is distinct, unhappy if it is indistinct. The width of the tray is gauged as a year, so time can be measured by dividing the sand into halves, quarters, or twelfths. Thus, questions about when the bad luck will pass, or when a romance will start, can be answered.

The time of a future event cannot be told in like manner by another widespread and ancient form of prediction—dice. Palamades is said to have invented dice in Greece about 1244 B.C., but there is evidence of their use before that. In earlier Egyptian civilizations, bone-like ivory molds—called *astragals*—were thrown to see what future events they revealed.

To consult the dice, a person tosses them inside a chalk circle drawn on a board or table. If one or any of the dice roll outside the circle, they are not included in the calculations—but this foretells a quarrel. If they fall to the floor on the toss, an estrangement is in the offing. The system is speedy and simple, although interpretations vary. Some say *three* means a pleasant surprise; *six*, the loss of something of value; *nine*, a wedding; *twelve*, an important letter on the way; *fifteen*, a warning of danger; *eighteen*, extreme good fortune. It is considered unwise to throw dice on a Monday or a Wednesday.

A most unusual novel of 1971, *The Dice Man* by Luke Rhinehart, is about divination by dice. In it, the leading character decides his every move by the throw of the dice, for

Predictions from Sand and Dice

Left: the sand painter scatters corn to call upon the help of the spirits in bringing about a cure.

Above: as the sick child sits on the sand painting, the medicine man chants his ritual invocation.

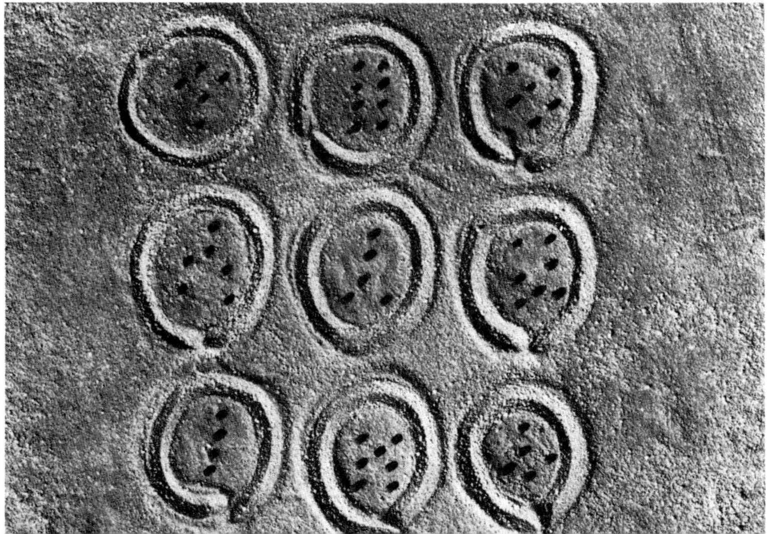

Left: shamans of Madagascar use sacred seeds to foretell the future. They drop the seeds into circles drawn on the ground, and find the answers to questions in the patterns the fallen seeds form.

The Casting of the Dice

which he sets all his own readings of the numbers. Thus he rampages through New York committing rape (his interpretation of *one*), murder (his reading of *three*) and other misdeeds.

People who are fascinated by numbers, as thousands are, may be inclined to choose the centuries-old system of reading dominoes to tell them of happenings to come. In the Western way of reading dominoes, all blanks are removed, and the remainder spread face downward on a table. All *ones* refer to travel, *twos* to social affairs, *threes* to romance, *fours* to finance, *fives* to work, and *sixes* to good luck. Using their left hands, two people alternately draw three pieces each. The two numbers on each domino are then read together. A *six* and a *one*, for example, means a fortunate voyage; a double *three* indicates an especially happy marriage; and a double *four*, a large windfall. The two pieces that no one wants to draw are the *three-one*, which foretells bad news, and the *four-two*, a sign that a disappointment is due. The Eastern Method of reading dominoes is somewhat more complicated. It employs the full domino set, and has 27 different and fuller meanings. It is thought to be unlucky to consult the dominoes more than once every seven days.

Reading pictures from the fire, or *pyromancy*, is the most personal of all the many different forms of divination. The formations of the coals project such different pictures and images to each person that it becomes impossible to tell any

Right: this South African witch doctor casts and reads the "wise stones" to see what the future might reveal for his tribe.

fortune but your own. To get the best results from the flames— and the clearest pictures— it is necessary to have a lively, roaring fire. This can be produced by throwing salt or sugar onto coals that may have burned down. Settled before the fire, you start by gazing into the flames for five minutes or so. If during this scene setting a piece of coal should leap out of the grate and land at your feet, the next 12 months will bring good luck and happiness.

The pictures do not necessarily have to be of shoes (which foretell of good news coming reasonably soon), or hatchets (meaning that disaster looms ahead), or anything as distinctive as that. Large circles or rings indicate a happy marriage, and double rings a hasty marriage that may fail. A shape like a three-leafed clover denotes the greatest prosperity, well-being, and success.

The language of the flames is almost identical to that of tea leaves. It depends much on personal interpretation. The tea leaf reader takes the cup in her left hand, and swirls the dregs and tea leaves in a counterclockwise direction three to seven times. If a man is giving the reading, he swirls the leaves clockwise. Next she or her querant gently turns the cup over onto a sauce, and on turning it up again, checks to see if any drops remain in the cup. If they do, they foretell the probability of tears in the next few days. This is a better sign than no liquid at all, however. The mass of dark leaves alone bodes trouble and sorrow.

Above: when people say "the die is cast," they probably don't know that they are referring to dice-throwing as an ancient form of fortune telling. (Die is the singular of dice). The Greeks of antiquity are said to have invented dice to help reveal the future. By the time of this 4th-century B.C. terra cotta statue, however, playing dice was more of a gambling game. Even so, the winner was the player who got the most favorable omen from the dice.
Below: playing dice is almost purely a form of gambling today, but the old idea of consulting them is not entirely lost.

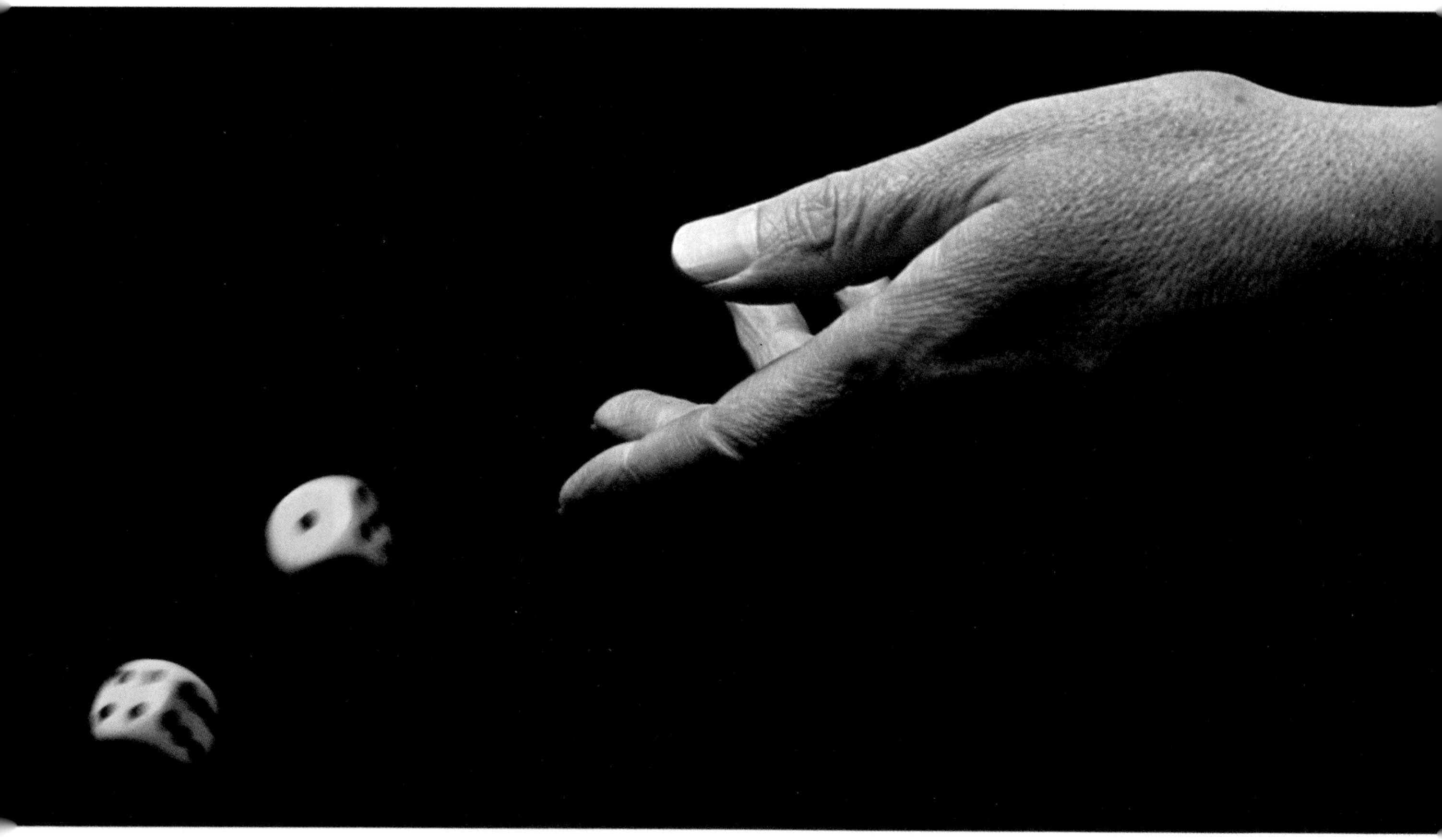

Who will I marry? This question has given rise to many customs involved with trying to see one's future spouse—especially if the questioner is an unmarried woman.
Above: in American lore, the unwed girl who looks into her mirror at midnight on Hallowe'en while holding a lit candle will, it is said, see the image of her husband-to-be peering at her reflection over her left shoulder.

Right: another old American practice made a kind of party game out of trying to get advance news of a marriage partner. Young men and women peeled an apple or potato without breaking the peel, tossed it over their shoulders, and read the letter the fallen peel most closely resembled. The letter was supposed to be the initial of the future spouse.

Folk Method of Prediction

By using her intuition and imagination, the reader will interpret the numbers and initials she will be able to see in the leaves. To obtain the most positive reading, it is best to use a plain cup rather than a patterned one, which can divert the mind. Always keep the handle pointing south, and remember that the bottom of the cup represents the distant future, the middle of the cup means time not too far away, and the upper part of the cup stands for immediacy.

The art of reading tea leaves is often passed on from generation to generation, but it can easily be self-taught, and the basic rules are quickly learned. The shapes most frequently formed are those of serpents, birds, and animals. A snake stands for evil and temptation, a mouse for financial insecurity, and a rat for danger. A horse is a symbol of a lover, especially to women, and a goat tells of enemies and misfortune, especially to a sailor. A spider is a lucky sign, and when surrounded by dots, means great wealth. A hen speaks of an addition to the family, and a peacock promises an addition of property.

Other shapes that form in tea leaves, and their meanings, include a hammer (triumph over adversity), a ladder (travel), scissors (a fight), a steeple (disappointments), an umbrella (trouble and annoyance), an apple (long life), and an acorn (good or improved health). Every so often, the face or hands of a clock appear in the leaves. While most of the hours that might be shown have no constant meaning, 7:00 or 9:00 implies that there will be a death in the family, and midnight signifies a secret and profitable rendezvous.

Arlene Dahl, actress and beauty expert, tells this anecdote about reading tea leaves. It happened while she was making a film in England a few years ago. "I came across a book that explained all the symbols to look for in the bottom of the tea cup," she says. "At first I took the book along to parties, but every time I had to check out something, I could feel I was losing my audience—so I started to improvise. But I was right too often and I got scared." It was while in London that her new "talent" got her labeled as a witch. "My hairdresser insisted that I read her fortune," she goes on. "Although I didn't know it, she and her husband had wanted a child for five years, and when I read a new arrival she was overjoyed. A few weeks later she ran in and called me a witch—she was

Far left: in old England, maidens in love placed nuts among the hot embers of the hearth, and whispered their loved one's name. If the nut jumped, it meant that the love affair would be successful.

Left: in another English custom, a small piece of wedding cake was passed through a wedding ring, and put under the pillow. This was supposed to bring a dream of the man the dreamer would marry.

Above: this African witch doctor will read fortunes from the marks left by a crab scrambling about in a bowl containing wet sand.

Above: some augurs read the signs by allowing birds to eat grains placed on the letters of the Greek alphabet, drawn on a circle. Words were formed from the letters left without grains, and the words thus formed gave the answer that was sought.

pregnant!"

Staying on the domestic scene for divination methods, it is possible to make a stab at telling the future with knives. All that is needed is an ordinary table knife and a round tray big enough to hold it. The tray is marked around the rim with various brief prophecies, which can be written on slips of gummed paper and stuck in place. Each person twirls the knife by its center three times—women using their right hands, and men their left. The message at which the blade points after the third twirl is the fortune. If the knife stops in a space between messages, this suggests that the coming days or weeks will be relatively uneventful. Nowadays divination by knives is a light-hearted game, but it was previously practiced in a more serious way by North American Indians.

Another common household implement that has long been a tool for telling fortunes is the mirror, the use of which goes back to the Iron Age. The so-called "magic of the mirror" was known both to the early Chinese sages and to the wise men and prophets of Greece, all of whom considered it an omen of death to dream of seeing your own reflection in water, copper, glass, or any other shiny surface. Extending this to waking hours, it was felt that gazing at one's reflection in water was forbidden by the "spirits of the lake." These spirits would, in fact, drag the gazer's soul down into the depths, and leave the physical body to die on the bank. The threat of a watery grave if one defied the water spirits was carried over as a threat if one gazed at oneself too much in any reflecting surface. Yet men and women defied the threat in the early practice of *hydromancy*, divination by water. They read their future fate by peering at their reflections in water. If the image was clear and remained undisturbed, it was an omen of serene and hopeful days to come. If the image was broken or got ruffled, it foretold of trouble—and perhaps even death. The idea of seeing into the future by studying reflections was later transferred to the use of mirrors.

The Egyptians, Greeks, and Romans spent a significant amount of their waking moments peering into bronze and silver mirrors, hoping to see pictures of the future. At the beginning of the 13th century, glass mirrors were first introduced in Venice, and then the art of mirror divination, or *catoptromancy*, thrived. The mirrors used were often handsomely encased. They were dipped into water to see whether a subject's reflection would show good or ill fortune. When the special ornate mirrors were not available, substitutes could include anything with the power to reflect—from polished stones to fingernails.

Health matters could be foretold by the mirrors, and it was not uncommon for them to be used to show the whereabouts of missing treasures or people, and the fate of nobles, leaders, and kings. In Europe in the Middle Ages, mirrors were used as a positive deterrent against wickedness, being said to protect their owners from the baleful influence of the Evil Eye. Among the Chinese of former times, small mirrors were placed about the house to frighten off evil spirits, which were thought to be terrified at the sight of their own reflections. For the young girls of old, however, mirrors had a more romantic and optimistic purpose: they were employed to reveal at what moment in the

Telling Fortunes

Left: because of the vagueness of the shapes formed by tea leaves, a good tea leaf reader has to depend a great deal on intuition, skill, and sensitivity.

Below: Moroccan girls at turn of century had such a strong belief in kites as an omen of the future that if theirs broke—which meant bad luck—they were plunged into a deep depression.

future love would come.

It was customary throughout Europe for a maiden to examine the moon's reflection in her hand mirror to see how many years would have to pass before her wedding day. The years were calculated mainly by the length of time that passed before clouds obscured the moon, or a bird flew across it. In the USA it was said that if a girl—especially a virgin— looked into a mirror at midnight on Hallowe'en, the reflection of her husband-to-be would be revealed over her left shoulder.

Maidens also had other sources for predictions about love and marriage. In the English county of Oxfordshire, it was long held that if a girl put an ivy leaf in her purse or pocket, she would marry the first man she met—even if she already had a husband. When a girl wanted to discover if her lover was faithful to her, she had only to place two nuts together on the bars of a grate. If they burned as one, her beloved was constant and true. However, if the nuts were forced apart by the heat, she would know beyond doubt that her man was faithless. In the North of England a willow wand was used as a magic guide to finding a husband. Holding the wand in her left hand, an unmarried girl had only to leave her house secretly, and run three times around it while she said: "He that's to be my good man come and grip the end of it." At the completion of the third lap, a likeness of her future mate would appear, and catch hold of the other end of the wand.

The list of ways humans have sought to learn the future ahead of time is by no means exhausted. Throughout the world and

The Shamans Power--Today!

the ages, peoples have tried divination by *belomancy* (arrows), *ornithomancy* (flight of birds), *sortilege* or *cleromancy* (drawing or casting of lots), and *ceromancy* (candle wax drippings). A notorious example of present-day use of sortilege is among the Mafia, whose members sometimes draw lots to decide who will kill a person who has tricked or betrayed them. However, of the ancient arts of prognostication, ceromancy is probably the one in most ominous use today. It has particular association with voodoo. Voodoo priests read candle wax drippings to advise others how to improve their love life, increase their money, or bring about the downfall of their enemies. Voodoo candle readings can last up to 12 hours, usually from 6 p.m. until dawn. During this time, wax drippings are allowed to fall into a shallow dish of cold water, and the patterns they form are interpreted by the priest or seer. If necessary, spells are cast. There are shops in New York City that sell wax figures to be used as fetishes for sticking pins into. Although the candles, wax figures, and dishes are on open sale, the all-important incantations that go with using them are not. No practicing Voodoo priest would ever sell or barter them. In this, he is like the shaman who opened this chapter: his art is a secret and personal art.

An example of the shaman's power became part of American Indian folklore in 1811. Tecumseh, the chief medicine man of the Shawnees, was greatly displeased when some 5000 Creeks refused to join his campaign to stem the US government's conquest of Indian lands. "You do not believe the Great Spirit has sent me. You shall know," he is quoted as saying. "I shall stamp my foot and the earth will tremble." This prophecy was realized two months later. On December 16, 1811, Tecumseh stamped his foot—and the first of three shocks tore through some 50,000 square miles of territory, including where the offending Creeks lived. Indians called it "the greatest earthquake in the history of man." It has been cited as an awesome example of the power of the shaman—who can not only foresee the future but, in some cases, make it come about through what magic no one else knows.

Although today the shamans of Asia are reprtedly losing their prophetic strength and their ability to engineer events, this does not appear to be the case among the American Indians. In 1962, a group of Indians were arrested for fishing near the Trinity River in northern California, and their relatives foretold of a "Great Killer Windstorm" that would strike the Pacific Northwest because of this. On Columbus Day of that year, a fierce storm in that region killed 50 people. Three years later, in November 1965, came the great electricity failure that blacked out the Northeast coast and turned New York into a city of darkness. The blackout was ascribed to the magical powers of the Indians by at least one person—Craig Carpenter, the tall, hawk-faced man active in the current, highly militant Indian Rights movement. "What everybody seems to forget about the Northeast's blackout," he states, "is that it started in a power relay station on land stolen from the Tuscarora Indians; and nobody yet has figured out *how* it started."

The following year, a drought hit Washington, D.C.

Below: this Blackfoot Indian medicine man, dressed for a healing ceremony, wears the mask of the particular evil spirit thought to have caused the illness. It was believed that with the right mask, the shaman could speak directly to the offending spirit and persuade it to go away.

Throughout the long, hot summer, the residents yearned for rain. Finally, a 107-year-old Hopi, Chief Dan Kachongva, was consulted. Through his interpreter, Thomas Banyacya, he said: "It will rain, don't worry." That night the rain started—and did not stop until 24 hours later, just as the interpreter had also predicted.

Not content with that demonstration of divination, Banyacya and other Indians marched on Niagara Falls in 1966. They said that the Great Spirit would reveal His powers there to show that when they told of an event in the future, they spoke the truth.

The Indians congregated at the Falls on September 17, 1966—New York State's official annual Indian Day. The following morning a front page story in *The Washington Post* said: "A flaming meteorite lit up the skies across the north central United States last night, frightening hundreds of persons who saw it before it broke up in bits of smoking debris over northern Indiana . . . Michigan Governor George Romney, flying in his private plane . . . said 'the meteorite almost hit us. It really frightened us—we thought we were under attack. All of a sudden the thing was coming and it was as bright as noon.' "

To most people it seemed incredible that Banyacya—or anyone—could have known that such a thing was about to happen. However, to those who had knowledge of the shamans, who understood and appreciated their powers of divination, and who accepted that such powers could be handed down, there was nothing extraordinary about the event. It was simply another indication that the future can be ours for the making—or, at least, for the predicting.

Above: was the New York blackout of 1965 satisfactorily explained by the scientists? American Indians strongly suggest that their magical powers were the cause of it.

Below: stranded commuters slept where they could, as this flash photo shows. How many would believe in a supernatural cause?

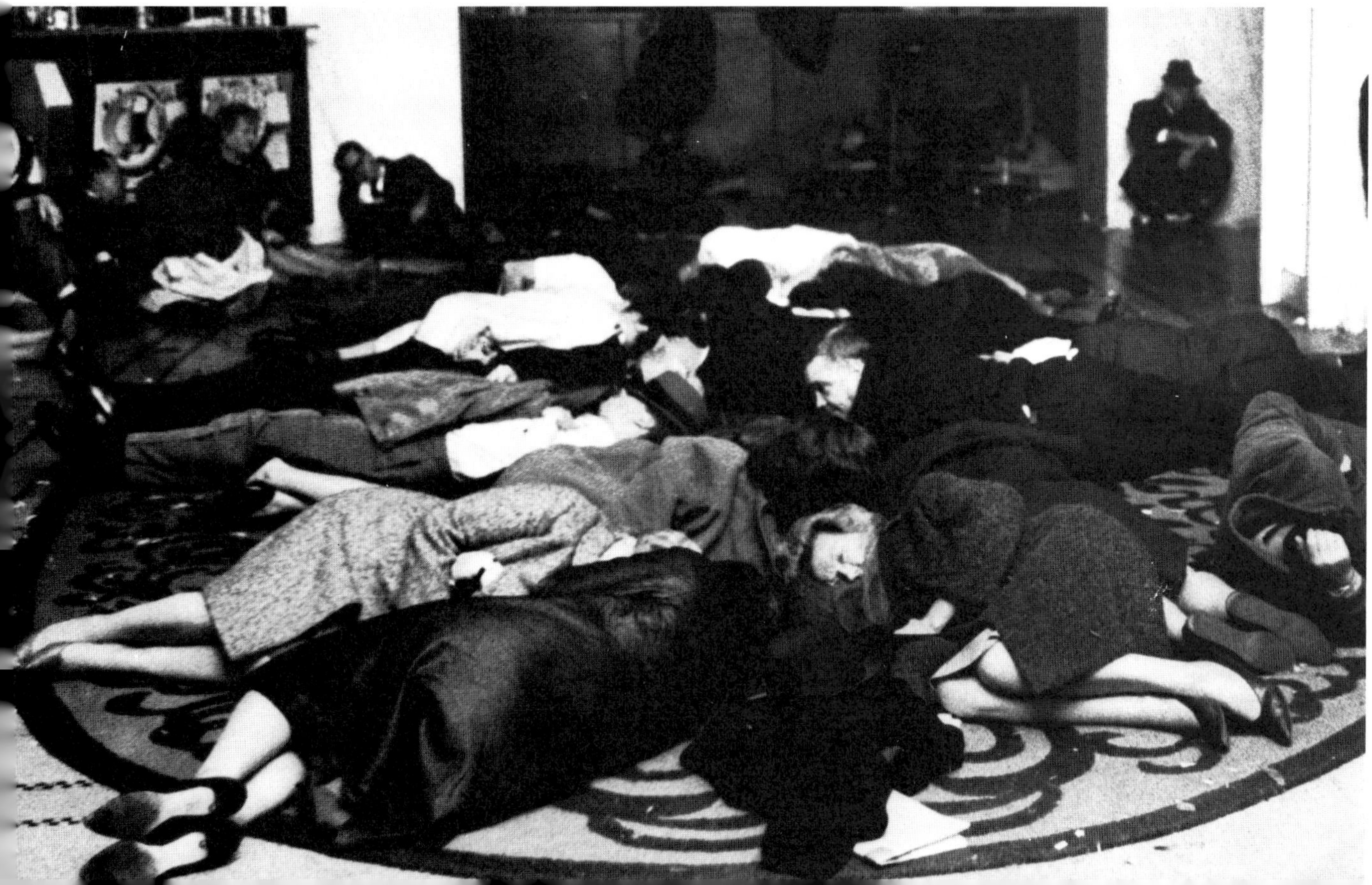

Chapter 3 Ancient Arts of Fortune Telling

What is the mysterious wisdom of the *I Ching*, which has attracted the devoted attention of philosophers and thinkers down through the centuries? How can casting the coins or the yarrow stalks lead to insights into motivation and alternatives, and suggest the proper course to be taken? Legend tells that an ancient Chinese emperor formulated the system, and Confucius certainly added his own commentary. But what has the *I Ching* to teach us now, in the 20th century? How can we learn to use the mystic hexagrams? And how can we apply the ambiguous messages to help resolve our complex problems today?

Confucius—the Chinese wise man and philosopher whose teachings helped shape his country's entire civilization—was almost 70 when, in 481 B.C. he stated, "if some years were added to my life, I would give 50 to the study of the *I Ching*, and might then escape falling into great errors." At the time, Confucius had already worn out three pairs of leather thongs that bound the tablets on which his copy of the world's "most revered system of fortune telling" was inscribed. As it turned out, he had only two more years to live instead of 50, but he spent them in deep and exhaustive study of the meanings and mystery of the *I Ching*, known as the *Book of Change*. This book, he said, had "as many layers as the earth itself." Hundreds of years later, when the Samurai warrior class ruled Japan, it was said that Samurai planned military strategy by consulting *I Ching*—and that they continued to do so right up to the 19th century.

No one can be sure of how old the *I Ching* (pronounced EE Jing) is, but it is believed to date from 2852 B.C. as the work of the legendary Emperor Fu-hsi. The contents of the book were systemized by King Wen in 1143 B.C., and his work was further clarified by his son, the Duke of Chou. Still later, Confucius edited and added explanatory notes to the *I Ching*. For all of this, the *Book of Change* remains full of symbolism with hidden and puzzling meanings.

Opposite: this illustration for *The Travels of Sir John Mandeville*, a book of the 14th century, shows Arab astrologers and soothsayers at their work of trying to find out what the future might hold.

Mysteries of the I Ching

The book contains 64 hexagrams shown by combinations of six solid and/or broken lines, as, for example:

Each hexagram symbolizes a specific human characteristic or condition of life, which is reflected in the symbolic name it bears. For example, hexagram 1 is "creative"; 11 is "peace"; 20 is "contemplation"; 37 is "the family"; 46 is "ascending"; 55 is "prosperity"; and 64 is "before completion." These hexagrams are formed by two sets of three lines, called trigrams, each of which also have their own name. The trigrams affect the reading of the *I Ching* by their own special qualities, images, and position —whether at the top or bottom of the hexagram.

It was King Wen who formulated the 64 hexagrams, gave them their names, and put the text message with them from the original work of Fu-hsi. After King Wen's death, his son Chou added notes to help explain the meanings of individual lines of the hexagrams, and the overall symbolism of them. The West owes its knowledge of *I Ching* to James Legge, a 19th-century specialist in Chinese studies. He translated the *Book of Change* into English in 1854, and his is the only thorough, scholarly translation of the entire book in English.

Below: one of China's greatest philosophers and scholars, Confucius was deeply interested in the mysteries of the *I Ching*. He thought it worthy of 50 years of study.

One of the most important things to remember about *I Ching* is that it is a whole system of philosophy. It is based on a code that embodies the traditional moral and mystical beliefs of the Chinese. Therefore, a querant cannot go frivolously to the *Book of Change*. Nor will he or she get an easy, direct "yes" or "no" answer. Questioners are thrown back on themselves for the interpretation of the answers, which are intended only as a guideline. As Raymond Van Over says in his edited version of *I Ching*: "It directs the questioner's attention to alternatives and the probable consequences of our actions if we choose one path instead of another. If the oracle wishes to direct our action in a specific direction or through a particular channel, it will tell us how a Superior Man would conduct himself. In this subtle way, our actions are directed toward a positive goal while still allowing us the free will to choose our own ultimate destiny. We can, of course, decide not to act as the Superior Man, and take any course we choose."

With the question in mind, there are two ways of consulting the *I Ching*: one by tossing three coins of any kind, and the other by throwing 50 yarrow stalks in a given sequence. The second method is long and complicated, and, since there is no proof that it gets any different results, can be left to the strict traditional or purist. Therefore, let us see how using the coins works.

The tossing of the coins reveals which hexagram the querant should consult as applicable in his case. A toss turning up two tails and one head is written as a solid line, ————. A toss of two heads and one tail is written as a broken line, —— ——.

Left: modern Korean followers of Confucius hold a procession on the philosopher's birthday.

Below: this 19th-century engraving shows someone about to throw the yarrow stalks that will lead him to the parts of the *I Ching* he must read to learn about his fate.

Right: it is simpler and just as effective to use coins instead of yarrow stalks to consult the *I Ching*. The coins shown here are Chinese bronze ones of old design, but any kind will serve.

Below and opposite: these sample hexagrams from the *I Ching* show the complexity, symbolism, and hidden meanings of the ancient text.

LÜ

10 TREADING CAREFULLY

Lü suggests the idea of one treading on the tail of a tiger which doesn't bite him. There will be progress and success. Hazardous position — no distress or failure.

TA YU

14 ABUNDANCE

Ta Yu indicates that there will be great progress and success. The superior man represses evil and gives distinction to what is good.

KUAN

20 CONTEMPLATION

Kuan intimates he should be like the worshipper who has made his ablutions, but not yet his offering. With sincerity and dignity he inspires trust and respect.

Hidden Meanings in the Hexagrams

Three tails are written ——x—— and three heads, ——o——. There are six tosses, and the first toss becomes the *bottom* line of the first trigram. Each succeeding toss is written as a line *above* the other until all six lines are drawn. Then, the questioner refers to a chart that gives him the name of the hexagram so indicated. Complications come in with what are called "moving lines"—three heads or three tails—which can refer the questioner to more than one hexagram. However, these do not always come up. In some cases, one or more individual lines of the hexagram are read as well as the text, commentary, and additional notes. In other cases, only the text is read. The coin toss says what to do in the way it forms the hexagram. In no case will the advice be immediately clear, for each hexagram has layer upon layer of meaning.

It has been said of the *I Ching* that, over the centuries, some 3000 scholars have tried to unravel its mysteries. This indicates that the book can hardly be regarded as just a fortune-telling system—more complicated and venerable than the horoscopes in our daily newspapers, perhaps, but no more important or valid than they are. When the book is studied for its ideas and ideals more than its prophetic properties, it can open the way to an understanding and finer appreciation of the universe's unceasing evolution and movement.

The more intuition used by the questioner of *I Ching*, the greater will be the range of choice open to him—for the book aims not to tell the future as such, but to determine whether or not the questioner is acting in accordance with his best interests. More than that, it can relate the individual's best interest to the

i

頤

27 NOURISHMENT

I indicates that with firm correctness there will be good fortune. We must look at what we are seeking to nourish and by exercising thought seek the proper aliment.

29 THE PERILOUS PIT

K'an, here repeated, shows the possession of sincerity, through which the mind is penetrating. Action will be of high value. Advance will be followed by achievement.

hsiao kuo

62 SMALL EXCESSES

Hsiao Kuo indicates progress and attainment but advantageous to be firm and correct. Action may be done in small affairs but not in great affairs — in this way good fortune.

Other Arts of the Ancients

wider world—even the universe. In fact, to become the Superior Man—which is one of the book's ideals—the questioner must necessarily follow the Right Path. He can only do this when he considers the fate and fortune of his fellow human beings.

Those who consult the *Book of Change*, either for themselves or as an interpreter for others, should look after their copy of the book with veneration and care—even if it is merely a paperback. When not in use, it should be wrapped in a piece of good clean cloth and placed on a shelf high enough that no one can look down on it. Just before using it, a person should wash his hands thoroughly in respect for the book. That done, he should place the *I Ching* facing south on a table in the center of the room and burn incense on another table that's lower. The seeker should prostrate himself three times on the floor while facing north. Only then, according to the strictest rules, is he ready to ask his question.

In the hexagram answers, the lines are based on opposites—starting with solid and broken for the drawing of the lines themselves. The solid lines stand for what is positive, light, active—all embodied in the Yang. The broken lines stand for the opposite of these: negative, dark, passive—the Yin. In Chinese philosophy, Yang stands for the hard, outgoing approach to life; Yin for the soft, shaded outlook. These two primary cosmic forces are like the two sides of a coin—one cannot exist without the other. Further, though they are in opposition to each other, they are also interdependent.

Below: the Romans believed that they could learn about the future from the internal organs of animals. In this ancient stone sculpture, the augur consults the entrails of a bull.

One of the most famous hexagrams in the *I Ching* is 4, entitled "youthful inexperience" or "youthful folly," which looks like this:

Anyone whose coin tosses refer him to this hexagram will discover that he is in need of a "proper direction." He is told that his immaturity and folly is the result of "uncultivated growth" and that he has rushed to the "foot of a mountain" where lies a "dangerous abyss." However, the *I Ching* goes on to say: "Yet such rashness may bring good fortune—fortune to be utilized when the moment comes . . . It is our sacred duty to correct the follies of youth through education." This can be interpreted to mean that the questioner has reached a given stage in his life, which is bound up with the universal situation. What the seeker must do is to decide whether he will advance or retreat, whether he will continue just as before, or alter his actions so that his course is not so rapid, so dramatic, so impulsive.

Whatever the questioner does, the decision—and the responsibility for that decision—are totally his. From this it

Above: the Assyrians used this kind of an instrument to make their astrological calculations.

Left: this 2nd-century Roman sculpture shows the casting of a horoscope. In this case, the subject is a tiny child. His future is being read by two women who are examining the celestial globe.

The Oracle of Delphi

Right: the Temple of Apollo in Delphi housed the most important oracle of ancient Greece, known as Pythia. Only the wealthy could afford the fees of the oracle, who also limited her appearances to given times. Yet many questions of state were decided by what the Delphic oracle foretold.

Above: proof that the high and mighty went humbly to the oracle at Delphi is found in this 5th-century B.C. Greek bowl. It depicts King Aegeus of Athens listening to the words of Pythia.

Opposite: this is how the supreme oracle of Delphi looked in the imagination of the 19th-century English artist Sir Edward Burne-Jones. The painting, which hangs in the Manchester Art Gallery, shows the oracle in front of the sacred flame. In her hands she holds the bay leaves that are the emblem of her priestly position.

might seem that the *Book of Change* is as remote and unfeeling as a recorded message on the other end of the telephone. However, this point of view is both an oversimplification and a misreading. The *I Ching* offers the advice of a wiser and older friend who looks at the problem broadly rather than from one person's narrow self-interest. In his updated version of the *Book of Change*, John Blofeld stresses the fact that the *I Ching* is unique because, in place of "rigid prophecies" it makes suggestions "based on an analysis of the interplay of universal forces, not about what *will* happen but what *should* be done to accord with or to avoid a given happening."

The *Book of Change* indicates that a man must not fight against the whirlpool when he is cast into it, but must *move with it* to survive. By continuing in what the *I Ching* calls the "course of righteous persistence"—one that harms no one and is in the public good—a person will eventually find his reward in this life rather than the next.

People's search for something to put them in touch with the rhythm and nature of the universe was in progress long before the *I Ching* was written. More than 5000 years ago in Mesopotamia, men and women sought signs of the future above their heads in the stars, or beneath their hands in the intestines of dead animals. Astrology was born in the Mesopotamian city of Babylon. Living in secluded monasteries near especially built high towers, Babylonian priests discovered five other planets besides the Earth, Sun, and Moon. Without the aid of telescopes, but with the blessing of unusually clear and cloudless skies, they succeeded in plotting the "workings of the heavenly spheres." These they related to the plagues, fires, earthquakes, and famines that beset the world. They asserted that everything was subject to the same set of celestial laws, and they drew up the first zodiac based on universal application of such laws. This zodiac was split into twelve parts in accordance with the number of lunar cycles in a year. Astrology replaced to some degree the Babylonian fortune-telling method called *hepatoscopy*, or inspection of the liver. According to the Babylonians, the liver of a man or a sheep was the "seat of life," and the coils and turns of a sheep's entrails contained messages about the future. The priests made clay models and tablets of livers and intestines, and said that these were the "prophetic books" of the gods.

Although astrology grew rapidly in popularity, hepatoscopy stayed in fashion until around 2000 B.C. At that time, reading the future from the liver lost favor because of the deduction by scholars that the heart was the true seat of life.

Astrology went from Babylonia to China and the Far East by way of the well-traveled smugglers' route of ancient days. However, the Chinese used a different set of stars and terms, and, instead of the zodiac, developed the Lo King. The Lo King is in the form of a disk on which there are six circles. These show the stars, the planets, and groups of other symbols. Providing the exact hour of birth was known, the disk could tell a person everything that would happen to him on earth and in the world to come. Besides being helpful to a ruler during his reign, the disk was invaluable in deciding exactly when he should be buried in order to flourish in afterlife. Marco Polo, the Venetian who spent many years in China during the 13th century, wrote of the Lo King: "I observed that when a Prince or great leader died, the magic disk was consulted as to whether the planets which governed his birth were in the ascendant. If they were, he would be buried without delay. If they were not, it was no uncommon thing for the corpse to remain unburied for up to six months before it was finally cremated or put in the ground. It all depended on the heavens and what they told."

The Greeks showed an interest in the stars later than the Chinese and the Babylonian innovators. For many years, the favored method of fortune telling in Greece was *cleromancy*, or divination by drawing lots. This simple system was widespread and important—even the all-wise oracle at Delphi was known to have a supply of beans used as lots. In seeking a glimpse of his future by cleromancy, an ancient Greek had to ask only questions that could be answered "yes" or "no." He would write this question on a strip of lead, which was then put into a jar containing black and white beans. The strip of lead was drawn out together with a bean, and the question on the strip was answered yes or no according to the color of the bean that accompanied it.

In their great desire to look into the future—a trait that seems to be common to humanity throughout history—the ancient Greeks grew dissatisfied with the simple system of lots, and developed the more sophisticated oracles. The oracles spoke only from certain temples throughout the country, the one at Delphi being supreme. They limited their appearance to once a month, and charged an extremely high fee for their services. Yet their influence was great, because they were often consulted by political leaders on questions of state.

The oracle was usually a young woman of common rank, said to have powers of prophecy and, therefore, known as a sibyl. The all-important sibyl at Delphi was called Pythia. In giving her prophecies, the oracle went into a trance during which she was the medium for messages from the gods—

Above: this illustration for Dante's *Inferno* was done in 15th-century Italy. It shows fortune tellers in hell with their heads twisted so that they look only backward all the time. This is their eternal punishment because, in life, they dared to assume the power of God by trying to see into the future.

principally Apollo. Her answers were so garbled and riddle-like that they had to be interpreted by a priest. This added to the mystery and solemnity of the occasion. Later, when Pythia spoke directly, some of her magic seemed lost.

The rising influence of consecutive philosophers such as Pythagoras, Plato, and Aristotle helped swing the Greeks away from the oracles and toward astrology. Aristotle, who was an avid student of astrology, declared that the earth was governed by the motions of a "far superior world."

To later Christians, there was a particularly striking instance of astrological power in the pages of the New Testament: it was a brightly shining star that led the three wise men to the newborn Jesus. The star they followed belonged to a constellation now known as Cassiopeia—the Woman and Child—from the Greek. Babylonians knew this constellation to preside over Palestine and Syria. Babylonian astrologers had also observed that the most prominent star of the constellation could only be seen once every 300 years—and then only when a future king had been born in Palestine.

From the Christian era on, astrology established itself among the main methods of fortune telling. One of the first big attacks against it came around the beginning of the 18th century from the caustic pen of satirist Jonathan Swift. Known for his biting comment against all he disliked, Swift was particularly opposed to "the bogus art of star-reading." In 1707, an almanac writer known as "Partridge" published his predictions for the year, and Swift was wildly incensed by Partridge's warning against the "outpourings of imposters."

Taking up his pen and, according to a colleague, "dipping it in vitriol," Swift quickly composed his own *Predictions for the year 1798, by Isaac Bickerstaff. Written to prevent the people of England from being further imposed on by vulgar Almanack Makers.* After supposedly studying the heavens, Bickerstaff

The Attack on Astrology

Left: this fantastic depiction of the universe was done in 16th-century Germany in the form of a woodcut. In it, a person has crawled through the rim of the universe, and has discovered the control mechanism for the stars.

(Swift) came out with some startling prophecies, including the imminent death of Partridge. "My first prediction is . . . to show how ignorant those sottish pretenders to astrology are in their own concerns: it relates to Partridge the almanac-maker. I have consulted the star of his nativity by my own rules," claimed Swift, "and find that he will infallibly die upon the 29th of March next, about 11 at night, of a raging fever." The fact that Partridge was still alive on March 30 was of no consequence to the "all-knowing, all-seeing" Swift. Again as Bickerstaff, he produced another pamphlet, *An Account of the death of Mr. Partridge, the Almanack Maker, upon the 29th instant in a letter from a Revenue Officer to a Person of Honour.*

To no avail did Partridge write or give denials of his death. He was stopped in the street by straight-faced wits who asked to be reimbursed for money they had contributed toward his coffin. An official of his parish church sent him a number of notes requesting that he "be a good fellow and come and be buried with the rest of the dead." The publishers of his almanac, the Stationers' Company, did him the worst injury of all: they marked him in their ledgers as "deceased," and refused to accept any further commissions from him! The unfortunate Partridge was forced at last to advertise in the newspapers that he was "not only now alive, but he was also alive on the 29th of March in question."

It was several years before Partridge managed to get his predictions printed again, but we do not know whether he ever managed to live down Swift's hoax—or whether he foresaw his own real death-date, just seven years later, in 1715.

As for Isaac Bickerstaff, his farcical "Predictions" continued to be taken seriously. The Inquisition in Portugal burned the Predictions because, beside forecasting the death of Partridge, they also pretended to forecast many disastrous events on the continent—including the death of King Louis XIV of France.

Below: 18th-century satirist Jonathan Swift attacked astrology by attacking an astrologer named Partridge. This woodcut of the period shows Swift—under the pseudonym of Bickerstaff—matching reason against superstition.

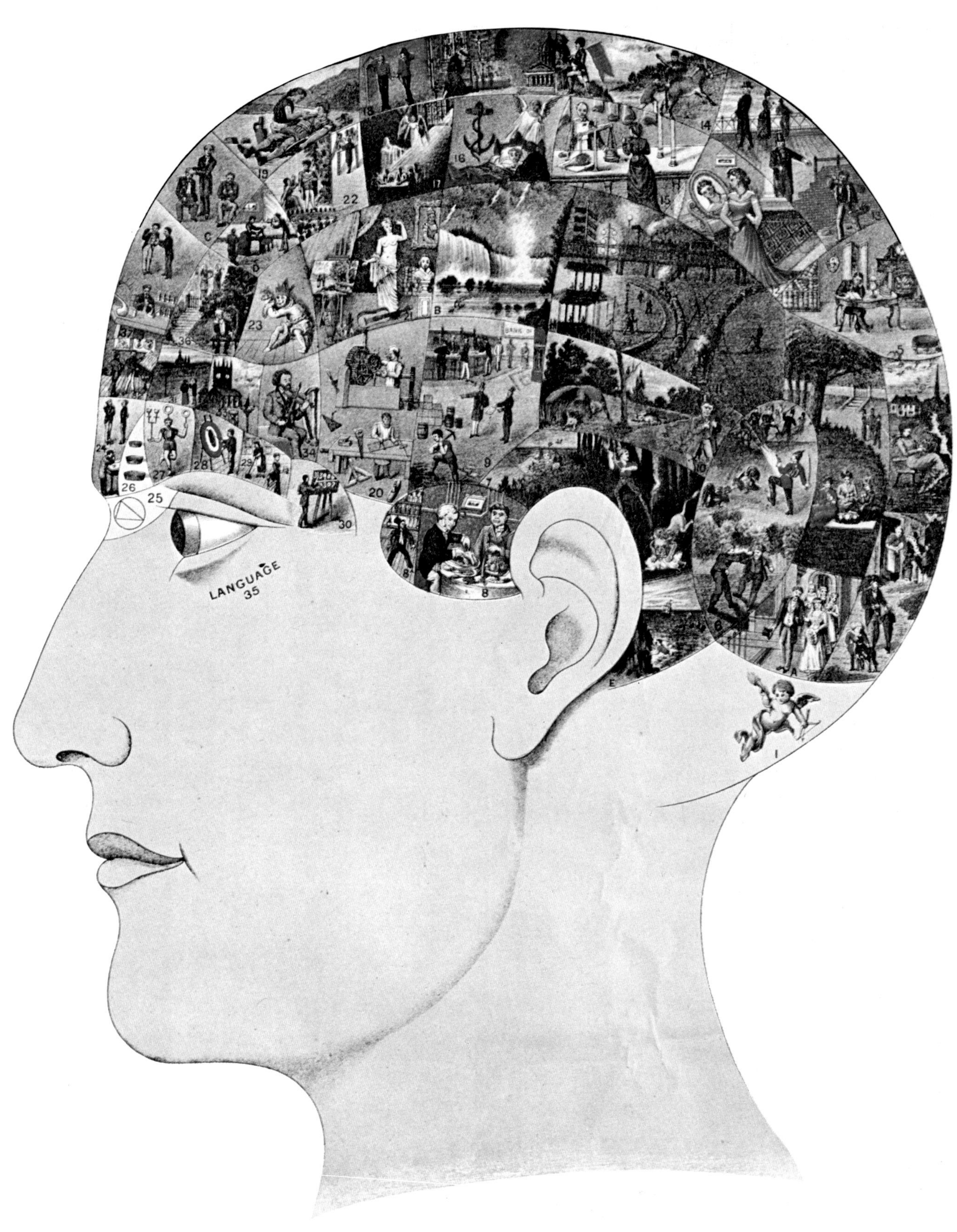
LANGUAGE
35

Chapter 4
What the Body Tells

We all tend to judge one another by appearance—but is it possible to read a person's character and future from his or her face? The demonstrated abilities of skilled men like Cheiro, the celebrated palmist, suggest that we carry in our hands a picture of our strengths and weaknesses, and a prediction of what our future may be. Other men theorized that the configuration of features on the face held an insight into character and likely fate, or that the bumps on the head were significant for an analysis of a person's potential. Is there any truth in these suggestions? How is it that palmists are so often proved right?

On a bright sunny morning in July 1894, the palmist Cheiro—whose clients were to include King Edward VII of England, the humorist and writer Mark Twain, the spy Mata Hari, and the film stars Lillian Gish and Mary Pickford—strode briskly through London's Whitehall on his way to the War Office. He had been summoned there by one of the most renowned soldiers in the British Army, Horatio Kitchener. Cheiro passed through the gloomy but imposing entrance, and was directed to a large, mahogany-paneled office on the first floor. There Kitchener stood nervously waiting, his hands clasped behind his back. He showed Cheiro to a chair, and, after a few moments of casual conversation, he leaned forward abruptly. He paused, fingered his full moustache, and said haltingly: "I want you to tell me about my future. There's something worrying me and I don't know what it is. Do you think you could put my mind at rest?"

By observing Kitchener's physique and bearing, and by noting his inability to remain still, Cheiro had already decided that here was a man of limitless courage and determination. But this man was also in danger of being undermined by something he probably loathed to believe in—Fate. The palmist then asked his client to put out his right hand, the one by which the future could be foretold. After studying it for some minutes, Cheiro raised his head and said quietly: "I can see nothing but success and honors for you in the next two decades. You will become one of the most illustrious men in the land, in the world indeed.

Opposite: phrenology enjoyed a great vogue in Europe and America in the 19th century, and was the most popular of all the psychic arts at one point. Early phrenologists classified the bumps on the head into 26 divisions, and read character according to how well or how poorly the bumps were developed. For example, a large bulge at the area marked 1 on this chart would signify a sensual nature, and an underdeveloped one would mean coldness. This detailed phrenological chart is of a period when 40 classifications were listed.

Kitchener's Hand Revealed his Fate

But after that your life is at great risk. I see a disaster at sea taking place in your 66th year. It does not, however, mean that you will necessarily die. If you do not travel on water in the year 1916, you will live to reap even more fame and riches."

At the time, Kitchener was aged 44, and, as Cheiro predicted, his major military achievements lay ahead of him. Four years later he captured Khartum. Then he distinguished himself in South Africa against the Boers. Then, at the outbreak of World War I, he was appointed Britain's War Minister. In 1916—and now Lord Kitchener—he was invited to visit Russia by the Czar to discuss Russia's role against Germany. Ignoring Cheiro's warning, and thinking only of the Allied cause, the minister sailed from a naval base in the North of Scotland, bound for the Russian port of Archangel. The cruiser carrying him—the *H.M.S. Hampshire*—was still in British waters when, at 7:40 p.m. on June 5, she struck a German mine and went down with the loss of most of her hands. Kitchener, who was in the

Above: Lord Kitchener had been warned not to travel by sea in his 66th year—when he drowned.

Right: Lord Kitchener was one of those drowned when the armored cruiser *H.M.S. Hampshire* was sunk by German mines in World War I. Cheiro had predicted this untimely end in the 1894 reading.

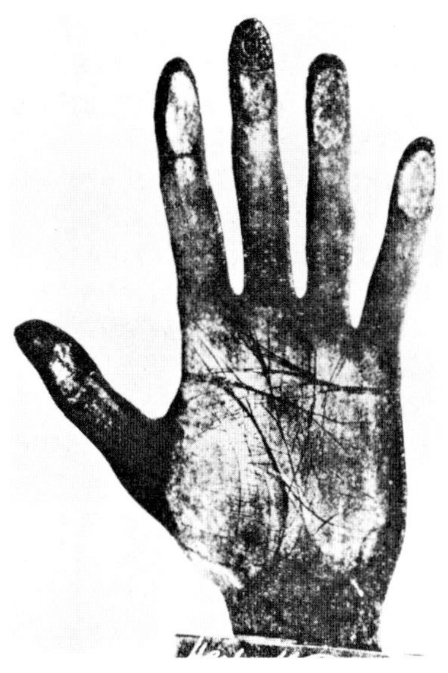

Far left: this hand print, described by the expert palmist Cheiro as showing an artistic bent, belonged to military leader Lord Kitchener—who, in fact, was an ardent student of literature, languages, and music. However, the lines also indicate the level-headedness and practicality that must have contributed to his army career. The impression was made in 1894 when Lord Kitchener, at the age of 44, was already widely known.

Left: Cheiro, whose real name was Count Louis Hamon, did much to make palmistry popular by his often reprinted books. Many of his clients were rich and famous.

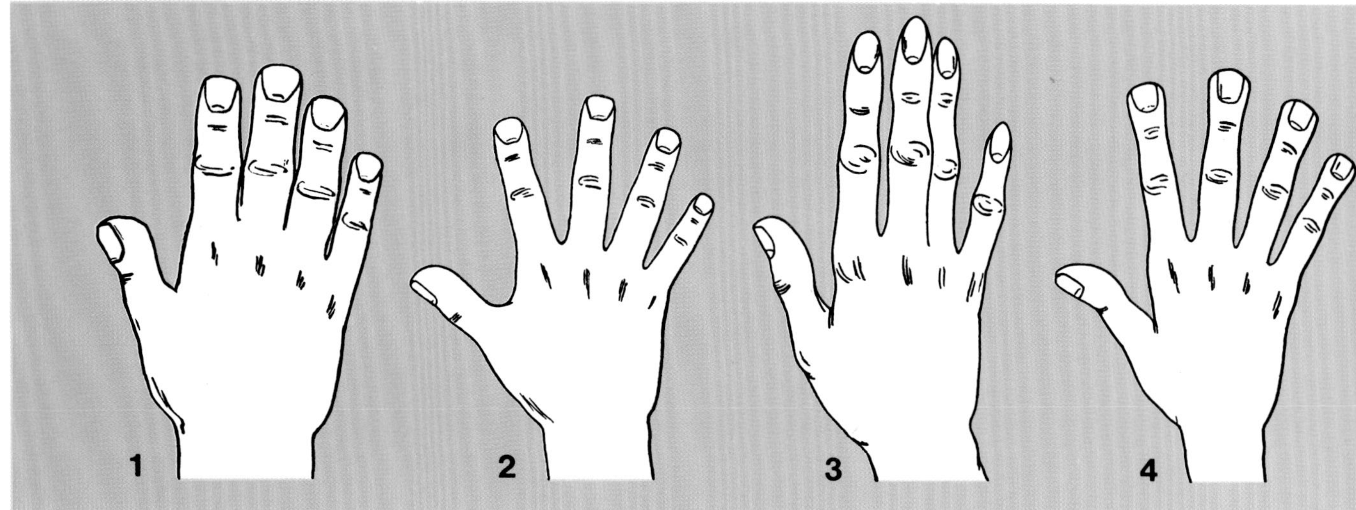

What Shape Is Your Hand?

What shape is your hand? These drawings appear in Cheiro's book *You and Your Hand* to illustrate the seven types of hands.
1 *The elementary hand* is short and thick, with stubby fingers and heavy palm. It indicates a slow thinker of stolid nature who is guided by his instincts.
2 *The square hand* is just that—clearly square in palm, base of fingers, and fingertips. It tells of a person who is level-headed, and very good in business.
3 *The philosophic hand* is long and angular with pronounced joints on long fingers. This type of hand denotes the deep thinker who may be hard to understand, and who is sensitive and dignified.
4 *The spatulate hand* has broad, flat fingertips, and a palm that is much broader at one end—either at the wrist or under the fingers. It points to energy, unconventionality, inventiveness, and love of action. Its possessor will be independent and original in anything he or she undertakes to do.
5 *The conic or artistic hand* is full and well shaped, either conic or round and with rounded, tapering fingers. Those with this hand love all things artistic, even if they are not creators of art. They are good conversationalists, at ease with strangers, and generous in money matters.

gunroom when the explosion sounded, disappeared into the Atlantic. His body was never found. Later, Cheiro gave his own account of his interview with the dead Field Marshal, stating: "The Line of Life gave the expectation of a long life under ordinary conditions, but my prediction . . . was based on the cross at the end of the travel line opposite the age of 66."

Cheiro, who was born Count Louis Hamon in Ireland in 1866, and took his name from the Greek word *cheir*—meaning hand—is still considered one of the leading authorities on palmistry. In making his reading for Kitchener, Cheiro followed the time-honored and basic rules of palmistry—which must be applied whether the reading is given in a tent, an office, or the privacy of one's home. He asked Kitchener no personal questions, but quickly turned to studying the client's right hand. (The left hand gives signs of a sitter's disposition and character.) Before examining the lines, however, he categorized the whole hand as one of seven main classes created by the French palmist Casimir D'Arpentigny: (1) elementary hands, with the short thumb and short thick fingers that indicate a manual worker rather than a thinker; (2) square hands, medium size and with strong well-developed fingers that speak of practicality, precision, moderation, and perseverance; (3) philosophical hands, with large thumb and palm, and knotty finger joints which reveal someone decisive and unemotional, who prefers reason to faith, logic to idealism, and who criticizes himself before others; (4) spatulate hands, shaped like a spade and with flat fingers, which show that the person is optimistic, self-confident, intelligent, and likely to rise to the top; (5) artistic hands that are pliable and have a delicate thumb and long tapering fingers, such as point to the poet, the artist, the musician; (6) psychic

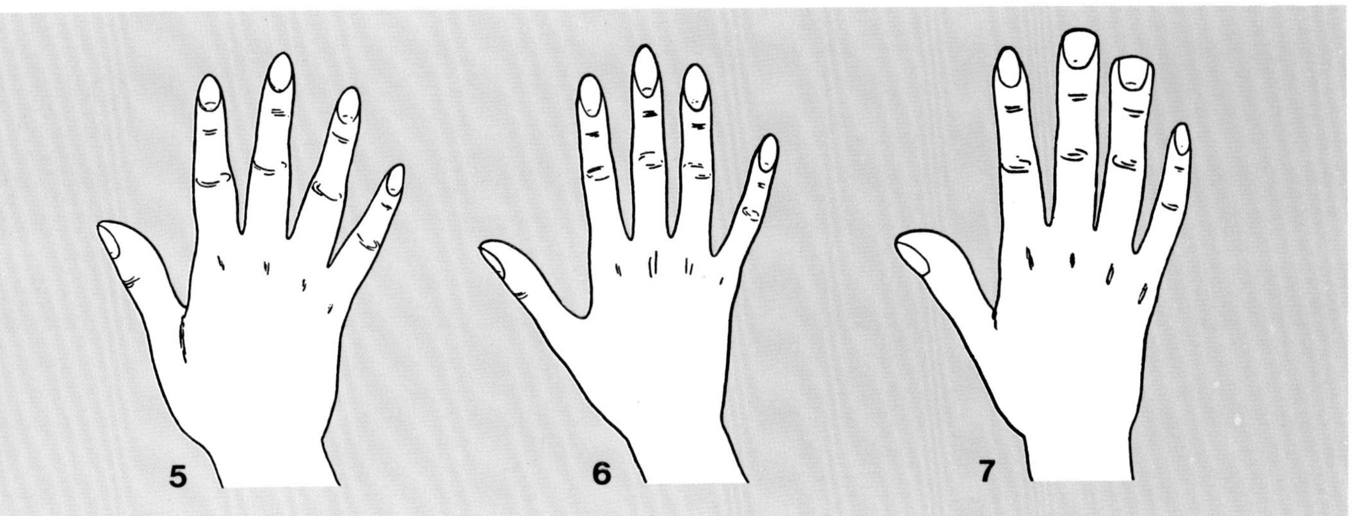

hands, the outward sign of a "dreamy" person who loves beauty, and who would rather go to a lunchtime concert than spend the money on lunch itself; (7) mixed hands, with fingers of different shapes, which bother the professional palmist, and confound the amateur.

Kitchener had mixed hands. The fact that he held them behind his back told Cheiro something else about the soldier: he was a cautious man who would painstakingly investigate a person or a situation before coming to any conclusion or decision. Had the soldier clasped his hands in front of him, it would have denoted dignity, calmness, and a slow-moving serenity. The most forbidding pose of all is when a subject lets his or her left hand dangle at the side, with the right hand level with the waistline, the palm uppermost, and the fingers partly clenched. Here is someone bloated with his own importance, who expects obedience and deference, and who feels that his opinions and wishes are the only ones that count.

After noting how a person holds his hands, Cheiro—or any budding palmist—would note the color of the hands, the texture of the skin, and the "feel" of the flesh. Pink and red hands tell of good health and energy. White hands are the opposite of this, while yellowish or sallow hands proclaim suspicion, irritability, bitterness, and the "blues." You don't need to be a Sherlock Holmes to realize that fine skin goes with refined natures, and that rough coarse skin points to the reverse. A palm that feels soft and offers no resistance belongs to someone who drifts uncaringly through life, and a palm that is firm reveals that its owner has a mature and rewarding balance between energy and rest. A hard palm that has no elasticity when pressed goes with the finger-clenching egotist—though

6 *The psychic hand* is long and slender, with tapering fingers and pointed tips. Its possessor is gentle, idealistic, and too easily deceived or imposed upon. It points to an unworldly person who is easily influenced and hurt.
7 *The mixed hand* has fingers from different types of hands, and no clearly classifiable shape. It shows great adaptability to work, people, and circumstances, but a lack of fixed purpose. One with this hand believes deeply in luck.

Left: the shape of the nail is an indicator of health. According to Cheiro, long wide nails (A, B) warn of lung weakness, and long narrow ones (C) of spinal weakness and general delicacy. Short nails of rounded shape (D, E, F) show a tendency for laryngitis, bronchitis, and general throat and nose ailments. Short broad nails (G, H, I) indicate bad circulation and heart trouble. Shell-shaped nails (J, K, L) point toward possibilities of paralysis.

Reading the Hand

Look at your hands. The line patterns, the mounds and valleys, the shape – each is wholly individual to you, and unlike anyone else's at all. It takes years of study and practice to read character from hands – and, perhaps, see the future. However, anyone can follow the major lines and features to get an idea of what you can see in the hand. This simplified guide is for beginners.

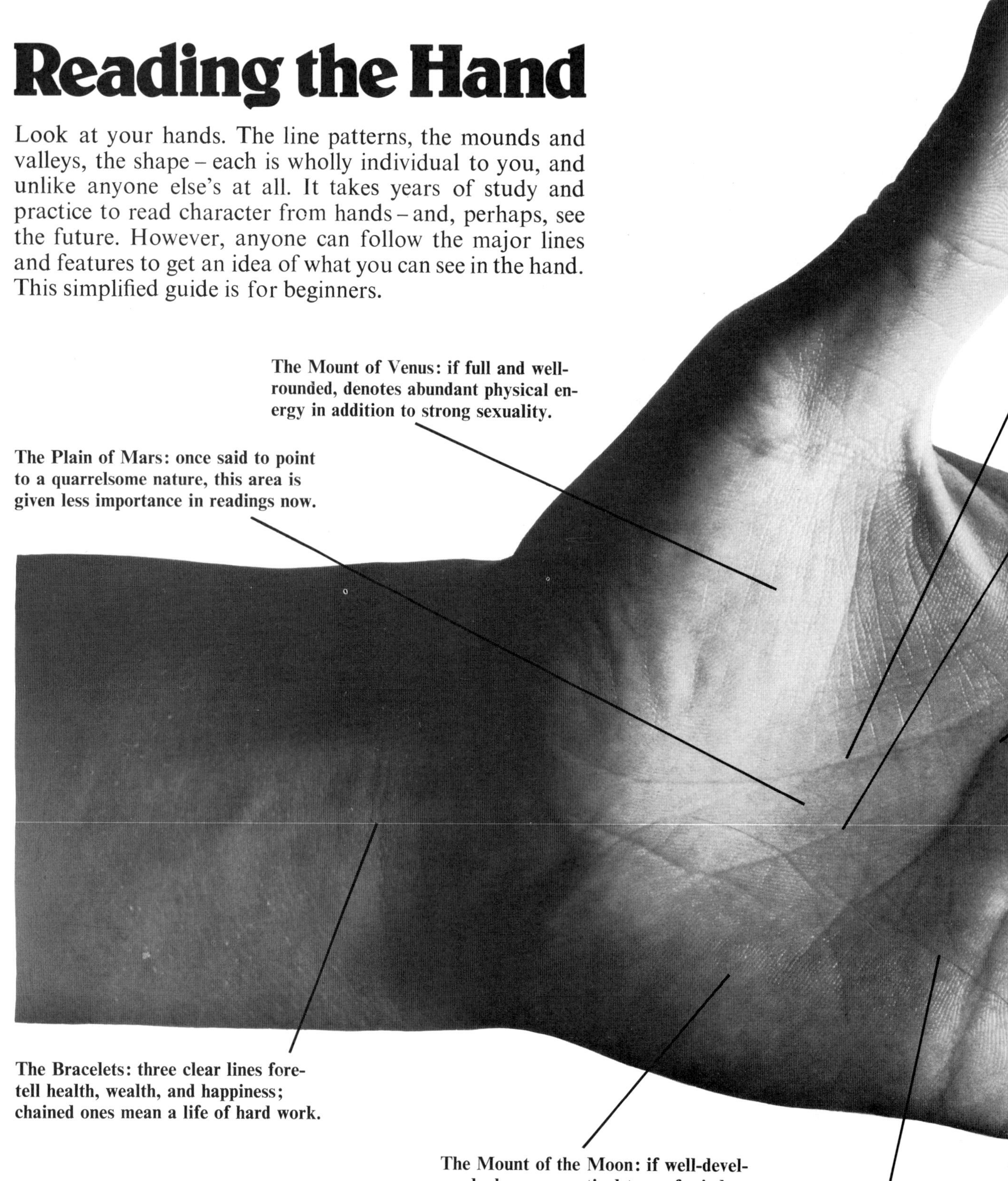

The Mount of Venus: if full and well-rounded, denotes abundant physical energy in addition to strong sexuality.

The Plain of Mars: once said to point to a quarrelsome nature, this area is given less importance in readings now.

The Bracelets: three clear lines foretell health, wealth, and happiness; chained ones mean a life of hard work.

The Mount of the Moon: if well-developed, shows a mystical turn of mind; if flat, it can indicate instability.

The Line of Intuition: points to intuitiveness. If present, and if strong, may denote possible psychic abilities.

The Life Line: shows physical vitality and pattern of life rather than length of life. A long, strong line indicates balance and stability; a chained or weak line can point to indecisiveness.

The Fate Line: indicates state of personality balance. Not on all hands, but if there, a strong line denotes a well-developed ego; a weak or broken line can mean a tendency to self-doubt.

The Heart Line: tells about emotions. A straight line points to strong independence; a line curving toward the index fingers shows a loving nature; a drooping line can mean insecurity.

The Head Line: shows intellectual and career tendencies. A straight, clear, and even line denotes practicality and reasoning powers. A gracefully curved one indicates an imaginative nature.

Finger of Jupiter (index): a long one means success; one shorter than the third finger may mean insecurity.

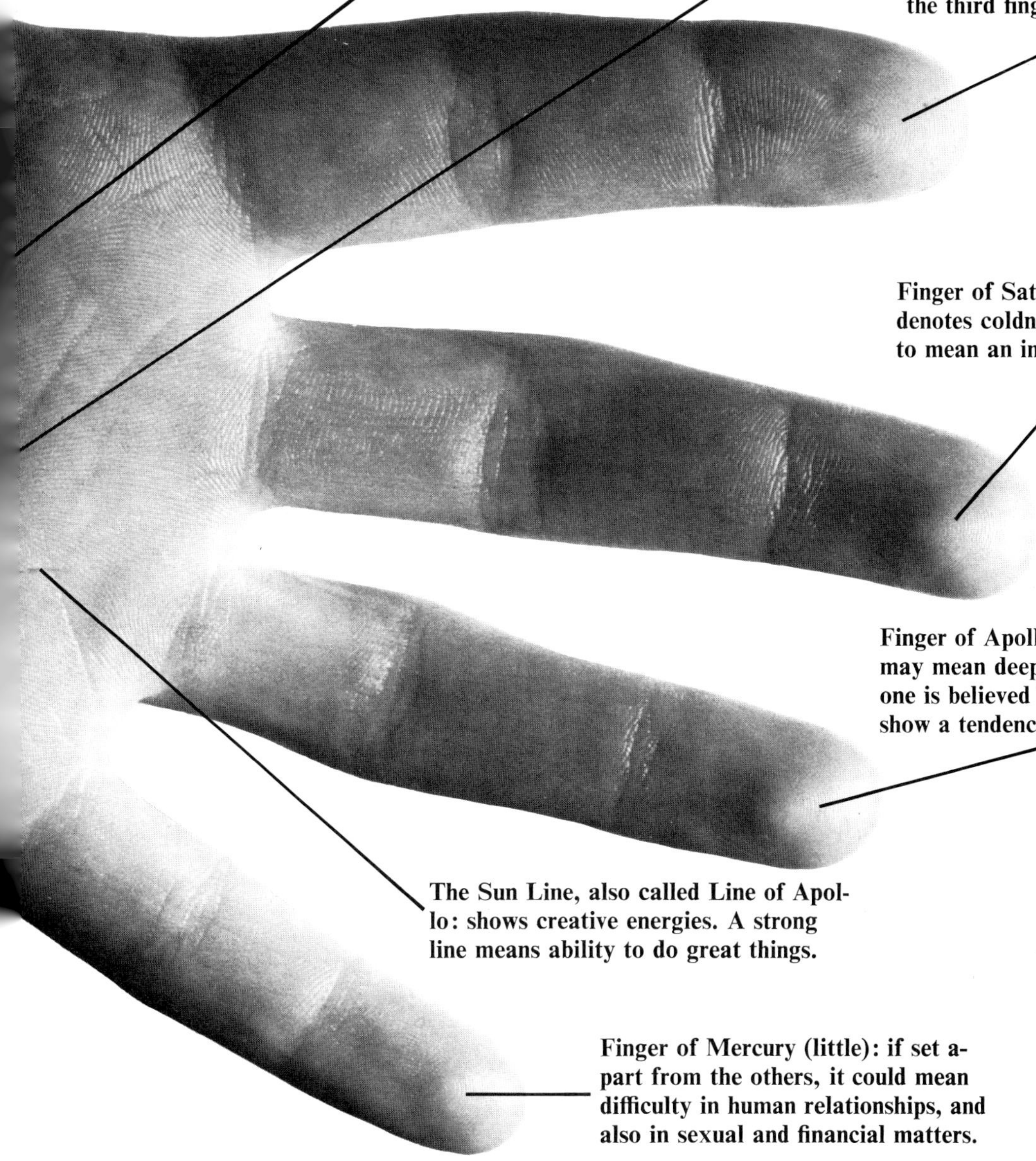

Finger of Saturn (middle): a long one denotes coldness; a short one is said to mean an intuitive, creative nature.

Finger of Apollo (ring): a long one may mean deep introversion; a crooked one is believed by some palmists to show a tendency to get heart disease.

The Sun Line, also called Line of Apollo: shows creative energies. A strong line means ability to do great things.

Finger of Mercury (little): if set apart from the others, it could mean difficulty in human relationships, and also in sexual and financial matters.

"Trafficking with the Devil..."

when both traits are present, the indication is that the person may have boundless resource and drive, but no proper direction. The length of fingers is also of significance, as is the shape of the nails (see diagram on pages 54–5). For example, long nails go with even-tempered people who are slow to anger; short nails with fault-finders and those fond of arguments; oval nails with those who feel sorry for themselves and have little push; round nails with those having fiery but usually short-lived passions; and square nails with disciplinarians and lovers of order.

It was the thumb, however, that most impressed Cheiro and his fellow palmists. "Know the thumb and you know the man," they said. They point out that, while the lines a person is born with are like so many finely traced roads along which a person will travel, it is the thumb that acts as the signpost. The fingers are no more than milestones along the path of life. Whatever qualities, characteristics, talents, inclinations, or skills someone has, it is the thumb that tells whether or not he or she will put them to full or only partial use. The thumb also tells whether an individual is likely to rush toward the danger that may await him, or if he will be more prudent, less hasty, and so avoid or minimize the lurking threat. Generally, the larger the thumb and the heavier its tip, the better it is for its owner. It is even more auspicious if the thumb joins the hand low instead of high. Thus, small thin-tipped thumbs set high on the hand are likely to be possessed by those who are lacking leadership, judgment, and will power, and whose uncontrollable emotions will lead them into trouble, misery, and pain.

When Cheiro was at the peak of his influence and fame, he was the first to admit and emphasize that the art of palmistry was one of the most contradictory ways of forecasting the future. "Just as no two painters use exactly the same technique, so no two palmists use the same methods, or even come to the same conclusions," he said. "I wrote my first book on palmistry when I was 12, and since then I have been astounded—if not dismayed—by the many ways in which both my predecessors and my contemporaries—to say nothing of my successors—have differed from me both in working methods and in interpreting what is contained in the hand."

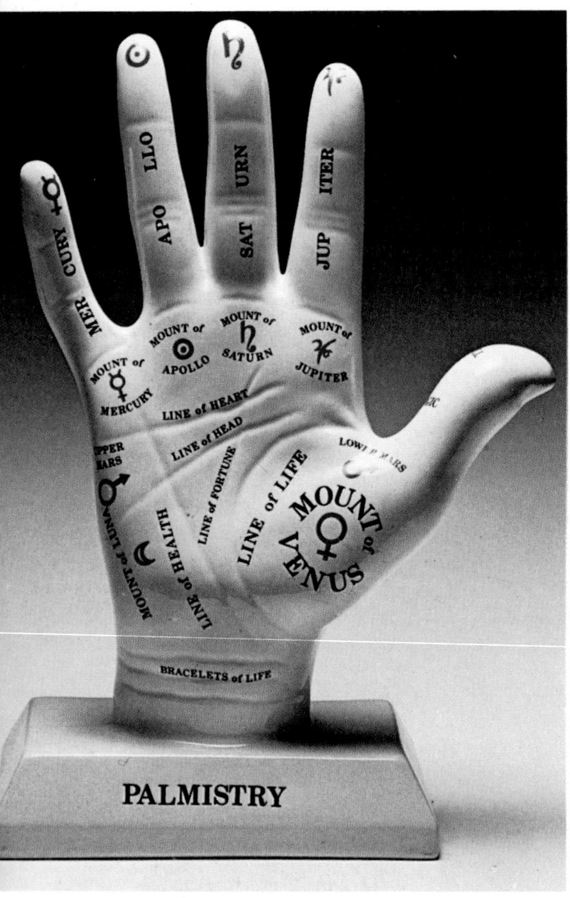

Above: this model of a palm shows the names of the lines and areas to be read in character analysis.

Apart from a reading made directly—which, ideally, should take place in a comfortable and relaxed atmosphere with good light—it is possible to make an imprint of a person's hand, and take it away for further study. Cheiro—who had a collection of 60,000 such prints—did this in the case of Lord Kitchener, bringing with him to the War Office some sheets of glossy paper, a rubber pad, a tube of fingerprint ink, and a roller of the type used by photographers. In making the hand print, the palmist pressed the hand firmly down so as to show fingers, tumb, palm, and "bracelets"—the three lines running across the wrists, which are favorable omens if clearly marked, and otherwise if not. He took prints of both hands.

Professionally, Cheiro was extremely fortunate. He was aware of this, and often told friends that, had he been practicing at certain times in the past, he would have been arrested and accused of "trafficking with the Devil." His knowledge of the

Above: since their appearance in Europe—probably about the 14th century—gypsies have been known for their fortune-telling skills. This early 17th-century painting shows a gentleman having his palm read.
Right: modern gypsies still practice palmistry as a way of earning money. Here they ply their traditional trade in Camargue, France.

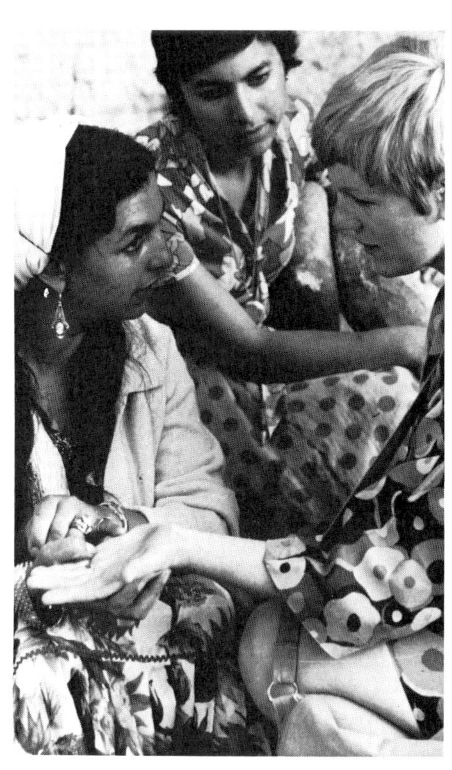

history of *chirognomy* (the telling of character from hands) and *chiromancy* (foretelling the future from hands) was extensive. In his research, he traced the related arts back to 1000 B.C., when mention of palmistry was made in the Vedic writings of ancient India. He also studied one of the "elevated and inquiring" books that the philosopher Aristotle wrote for his pupil Alexander, later Alexander the Great. According to the philosopher, it was based on an Arabic treatise he found "graven in letters of gold, upon an altar dedicated to Hermes [the messenger of the Gods]." The oldest palmistry manuscript known in England was the *Digby Roll IV*, dating back to 1440, and the first book to be published in Europe came some 35 years later with Johan Hartlieb's *Die Kunst Ciromantia (The Art of Chiromancy)*, printed in Augsburg after his death.

In the last decades of the 14th century, an Italian named Andreas Corvus made a name and a fortune for himself as a "practical palmist." He caused a sensation by his warning that a certain citizen of his native Bologna would commit a

Character Reading from Heads

"detestable murder" on September 24, 1504. The prophecy came true when that very person—either to oblige or out of malice—struck and killed Corvus himself on the day in question. An equally bizarre fate befell the palmist Tibertus Antiochus, who took Corvus's place. He predicted the violent death of a military adviser called Guerra. When asked how he himself would die, he answered: "It has been decreed from all eternity that I shall end my days on the scaffold." Sure enough, Guerra was stabbed to death by someone, and Antiochus, falsely accused of the crime, was sentenced to be hanged. Thus his prediction came true.

These macabre happenings led many people to keep their hands to themselves, and out of the way of palmists. A series of attacks was launched on those who made easy money—and made people uneasy—by reading palms, and wandering bands of gypsies were soon in the front line of fire. In 1530, King Henry VIII of England acted against "an outlandish people

Although J. K. Lavater did not succeed in his goal of making physiognomy an exact science, he gained fame for his skill in reading character from a person's appearance, especially the face. His book *Physiognomical Fragments* was published in the 1770s, and would be called a best seller in today's terms. In his book, Lavater gave these examples of how to read faces.
1 No strength of mind, shown most clearly in the area around the eyes. Also shows commonness.
2 None of the features point to strength of mind, but none can be pinpointed as showing weakness.
3 A resolute, industrious, and enterprising person, ready and able to undertake big projects.
4 The eyes and nose in particular tell of sincerity, frankness, and sensibility. A benevolent person.
5 There is something of the eager inquirer left in this face, but it has distorted and become gross.
6. Quick perception, charm, and grace. The forehead, eyebrow, and poetical eyes are the sure signs.
7 A terrifying face because the qualities of power, daring, and eloquence are void of grace.
8 The eyes denote a thinker; the nose, an accurate investigator; the mouth, eloquence.
9 A face of noble character, including sincerity, fortitude, humor, perseverance, harmony.
10 Understanding and originality mark the face of a poet. There is also tranquillity and taste.
11 Another person of poetic genius, but more vigorous than elegant. Strength, fidelity, and sweetness.
12 Lavater's face, on which he says: ". . . the commentary is before the world—in this book."

Above: this 19th-century English ceramic head shows the divisions of the brain as used for phrenological readings of people.

Above left: the 20th century seems to have a machine for everything. This mechanical device of 1907 was meant for use by phrenologists.

calling themselves Egyptians . . . who have come into this realm, and gone from shire to shire in great companies, and used great subtle and crafty means to deceive people, bearing them in hand that they, by palmistry, could tell men's and women's fortune, and so many times, by craft and subtlety, have deceived the people of their money and have also committed many heinous felonies and robberies." James I, when he came to the throne a century later, added his venom against the "devil dealers." In 1664, the English writer Richard Saunders warned his readers against palmists in London, stating, "(there) lurk in obscure corners, in and about this famous city, many illiterated pieces of nonsense and impudence . . ."

The odium in which palmists were held spread to France. There they were condemned by the Church, and it was stated that, "now no man professeth publicly this cheating art, but thieves, rogues, and beggarly rascals." Despite this, however, it was in France in the mid-18th century that the palmist Johann K. Lavater was most popular. A clergyman from Zurich, Lavater was also a *physiognomist*—one who reads character from faces. He anticipated the forensic science of fingerprinting when he announced that "the hands of man are equally diverse and dissimilar as their faces . . . just as it is impossible to find two faces perfectly alike, so it is impossible to find two people whose hands resemble each other perfectly."

His views were echoed by true scientists of the 19th century. These included the naturalist Charles Darwin, who wrote

Criminals and Physical Types

a study of the *Expression of the Emotions in Men and Animals*, and the Italian anthropologist Paolo Mantegazza, who concentrated on the difference between eyes, noses, and upper lips, and made them the basis of his "abbreviated portrait of all faces." He, and those who later carried on his work, divided the face into three sections: the forehead, the nose, and the area from the base of the nose to the point of the chin. In reading each of these divisions, he stated that the longer the forehead, the brainier the person; the longer the nose, the more energetic and forceful the person; the longer the mouth and chin, the more determined and dogged the person. From there he moved to the eyes—"the windows of the soul"—saying that large eyes denote someone eager and observant, while small eyes denote someone calculating and shrewd; wide-set eyes indicate someone reliable and trusting, and close-set eyes belong to a man or woman who is suspicious, cynical, and on the defensive.

To some extent, Mantegazza's work inspired the Italian criminologist Cesare Lombroso, who believed that criminals fell into definite physical types. These types included those possessing handle-shaped ears, outsize jaws, and high cheekbones. Taking such features into account, Lombroso said that he could predict who would become a thief or a forger. Along

Below: this 19th-century cartoon jokes about phrenology. As the lecturer whips off his wig to reveal the bumpiest head imaginable, the members of his audience register wonderment and awe.

with most palmists of the time, he believed that a potential killer could be spotted by his "murderer's thumb"—one with a bulbous nail-bearing joint. His work was much ridiculed, and Lombroso became embittered by failure.

Recently, American researchers have suggested a link between abnormal palm prints and congenital physical defects and disorders. They think it possible that the so-called "simian line"— in which the heart and head lines appear as one—and a broad Y-shape on the palm running from the wrist and branching out toward the index and little fingers, can be signs of mongolism or some other mental retardation.

In his final years, Lombroso turned to spiritualism for solace. In some ways, his career and fate paralleled that of the German physician Franz Joseph Gall, who was the founder of the system of *phrenology*—reading of character by bumps on the head. According to Gall, he was a schoolboy when he first noticed that the most outstanding scholars were those with "prominent eyes and, even more significantly, certain peculiarities in the shapes of their heads, the shapes caused by variations in the development of certain areas on the surface of the brain." On graduating from university, he spent several years visiting schools, prisons, and lunatic asylums, where he studied, felt, and

Character Shown in their Faces

J. K. Lavater, 18th-century pioneer of physiognamy, laid down exact rules for reading character from the face. Here are three of his interpretations: The face above reveals a despicable nature. Greed, craftiness, and viciousness are fully shown in the mouth, eyes, and facial contours.

This face shows up a cheat or con man, even though the pointed nose and chin indicate a winning personality. The long and wide forehead points to a deep thinker; but taken in all, the face is of an untrustworthy man.

The man with this face is a heavy drinker, and this is seen in every one of its features. The nose, the lips, the wrinkles—all suggest an "unquenchable thirst." There is a lack of energy in the look, and the whole face has been altered. It is puffy, wrinkled, and very ruddy.

The Mysterious Meaning of Moles

The study of moles for fortune telling takes into account the shape, color, and location of them on the body.

Round moles point to goodness of nature; angular ones stand for good and bad characteristics; oblong ones denote a degree of material well-being. Light moles are thought to indicate luck; black ones tell of difficulties to overcome before final success will be achieved.

Some of the meanings of moles by location are as follows:

Belly—a tendency to self-indulgence. Watch out for overeating, overdrinking, and overspending. Marry someone calm and understanding.

Buttocks—lack of ambition. The tendency is to accept whatever comes along, even if it's poverty.

Chin—a first-rate character and personality. A host of good qualities, such as generosity, lovingness, competence, responsibleness.

Finger—dishonesty. This comes mainly from an inclination to exaggerate because of inability to face reality.

measured hundreds of skulls. Calling his system a "scientific form of divination," he used his calipers to discover whether or not a subject had an "underdeveloped organ of benevolence" or an "overgrown organ of theft."

On one notable occasion, Gall received a box of skulls from a prison doctor, and selected one with abnormally wide temples. "My God"! he exclaimed, "this is the cranium of a thief"! His diagnosis was correct, and he might have made a name for himself. However, his system was abused by scores of quacks and charlatans who toured the salons and fairgrounds of central Europe. Gall himself was attacked and ridiculed by priests and fellow doctors. His lectures in Vienna were shouted down by his opponents, and, when he later settled in Paris, he again saw his new "science" mocked and ignored.

The English poet and mystic William Blake, who was of the same era as Gall, also believed that a person's face said what a person was. As a schoolboy of 13, Blake was taken by his father to see an engraver named Ryland. Leaving the engraver's premises, William turned to his father and said: "I don't like that man." "Why not?" asked his father. "His face," replied the boy, "looks as if he will yet be hanged." Twelve years later, in 1783, Ryland was hanged for forging banknotes, and for the rest of his life, Blake tended to judge people by their features and physical appearance. In this, he agreed with the essayist Joseph Addison that "a good face is a letter of introduction."

In the 19th century, the art of palmistry began to stage a comeback in Paris. Encouraged by the silence of royalty and the new and apparent broadmindedness of the clergy, a cluster of palmists appeared on the scene. They worked on the theory that each person "knows" his own future, whether he realizes it or not, and that the lines on his palms can help him get at this knowledge. So popular did they become that they had to turn clients away.

Prominent among this latest breed of fortune tellers was the stout and bespectacled Madame Adele Moreau, who announced that she would receive querants "every day except Sunday and Feast Days, between the hours of nine and six." For those who either couldn't gain entrance or come in person, she would "take consultations by post in the form of photographs and prints." Her autobiographical book about her career was a best seller, with its intimate and revealing accounts of the people—both famous and unknown—who came to her with problems that would have taxed a present-day psychiatrist.

Madame Moreau's male counterpart was the same Casimir D'Arpentigny who formulated the seven types of hands already described. He also designated two main classes of hands—the "smooth" and the "knotty." The hand with smooth fingers he found embodied "impressionability, caprice, spontaneity, and intuition, with a sort of momentary inspiration . . . and a faculty which gave the power of judging at first sight." It was invariably the sign of the artist. Compared with this, a hand with knotty fingers reflected "order, aptitude for number, and an appreciation of the exact sciences . . . mathematicians, agriculturists, architects, engineers, and navigators; all, in short, who were led to the application of acquired knowledge."

Signs on the Body

A hero of Napoleon's army before he retired at the age of 48, D'Arpentigny laid the foundations for those who were to bring palmistry into the 20th century, both in Great Britain and the USA. His findings and working methods were discussed throughout Europe, and it was written of them that: "As water falling drop by drop upon stones makes, in the course of time, a visible impression . . . so the mind, acting at every instant of time upon the plastic susceptibility of the hand, leaves ultimately signs which are accepted by the chiromancist as the visible records of the impulses emanating from the great nervous center."

In April 1889, the English Chirological Society came into being in London with the express purposes of, "firstly, raising the study of the hand to the level of scientific research; secondly, for promoting the study of Palmistry in all its branches; thirdly, as a safeguard to the public against charlatans and impostors." This was the climate in which Cheiro first opened his consulting room in England—although he soon found that "the hands of men of God" were turned against him.

"I had not been in London one month," he wrote, "before a Catholic priest refused to give absolution to an entire family because they had consulted me against his orders. In America, during my first year, I was visited by two clergymen, with the object of persuading me that my success was due alone to the agency of the devil. One went so far as to tell me that God had sent him to offer me a clergyship—at a small salary, of course—if I would only give up my relations with the Evil One."

Apart from his supposed association with the devil, Cheiro

Below: one of the less well-known psychic practices is the interpretation of lines on the forehead. It dates from the 16th-century.

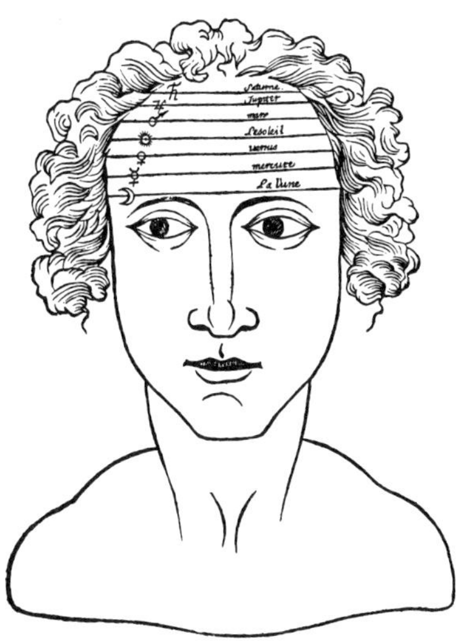

Left: a woman who laments about a mole on her face might be happier if she knew it could foretell good things—depending on its position. Instructions for telling fortunes from moles were usually included in the dream books of the late 19th century.

The Warning in Wilde's Hand

gained more ecclesiastical enemies by contending that biblical scholars had mistranslated the seventh verse of the 37th chapter of Job. In the accepted English version, it read: "God sealed up the hands of men that all men may know God's work." The palmist insisted that, in the original Hebrew, it went: "God placed signs and marks in the hands of all the sons of men that all men might know their works." Cheiro's version was accepted by his thousands of clients and disciples, who felt as he did that the Church was "too obstinate" to admit that forecasting the future by palmistry was divinely inspired. Another aspect of Cheiro's system dealt with the time at which changes would occur in a person's life. He based his system on the ancient Greeks, who, in their study of the hand, considered that a person did not enter into the "battle of life" until he was 21. Cheiro placed the period of 25-to-35 years of age as the critical one in the "struggle for existence." "It is in reality the foundation on which man builds for the following 35 years," he stated. "If he has not by the middle of his life done something to warrant his existence, it is not to be expected that he would make much out of the remaining half."

In his first season in London, Cheiro was asked to read hands from behind curtains as a test of his skills. Unable to see the subject's face or general appearance, he was still able to make predictions that sometimes startled the client, and even shook society. Such was the case on the day he was invited to a large reception and asked to read "a somewhat soft and flabby" pair of hands without seeing or knowing who their owner was. "You are a famous man," said the palmist after studying the hands, "and are at the very height of your success now. However, your Lines of Fate and Success are broken just seven years further on. You must beware of taking any precipitate action then. If you do it will be the ruin of you." At this the client—the Irish playwright Oscar Wilde—pulled his hands away and

Below: Cheiro's consulting room was richly furnished, and had the atmosphere of the occult about it.

said gravely to the assembled guests: "Cheiro may be right. As fate keeps no road-menders on her highways—*Che Sara Sata*—what is to be, will be." Seven years and two trials later, Wilde was imprisoned for homosexuality after a notorious legal battle. "This otherwise clever man," said Cheiro of Wilde, "could not realize that the 'road-mender' was in himself. He made no change in his habits, and so he went headlong to his doom."

Throughout his long and prosperous career, Cheiro repeatedly said that actually seeing into the future was only one, and perhaps not even the most significant, aspect of divination. Most important was what a person did or did not do when coming events were revealed to him. For, said Cheiro, although the event itself may be predestined, its effects were not, and it was in the power of the individual to make its effects either beneficial or harmful. As Cheiro typically and dramatically put it in his book *You and Your Hand*:

"An engine driver may receive a warning in advance that a broken bridge some 10 or 20 miles ahead spells catastrophe for himself and the train he is driving. If he is a sensible man he will accept the warning—wait for the bridge to be repaired—and so save his life and the lives of others. If, on the contrary, he is too stupid or headstrong to be guided by the knowledge he has gained he will dash on to destruction . . . In all such cases the 'broken bridge' might have been repaired—but those terrible words 'too late' too often turn life into a tragedy instead of the beautiful creation it might have been."

Like many others in his field, Cheiro was intrigued by the study of murder, especially of deciding which person was likely in the "right circumstances" to kill, and which person was not. "The fact that one man kills another in a fit of uncontrollable passion or blind fury," he wrote in *You and Your Hand*, "is no more or less an accident that may occur to anyone who has not cultivated self-control. In such cases the Head Line is generally short and coarse-looking, with a brutal looking thumb . . . There is, however, another class of murderer—that of the brooding, melancholy type. In this class the Head Line is generally shown in a kind of jumble of Head and Heart Lines with a sloping line from this formation to, or toward, the Mount of Luna. In this case the man would brood for years over some real or fancied wrong, generally proceeding in some way from the affections. Examples may be read in the newspapers almost every day of men who murder their wives and sometimes their entire family. From the standpoint of study, the most interesting class of murderer is the poisoner. Here calculation, patience, caution, intelligence all play their role. In consequence, the Line of Head would naturally be expected to be long, finely marked, and connected with the Life Line to give it extreme caution."

The infamous Doctor Crippen, who poisoned his wife and dismembered her body in their North London home, was a clear example of the second kind of killer. Cheiro—who was also a numerologist—worked out a complicated chart which showed that the numbers 4 and 8 had proved fatal to Crippen. He was born in 1862, which adds up to 17, which in turn

Above: Oscar Wilde was the subject of a test for Cheiro, who, at a society party, was challenged to read the famous writer's hand from behind a curtain. If Wilde had listened to the palmist's warning of ruin from "precipitate action" in seven years' time, he might have saved himself from imprisonment and public scorn.

Left: this is the hand print of one of history's best-known women spies—Mata Hari. It shows where her life line was crossed and cut in her 37th year—when she died. Cheiro made this imprint of her hand 17 years before she was executed for spying by the French.

Right: Mata Hari wore a skimpy costume when she did what she called a Javanese dance. She performed at private parties where she met the rich and influential men of Paris. Her real name was Lady Cresta Macleod.

ultimately adds up to 8; he killed his wife on the 31st (4); her mutilated remains were discovered in his cellar on the 13th (4); and while trying to escape, he used the name Robinson (8 letters). He was recognized and arrested aboard the ship *Montrose* (8 letters) on the 22nd (4), and was brought back to England on the *Megantic* (8 letters). Crippen's formal arrest took place on the 31st (4), his trial ended on the 22nd (4), and he was hanged when he was 48 years old.

Cheiro was not personally involved in the Crippen case, so it took another murder case to bring the palmist to the notice of the public. This was the case of the killer physician, Dr. Meyer. Impressions of Meyer's hands were given to Cheiro during his first visit to New York, when reporters from the *New York World* sought to test his powers. Without knowing whose prints they were, or anything about Meyer, Cheiro stated: "Whether this man has committed one crime or 20 is not the question. As he enters his 44th year he will be tried for murder and condemned to death. It will then be found that for years he has used his intelligence and whatever profession he has followed to obtain money by crime, and has stopped at nothing to achieve his ends. He will be sentenced to death, yet his hands show his life will not end in this manner. He will live for years—but in prison."

Meyer, who was then 44, had at that very time less than a week to go before he was to be strapped into the electric chair in Sing-Sing prison. One of his last requests was to speak to the celebrated palmist, and Cheiro obligingly went up to the jail. There he met the "completely broken" man, who gasped: "For God's sake, tell me if you stand by your words that I shall escape the chair." Cheiro calmed the condemned man down, telling him that his Line of Life went on "clear and distinct" well past his 44th year, and that it showed no sign of a break. With that, Cheiro returned to his hotel.

"Day after day went past," he recorded in his last book *You and Your Hand*, "with no news to relieve the tension. The evening papers, full of details of the preparations for the execution fixed for the next morning, were eagerly bought up. I bought one and read every line. Midnight came. Suddenly boys rushed through the streets screaming 'special edition.' I read across the front page, 'Meyer escapes the chair. Supreme Court finds flaw in indictment.' The miracle had happened—the sentence was altered to imprisonment for life. Meyer lived on for 15 years. When the end did come, he died peacefully in the prison hospital."

As with all forms of fortune telling, palmistry is concerned with death—how, when, and where one will die. It is a question that is frequently asked, and infrequently answered. The majority of palmists know the danger of revealing such information to a client, especially if the person is nervous or emotional. Subconsciously, such a querant may bring about his or her own doom by behaving in a rash or suicidal way. "In such instances," said Cheiro, "it is better to remain silent, and to risk being called a fool or a fraud. The most important quality a responsible palmist can have is humility, the humility to know when it is kinder and more Christian not to speak."

His Palm Said He Wouldn't Die

Below: this is the hand print of Dr. Meyer, a notorious poisoner. Cheiro read it without knowing who it belonged to, and, because the life line was unbroken at that given point, predicted that its owner would not be put to death. Cheiro was right: Dr. Meyer was pardoned at the eleventh hour.

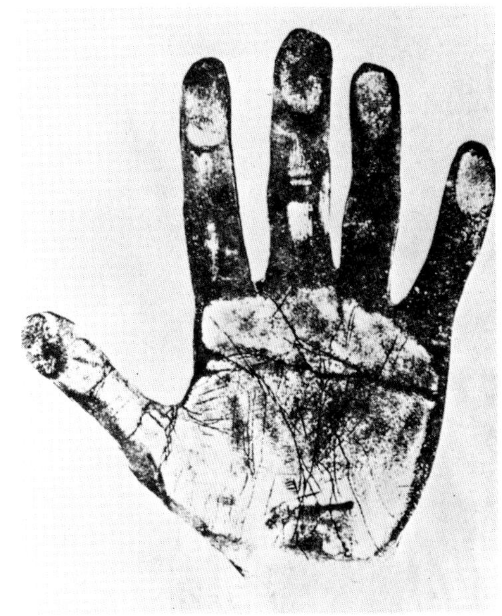

XIII
TROMPS
נ Death ♏

Chapter 5 Revealing the Tarot's Secrets

Is it possible to tell the future from the cards? What is the mysterious origin of the Tarot deck, with its strange picture cards carrying memorable titles: the Fool, the Wheel of Fortune, the Hanged Man? Some have claimed that the Tarot deck came from ancient Egypt. Others say that the gypsies invented them early in the Middle Ages. The Tarot cards appear to capture the imagination as effectively now, with their apparent power to show the future and answer the innermost questions of the querant's heart. How can the cards be used to interpret the unfolding of fate?

Opposite: in this modern version of the Tarot death card, a skeleton does a whirlwind dance while brandishing a scythe. It was designed by Aleister Crowley, one of the most colorful occult figures of the 20th century. Crowley believed that the Tarot dated from ancient Egypt, a theory he explained and defended in his last work, *The book of Thoth*.

Two hours before attempting to beat his own world record, British motorboat racer Donald Campbell decided to tell his fortune by the cards. He shuffled a pack and drew two cards that made him grow pale and shake his head—the Ace and the Queen of Spades. "These are the same cards that Mary Queen of Scots turned over on the night before her execution," he told watching friends. "I think that someone in my family will die soon." This scene took place on the morning of January 4, 1967. Those present were horrified when, a short time later, Campbell's jet speedboat *Bluebird* reared up on her tail while skimming over Coniston Water in the English Lake District, and turned a back somersault at almost 300 miles per hour. The boat plunged 140 feet to the bottom of the lake, and, although Royal Navy divers later brought up sections of the hull, Campbell's body was not recovered. "If he'd heeded the cards," one of his friends said later, "he would be alive now." A superstitious person for most of his life, Campbell read cards much as others read the daily newspaper. He believed that the future could be seen in them. What he probably didn't realize was that the ordinary pack of 52 playing cards he used was based on the 78 cards of the Tarot, a set of mystical cards hundreds— perhaps thousands—of years old.

Although the origin of the Tarot has never been fully explained, the colorful cards have a long history. One of the earliest proven dates of their appearance is 1329, when there

Death in the Cards

is a record of them in Germany. However, some occultists believe that the Tarot dates back to Egyptian civilization, and others find evidence for their existence between these two periods. With no one able to disprove their claims, such different groups as gypsies and the crusading Knights Templar asserted that the Tarot was their creation. Whichever of the many theories is accepted, it is indisputable that the cards have long endured—both as a fortune-telling method and as a game.

The word itself derives from the use of the cards for play. In 14th-century Italy, they were the basis of a game called *tarocco*. When France adopted the game, they also adapted the name, which became *tarot* in French. Even though it is the French name that has stuck, it is more likely the Italian deck from which the present-day deck of playing cards has been developed.

The traditional Tarot deck has 78 cards, and the symbolic pictures on them are much the same as they have been through

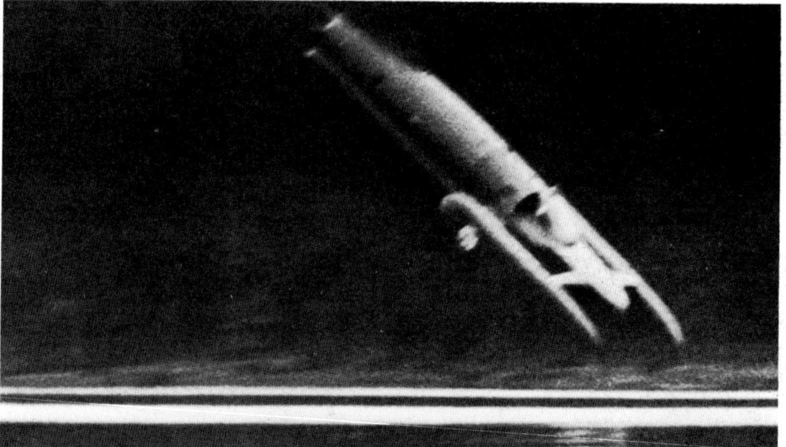

Above: the speedboat *Bluebird* reared into the air at the start of the accident that took the life of Donald Campbell, then the world water speed record holder. It happened on Coniston Water in the Lake District of England.

Above right. the racing boat then turned a complete back somersault.

Far right: from the somersault, *Bluebird* plunged into the water and sank. It went 140 feet down.

Right: Donald Campbell, dressed in his usual way for boat racing. A believer in signs, Campbell had told his fortune from the cards just before his final race—and had drawn two cards of bad omen.

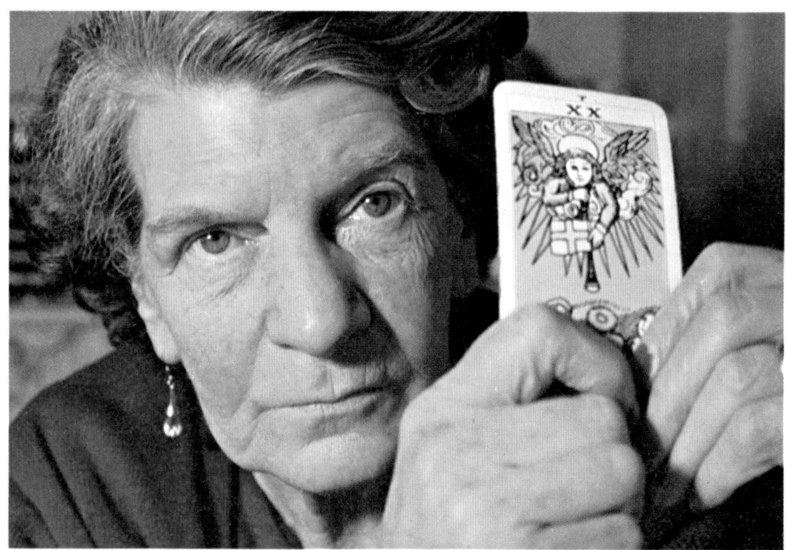

Left: Madame Nicole reads Tarot cards in a lean-to shed behind one of the busiest streets of London—and earns a good living. She's been doing this work since she was 17, and says: "It's noble work, if you do it religiously."

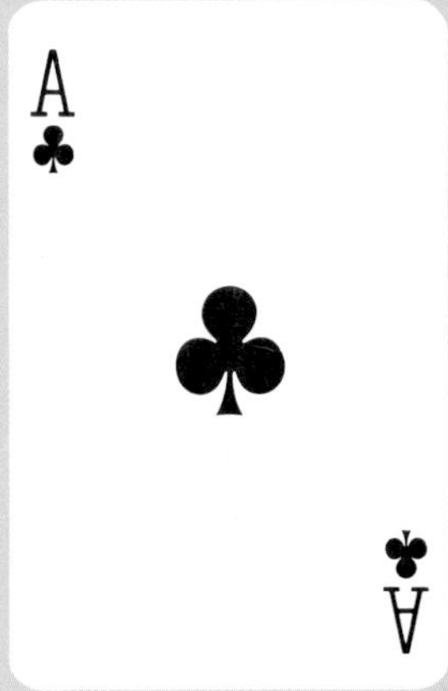

The Tarot suit known as Batons, Scepters, or Wands is Clubs today.

From the Tarot's Cups or Coupes has come the modern suit of Hearts.

Above: modern playing cards developed out of the 56-card Minor Arcana of the Tarot, which has four suits containing nonsymbolic picture cards and plain cards. The number of cards was reduced to 52 by the combination of the knight and the page into a jack.

Below: it doesn't have to be a Tarot deck for fortune telling by cards. This French engraving shows playing cards being used.

the ages. There are 22 picture cards called Major or Greater Arcana, Trumps, Triumphs, or Atouts. Generally speaking, they represent the spiritual and cosmic forces affecting mankind, such as power, faith, death, and courage. Each of these symbolic picture cards has a title, most of which express mightiness. Among them are Jupiter, The World, Justice, The Empress and The Emperor, Death, Star, Moon, and Sun. They are also numbered, except for The Fool. This card has no number, but is nonetheless essential to the deck.

Another 56 cards, called the Minor Arcana, are divided into

The Swords or Epees of the Tarot has developed into the present Spades.

What was Coins, Pentacles, or Deniers in the Tarot is now Diamonds.

"Key to the Mysteries"

four suits. Picture cards also appear among these, but they are familiar rather than symbolic—King, Queen, Knight, and Page. The Tarot suits are swords or epees; batons, scepters, or wands; cups or coupes; and coins, deniers, or pentacles. These cards broadly represent occupations or careers and social position.

Another distinctive feature of the Tarot cards is that they are not the same when turned from top to bottom, and can best be read in the upright position. If they appear inverted during a reading, their meaning is altered—or even reversed.

The playing cards used today came from the 56 cards of the Minor Arcana, plus The Fool. Because the Knight and the Page were combined into the Jack, the modern deck has only 52 cards. The Fool has become the Joker, but it is very much an extra, being important in only a few games. As for the suits, spades has its source in swords, clubs in batons, hearts in cups, and diamonds in coins.

The Tarot as a means of telling fortunes is said to contain an entire symbolic system that provides a "key to the mysteries," and "holds the secret of the true nature of man, the universe, and God." Those versed in the use of the Tarot believed that there was nothing about man and his destiny that could not be revealed by these cards. The acceptance by many people of the Tarot's powers meant that it would eventually come into conflict with the Church. It did so, and in 1377, a Swiss monk came out with the first recorded diatribe against the Tarot in particular, and playing cards in general.

However, the production and use of playing cards grew. Only two years after the Swiss monk's public condemnation of cards, the ledgers of the Belgian Duke of Brabant contained the first recorded purchase of cards in his country. Later that same year of 1379, playing cards was described as a pastime at a fete in Brussels.

The Tarot appeared in splendid forms at royal courts, in noble castles, and in rich manor houses. In 1392, King Charles

VI of France commissioned the painting of three packs of cards that became famous as near works of art. They were done by the artist Gringonneur. He painted them on gold-edged, silver-backed vellum, using lapis lazuli for the beautiful sky blue color, and a rich red pigment known as "mummy's dust." Seventeen of these unique cards still survive, and are preserved in the Bibliothèque Nationale in Paris.

The Gringonneur cards deviated from the original spirit of the Tarot in that the pictures were more on the pretty side than powerful and brooding. In the following century, similar cards were painted for the Duke of Milan and other powerful

The second card of the Major Arcana went through a change from a Lady Pope to a High Priestess.
Above: in the early Italian Tarot packs of the 14th century, the card showed a female pope in both name and garb—probably based on the legendary Pope Joan of five centuries previous.

Right: in more modern Tarot decks, this card is illustrated by a priestess in both name and dress. The 1910 design of the High Priestess by occultist A. E. Waite has robes that hint strongly of origins in ancient Egypt.

families of Northern Italy. Despite their cost and the artistic effort that had gone into them, the Tarot cards were again condemned—this time by St. Bernadin of Siena in 1423. His attack resulted in the burning of numerous packs, among them some choice ones.

After this, both political and religious rulers of Europe made efforts to stifle the growth of the Tarot cards. The pious considered them as a "pagan challenge" to the Church, and forbade their use on grounds of their being unholy. It was on economic grounds, however, that the Venetian authorities in 1441 and the English king in 1463 banned their importation. In time, these prohibitions worked against the popularity of the Tarot, and people sought other, easier ways of trying to see into their futures. To consult the Tarot became a harmless game or pastime, like playing ordinary cards. It wasn't until near the end of the 18th century that the Tarot was again taken seriously as a means of reaching out into the future.

The Tarot Revival

The man responsible for this revival was the learned French writer Antoine Court de Gebelin, whose lifework was the preparation and publication of a mammoth book *The Old World Analyzed and Compared With the New World.* Nine volumes of the uncompleted work appeared between 1773 and 1784. Volume eight, which came out in Paris in 1781, contained a section called "The Fame of Tarot." In that section, Gebelin wrote: "If one were to know that in our days there existed a work of ancient Egypt, one of their books that escaped malicious destruction . . . a book about their most pure and interesting doctrines, everybody would be eager no doubt to know such an extraordinary and precious work."

Gebelin himself had been introduced to the Tarot at a friend's house, and with his usual display of wide knowledge, declared that the cards had "doubtless originated in Egypt." He felt confirmed in this point of view after further research, when he stated that the Tarot was no less than the remains of the famous Egyptian book of magical learning, the Book of Thoth. "There is no doubt whatsoever in my mind," he stated, "that the Tarot images and symbols contain the answers to the occult powers and wisdom of the ancient world. And what had validity and was in force then is also present in our modern times."

His imaginative view of the Tarot's origins was largely disproved after the discovery of the Rosetta Stone in 1799, which led to the deciphering of early Egyptian writing. Meantime, however, his ideas were ardently taken up by a Parisian wig maker and barber named Alliette, who proceeded to restore what he said were the original Egyptian designs to the cards. Declaring that both the pictures and their meanings had been distorted over the centuries, Alliette brought out a series of extremely popular books about the Tarot. "I have studied the mysteries of the cards for more than 30 years," he said, "and it is only now that I am beginning to understand them at their truest and deepest level."

Despite the intellectual exertion required to learn and read the mysteries of the Tarot, it found thousands of new followers during the time of Napoleon. The emperor was well known as a firm believer in fortune telling. He even had his own personal

Below: the stories about Pope Joan—now believed highly unfounded—were picked up by English Protestants in the 17th century for anti-Catholic propaganda. This frontispiece of a book published in London in 1675 shows the discovery of Pope Joan as a woman when she has a baby during a holy procession. Some Tarot authorities believe that Pope Joan was the source for the Lady Pope card.

The Changing Face of the Tarot

Below: this artistic representation of The Sun was part of the Tarot deck painted by Gringonneur for King Charles VI of France in the 14th century. The few cards that remain from this deck show it to have been a near work of art.

and highly complicated Book of Fortune, which he consulted before each of his battles. The Little Emperor was impressed by the talents of Marie Lenormand, who used a set of Tarot cards of her own design, and by which she predicted his marriage to Josephine. Later, she was appointed as an attendant to the Empress. Even so, Napoleon twice imprisoned her for making prophecies not in accordance with his plans, and became violently angry when she told him that the cards foretold of his death by either rope or bullet. (His disposition was not improved when the seeress also lost her temper and threw her Tarot pack in his face.)

For the next few decades of the early 19th century, Tarot readers continued to turn up The Hanging Man, The Juggler, The Fool, The Devil, and all the other traditional card symbols throughout the fashionable salons of France. Their influence was not as strongly felt in any other European country, however. For example, there had been no recorded use of the Tarot in England since the late 16th century, when Henry Cuffe, secretary to the Earl of Essex, had consulted someone to read the cards for him. That card reader told Cuffe to draw three cards from a Tarot pack, and to place them face downward on a table. Cuffe did so, and then, as instructed, turned over the cards in the same order he had drawn them. The first was a full-length picture of a man under the escort of armed soldiers; the second showed a grim-faced judge; the third a gallows. At the time Cuffe laughed at the clear omens—especially that of the hangman. However, on March 13, 1601, he was found guilty of treason against Queen Elizabeth I. He was then taken to the Tyburn, the public hanging place of London, and "hanged by the neck until he was dead."

Interest in the Tarot held fast in France during the 19th century. One of its leading practitioners was Alphonse Louis Constant, who used the pen name of Eliphas Lévi. Lévi bought a deeper meaning to the use and interpretation of the Tarot. After being educated at a Catholic seminary and being ordained as a deacon, he left the church to marry a girl of 16. When she deserted him—taking their two children with her—Lévi turned to the study of the occult for consolation. He showed a particular interest in the Tarot, which he regarded as being linked with the Cabala. This occult system of thought originated with Jewish mystics of the 2nd or 3rd century, and is one of the oldest schools of mystical belief in the world. For many centuries, the Cabala was regarded as the true key to all the mysteries of the universe. It influenced almost every philosopher from the period of its founding to the late 13th century. It had many advocates in later eras, and still has today.

In 1856, Lévi published a book entitled *The Ritual of High Magic*. In it he states: "The universal key of magical works is that of all ancient religious dogmas—the key of the Cabala and the Bible. . . . Now, this Clavicle [The Tarot], regarded as lost for centuries, has been recovered by us, and we have been able to open the sepulchres of the ancient world, to make the dead speak, to behold the monuments of the past in all their splendor, to understand the enigmas of every sphinx, and to penetrate all sanctuaries. Among the ancients the use of this key was permit-

Above: the traditional in Tarot design is represented by this card from the Swiss IJJ deck, said to be some centuries old.
Center: another traditional design from the Marseilles pack.
Right: A. E. Waite's design of 1910 was more romanticized.

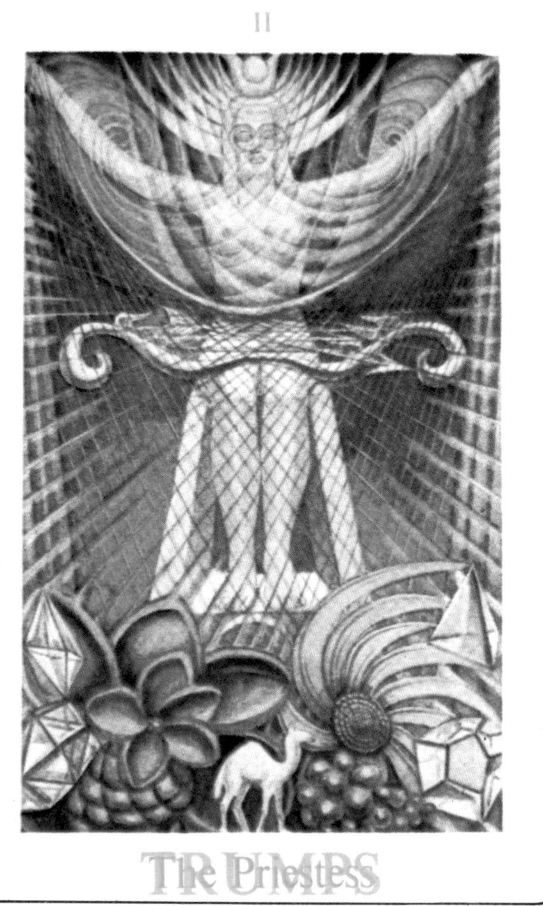

Left: Egyptian themes dominate Aleister Crowley's Tarot design.
Above: this new Tarot card of the Magician was especially commissioned for a James Bond movie.

"Bible of Bibles"

ted to none but the high priests, and even so its secret was confided only to the flower of initiates."

Even though he considered himself a "flower of initiates," Lévi never had the time or patience to design a complete set of Tarot cards in line with his ideas. Such a set would have had to include "the Sacred Tree," a cabalistic diagram of the "anatomy of God." It consists of ten circles joined by 22 lines—the circles being spiritual states, and the lines paths to them. The design on which most modern European packs are based was bequeathed by a follower of Lévi's named Oswald Wirth, and his ideas were later spread by Dr. Gerard Encausse. Like Lévi, Encausse believed that the Tarot had come to Europe by way of the gypsies.

Encausse followed the example of the majority of Tarot experts of the 18th and 19th centuries by writing under a pseudonym. This was probably done both as a bit of showmanship and as a way to protect themselves and their relatives from possible ridicule and abuse. Encausse used the name Papus in his writings on the Tarot, which he described as the "Bible of Bibles." He and Lévi were largely responsible for the popularization of the Tarot in the central countries of Europe. As far as the United States and Britain were concerned, the cards were in other prophets' hands.

In 1887, London saw the founding of the Hermetic Order of the Golden Dawn. This group followed Lévi's teachings in some respects, but differed greatly from it in others. The Golden Dawn was put on the occult map mainly through the efforts of a man who called himself MacGregor Mathers, or Le Compte de Glenstrae. Its system was also based on that of the Cabala, and held that the Sacred Tree could be climbed by man until he comes into some form of contact with God. The 22 cards of the Major Arcana were linked both with the 22 paths of the Sacred Tree and the 22 letters of the Hebrew alphabet. In this cabalistic formulation of the cards, the attempt was made to show the relation between God, Man, and the Universe. Mathers and other members of the Golden Dawn also made changes in the design of, and gave different meanings to, the Tarot.

The various designs and conflicting interpretations can make things difficult for the student of the Tarot, especially if he or she is a beginner. However, by dispensing with the Minor Arcana and making a formal, straightforward spread of the Major, it is possible for the amateur to give a not unsatisfactory reading of the cards. This stems from the activation of the subconscious, which, according to Tarot expert Richard Gardner, frequently brings about quick results. "The merest amateur, who has still to look up lists of card meanings while reading a spread, will often give a little message that is quite valid or useful," he stated.

Before the cards are laid out, however, there are other conditions that must be observed, and other factors that the would-be diviner must bring into focus. In his comprehensive book, *The Occult*, Colin Wilson suggests that, for utmost impact, the student should be imbued with a feeling for the Middle Ages. "The mind," he writes, "should be full of images

Below: Napoleon and his wife Josephine are constantly described as deep believers in all kinds of fortune telling. Mlle. Lenormand, here shown reading cards for the Empress, was said to have a great influence with the couple.

Above: Napoleon is shown with an Egyptian soothsayer who, according to many reports, predicted his divorce and his later exile.

Below left: in this engraving, Napoleon consults an Italian astronomer.

The Major Arcana of the Tarot

There are altogether 78 cards in the Tarot deck, but the most important of them, with the richest significance, are the 22 cards of the Major Arcana. Traditionally, in reading the Tarot cards, the Major Arcana represents the physical and spiritual forces that act upon mankind. Unlike the ordinary double-headed playing cards, Tarot cards have a single picture which alters in meaning if inverted. Here the interpretations are given for both upright (▲) and inverted (▼) cards.

The Fool

The unnumbered card.

▲ Immaturity, lack of consideration, thoughtlessness. One drawing this card should take care to exercise will power in order to overcome foolishness, and to make the correct choices in life.
▼ To make the wrong choice; to stop or hesitate in life's progress. Apathy or negligence.

The Emperor

▲ The card that symbolizes worldly power, competence, skill, and the domination of intelligence and reason over emotion and the passions. Realization of goals.
▼ Immaturity; lack of strength; weak character. Feebleness in action, a failure to control emotions, to get to grips with things.

Jupiter or The Pope

▲ Here is the symbol of mercy; a religious or spiritual person. Humility; kindness; leniency; or compassion. A person to whom other people go for help. Servitude; ritual; conformity; or forgiveness.
▼ Overkindness; the foolish exercise of generosity; frailty; also unorthodoxy, unconventionality.

The Lovers

▲ Not only the symbol of love, but of reconciliation. The necessity for testing, putting to the proof. Possible predicaments. Compatibility; harmony; beginning of a possible romance.
▼ Failure when put to the test. Unwise plans; infidelity; fickleness. The possibility of a wrong choice.

The Wheel of Fortune

▲ Symbol of the unending cycle of a changing universe. Advancement for better or possibly worse. Good fortune; luck; unexpected events. The full circle points to the course of events from start to finish.
▼ Bad luck. Sudden ill fate; a broken sequence; a break or inconsistency in what is expected.

Strength

▲ Courage; fortitude; energy; the needed strength to endure in spite of obstacles. Triumph of love over hate; hidden forces at work. Self-reliance; heroism. Strength and power, both physically and spiritually.
▼ Weakness; discord; the abuse of power; lack of faith. Overbearingness leading to tyranny.

The Hanged Man

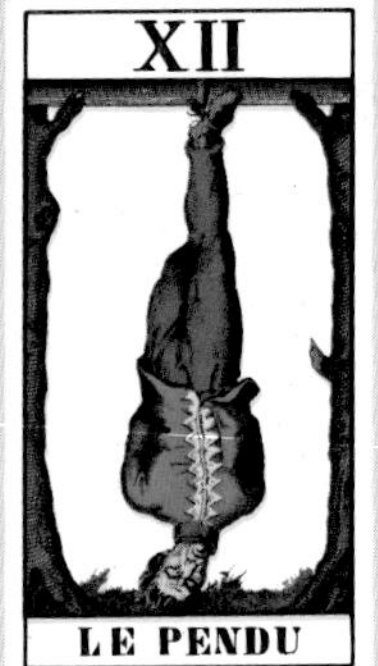

▲ A life suspended; a point of transition; the changing of life's forces. Sacrifice; readjustment; rebirth. Effort and sacrifice may be called for to move toward a goal that may nonetheless not be reached.
▼ A lack of sacrifice; failure to give of one's self. Self-preoccupation.

The House of God or The Lightning Struck Tower

▲ A card that can mean catastrophe, but that also points to a better future. Breaking down of existing forms to make way for the new. Havoc. Breakdown. Terrible danger. Bankruptcy; loss of security. Loss of stability.
▼ Inability to make a necessary change. Continued oppression. Trapped; imprisoned.

The Star

▲ A card symbolizing hope, faith, trust. A good omen; promise of opportunity; a bright future; optimism; favorable prospects. Insight; satisfaction; spiritual love.
▼ Hope unfulfilled. Bad luck; pessimism; a lack of opportunity; stubbornness. Possible harmony, but only short-lived.

The Moon

▲ The crayfish that creeps toward the girl symbolizes something that comes out of the unknown depths. Deception; trickery; insincerity; dishonesty. False friends; unknown enemies. Disillusionment.
▼ Minor deceptions, trifling mistakes. An uneasy peace after paying the necessary price.

The Magician or The Juggler

▲The magician symbolizes originality and imagination, the ability to set one's own course, and the determination to see a chosen task all the way to completion. Mastery; self-control; skill; or subtlety.
▼Weakness of will or insecurity. Limited interest; delay; lack of imagination. Using skills for evil ends.

Juno or The High Priestess

▲This card represents wisdom united with common sense; knowledge; intuition; understanding; education. She is a symbol of a good balance of intelligence and foresight.
▼Ignorance; shallowness; conceit; selfishness. One drawing it is apt to be satisfied with superficial knowledge.

The Empress

▲The symbol of feminine productivity and action. Feminine progress; evolution; material wealth; fertility; marriage; the love of the good things in life.
▼Vacillation and indecision. A lack of concentration, leading to inaction and delay in getting things done. Anxiety.

The Chariot

▲Trouble and adversity (which may possibly have been overcome already). Ordeal; obstacle; a great effort against overwhelming odds. Victory; triumph; greatness.
▼Defeat. Failure at the last moment to succeed; the sudden collapse of plans. Overwhelmed; a failure to meet and face responsibility.

Justice

▲The pillar of moral strength and integrity, meaning justice; fairness; reasonableness; moderation; virtue; virginity; self-satisfaction in accomplishments.
▼ Bias; intolerance; false accusations; abuse; bigotry; severity in judgment; unfairness.

The Hermit

▲A card which represents wisdom and prudence; self-denial; thriftiness; withdrawal; silent counsel. It can indicate regression; desertion; or annulment.
▼Lack of patience, or possibly over-prudence that can cause unnecessary delay. Immaturity; childishness; imprudence; foolishness.

Death

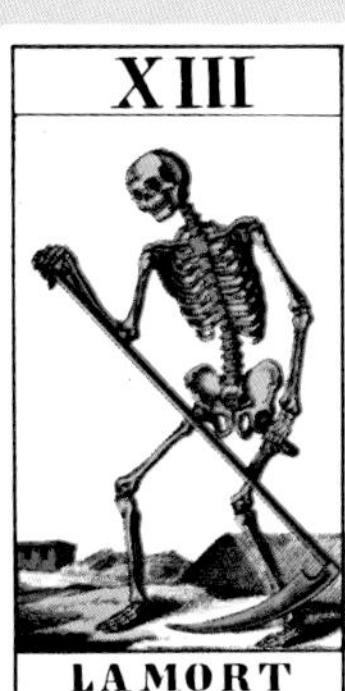

▲The unlucky number 13 points to change and renewal rather than death itself. Clearing the way for transformation. Death of the old self, though not necessarily physical death. Ruin, end.
▼Stagnation; inertia; immobility. Change, but only a partial and incomplete one.

Temperance

▲Moderation; temperance; self-control. Friendship; mixing or bringing together into a successful union. Reflection; harmony; compatibility; consolidation, fusion, patience; frugality.
▼ Discord. Sterility; stubbornness; lack of patience; inability to work with others. Desires unfulfilled.

The Devil

▲Bondage; subordination; black magic. A card of suffering, ravage, violence, shock, fatality—sometimes self-punishment.
▼Release from bondage; the realization that the ties can be broken. The first steps toward enlightenment; the beginning of spiritual understanding, of overcoming fear.

The Sun

▲A card of triumph and achievement. Satisfaction; success; rewards through work. Engagement or a happy marriage. Moderation in life. Success in work; delight in daily life.
▼Triumph delayed, but perhaps not lost forever. Canceled plans; a broken engagement.

Judgment

▲The rising figures suggest revival and reawakening. Rejuvenation; rehabilitation. A change of position. Readjustment; improvement; development; promotion.
▼Delay; failure to face facts. Separation, divorce. Indecision; procrastination; failure to find happiness.

The World

▲The summing up of what all the other cards have said. Attainment; ultimate change; completion; success. The admiration of others. Triumph.
▼Imperfection; lack of vision. Failure to finish what has been started. Refusal to recognize the meanings given by the other cards.

The Three Card Spread

of Gothic cathedrals, of medieval stained glass . . . of small towns surrounded by fields, and artisans at their everyday work. Without this kind of preparation, the skeptical modern mind is likely to attach its own associations to cards like The Pope, The High Priestess . . . and The Devil." Whether or not this medieval state of mind can be achieved, it is essential for the diviner to empty his head of everyday thoughts, and to concentrate on the mystic symbols. Once the meaning of the various cards has been learned—or jotted on the backs of the cards if necessary at the start—the reader will be ready to receive his first questioner. It is considered too introspective, and, therefore, too dangerous to tell your own fortune by means of the Tarot, because the magic of the cards can easily work against you.

By the time you give your first reading, your Tarot pack should have become personal to you, much as a pet becomes a kind of extension of its master. Two-way vibrations pass between the pack and its owner, and to protect this sensitive feeling, it is necessary to keep the cards away from anyone else. As a reader, you must become as familiar with your pack as possible, never using a new one for a reading. You should handle and study your Tarot pack as often as possible, so that a bridge is constructed between your subconscious and the Tarot symbols.

When not in use, the cards should be wrapped in a square of black or purple silk, and kept in a closed wooden box. As with the *I Ching* (see Chapter 3), the cards must be accorded a

Right: all Tarot readings are highly personal, and it is difficult to lay down precise interpretations of each card. Until practice has sharpened a reader's intuition, an amateur card reader is probably well advised to start with the simplest of the Tarot spreads, which is the three-card spread. Here is a sample of what might come up in such a card reading.

place of honor in the room. They should be kept on the side facing east—the direction from which the "light of inspiration" appears. The very fact that an object is regarded as having special powers can help the person believing in them to approach these powers himself. To increase your state of sensitivity, it helps if the room in which the reading is to be given is filled with incense. After a short period of meditation—perhaps ten minutes for beginners—some readers say in prayer, "God speaks through me." They ask their querant to observe a similar solemnity, for nothing can doom a Tarot reading more than a questioner who is merely out for a quick laugh.

You settle in a comfortable chair, and the querant sits across a table, on the south side facing north. Your seat opposite him is in keeping with the concealed currents of the earth, which are said to flow from north to south, from south to north. If you notice that the querant seems too stiff and awkward to allow a satisfactory reading, try to loosen him up with a cup of coffee or tea. If he seems too relaxed, try to impress on him the need to be alert and concentrated.

Providing the question has been serious and meaningful, the answer should be constructive. Again much depends upon you as the reader—how you interpret the inverted cards; whether you disbelieve the value of any sequential relationship; what value and significance you place on pairings. (For example, The Empress and The Emperor together can suggest either harmony or opposition.)

In doing your reading, you would be advised not to try

Below: the querant sought an answer to the question, "Will I be able to provide for my family financially in the future?" In reaching an answer, the first card showed that the querant had experienced past financial difficulties of a serious nature. The second card said that those problems seemed to have been resolved, and the querant was at present financially stable. The third card indicated that further setbacks will come, but that these will be surmounted if the querant exercises caution.

forcing the cards, for they will fall as they will. By cooperating with the cards fully, you will sometimes find that the seeker's question was not the one he really wanted to ask, but a cover for some deeper underlying problem that was his true reason for consulting the Tarot. Having exposed this mental block, you can then coax him to talk about his basic worry—rather as a skillful doctor will ease the truth out of a patient who tries to minimize his symptoms. It is then that you can fully use the psychic energy at your disposal, and interpret the messages contained in the pack. "The cards," writes author Fred Gettings, "bear some resemblance to a highly refined Rorschach test in which the formless ink blots have been replaced by archetypal images which help the hidden truth in the spirit to reveal itself."

This is the Celtic Cross spread, said to be easy and interesting. The querant is a young woman who asked, "Will I succeed in my career?" Her significator, the Knight of Cups for a light-haired person between 18 and 30, is hidden under card number 1.

1 The querant obviously wants to know if her accomplishments will be recognized.

2 The threat to her ambition is a tendency to be indiscreet and somewhat unmindful of others.

3 In the past, her abilities have been put to the test, and she has been proved worthy.

4 This card says the querant has been underhanded in her effort to get ahead.

5 There is a possibility of disappointment in her ambition.

6 In the near future, she will have a period of stagnation, and even sacrifice will go unnoticed.

7 She herself fears that impulsiveness will impede progress.

8 Friends are worried that the querant will sustain losses.

9 There is hope of success in her work if she shows more appreciation of her co-workers.

10 The egoism indicated by previous cards will be difficult to overcome, but her hopes can only be realized if she does.

3 Specific Goal

1 Present Influence

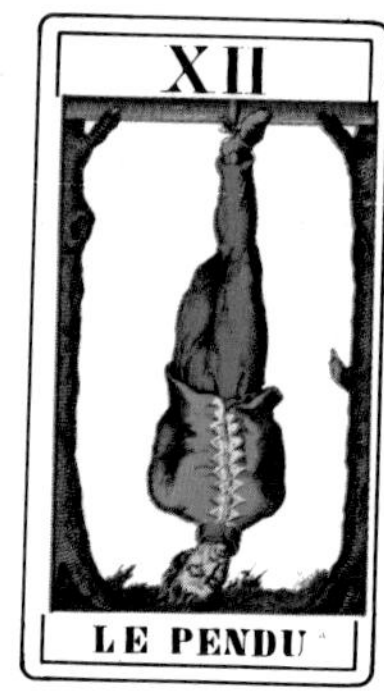

4 Past Foundation **2 Immediate Obstacles** **6 Future Influence**

5 Past Events

Now you start the reading. You take the 22 cards of the Major Arcana from their cover, spread the silk square over the flat surface of the table, and then carefully shuffle the pack so that there is an adequate mixture of upright and inverted designs. Remember that the cards must not be laid on anything but the silk. The querant is requested to give a final shuffle, and you deal the spread you have chosen for the reading.

The first and most important card to be decided in a Tarot reading is the Significator, which is used to represent the questioner. This can be taken from the Minor Arcana. The choice is arbitrary, but should be made in keeping with the querant's personality or appearance. For example, the cups represent people with light brown hair or an indolent nature; the swords are for dark brown hair or tempestuousness; the wands for blonds or the active; the coins for the dark or the lazy. As far as age is concerned, the King or Queen fits someone who is over 35; the Knight, anyone between 18 and 30; and the Page, those under 18. The Significator is generally put face up in a central position on the table, and the spread is laid out face down beside it. Most beginning readers find that their strength and inspiration starts to drain after about a half hour, so they should choose one of the simplest spreads at first.

The least complicated of all the Tarot spreads is the three-card spread. This was the one used by the reader who predicted Henry Cuffe's fate. Of the three cards laid down in a row, the center one represents the querant in the present, the left one stands for the past, and the right one shows what might happen in the future. (Directions referred to are from the reader's point of view.)

Although it looks much more complicated, the Celtic cross spread is considered to be one of the easiest to master. It has the additional advantage of being interesting and rewarding. In this spread, 10 cards are used in total. Six of them are laid out in the form of a cross, and four go to the right in a straight up-and-down line. Instead of being face up, the Significator is covered by the first card. After the cards have been read in a sequence to show past and future influences, the answer to the specific question asked by the querant is revealed in the last card turned up.

Another spread that a beginner could try with fairly certain success is the seven-card spread. This is said to be particularly good for answering a "yes" or "no" question. All seven cards are laid out in a straight left-to-right line. Two cards stand for the past, three for the present, and two for the future—and the last card turned over gives the answer to the question asked.

The Tarot session is not over until the reader has completely dismissed the images from his conscious mind. Then, in accordance with tradition and occult protocol, he will go through the opening stages in reverse until the cards are safely back in their closed box pointing toward the sunrise. The beginning diviner and the querant may find themselves suffering from shyness or embarrassment. There is no valid reason why this should be so, but it might help if they think of eminent people in all professions and fields of endeavor who have found that the Tarot satisfied their desire to get an advance hint of the future—

The Celtic Cross

10 Final Result

9 Inner Emotions

8 Environmental Factors

7 The Questioner

Above: the seven-card spread is supposed to be particularly good for a "yes" or "no" answer. The question in this case was, "Will I marry and be happy?"

whether or not the hint was a favorable one.

Novelist Dennis Wheatley is a case in point. More than 40 years ago, he bought a Tarot pack and asked his wife—a gifted fortune teller with ordinary cards—to give a reading for him. The spread she laid was involved and complicated, and she puzzled long over it. Finally, Wheatley himself twice cut the pack, strictly against the Tarot code. Twice the Tower Struck by Lightning turned up, as though to tell him he would have to pay for his disregard of tradition.

"At worst," he related in his book *The Devil and All His Works*, "this card means violent death; at best when it is upside down, as was the case with both my cuts, it means heavy financial loss and possible imprisonment. I should have been greatly worried but, having no reason to anticipate such misfortune, laughed the matter off. However, a year later I had ample cause to recall this sinister indication of misfortune. For then, not only was I accused of fraud and faced with the threat of criminal proceedings; I might well have been sent to jail if an accountant had not, almost at the last minute, unearthed a document that exonerated me completely.

"It is by no means unusual for the Powers-that-Be to decree that we must suffer ill-fortune in order that our way of life be ultimately changed for the better. During the agonizing months that I could not go to my own office, and was debarred from taking a job with any other firm, I resolved to do my utmost to divert my mind from worry, so I wrote an adventure story, *The Forbidden Territory*, and *A Private Life of King Charles II*. Both were published in 1933. They are both still widely bought and read."

Judging from Wheatley's experience, it can be seen that the effects of the Tarot predictions can be short-term. This is welcome news for those beginning their association with the

1 Past relationships failed because of her lack of tolerance.
2 She has become more easy going, so recent relationships have been more satisfactory.
3 New understanding enables her to enjoy platonic friendships.

Past

Present

LA JUSTICE

VIII

Distant Past

Immediate Past

Present Influences

Presen

so-called "Devil's cards." The relationship between the reader and his pack is like that of a modern computer and its operator—a balance of input and feedback, the one dependent upon and stimulated by the other. The Tarot is to be respected, but not feared, listened to, but not panicked by. On the highest level, and in the words of author Eden Gray, the skillful Tarot reader must:

"Go deep within in meditation; find your own divine center, and you will understand by direct intuition that which the Tarot only hints at—that which the mystics and philosophers who first designed the cards have been trying to convey to you in these picture-symbols."

In a more lighthearted vein—but not frivolously—America's "leading self-confessed witch" Sybil Leek sees the day when a Tarot pack will be as much a part of an average home as a dictionary, a refrigerator, or a vacuum cleaner. For the woman who wants to throw the party that has everything, a half-hour session with the Tarot will be obligatory.

"The fears of being thought 'odd' no longer apply to the hostess with a Tarot pack among her canapés," she asserts in *The Sybil Leek Book of Fortune-Telling*. "When prophecy takes place in the familiar, comfortable surroundings of a house, fear of being laughed at is dispelled . . . Perhaps only when we see the serious aspects of life as a game can we feel free to enjoy it . . . This may be the case with the Tarot cards. Once they were treated seriously throughout the world, then neglected and forgotten except by a chosen few in each generation who kept the art alive.

"Now they are finding favor as a parlor game. Those who know the occult significance of the Tarot cards can only hope that understanding is the next step in their exciting history." For the long-lived Tarot, this would merely mean a return to its former glory.

The Seven Card Spread

4 If she keeps her present outlook, it appears that she will make a happy marriage.
5 She must resist the temptation to be emotional, and also avoid purely physical affairs.
6 She will have to work to keep her marriage interesting.
7 The final answer is "yes," but with a caution to heed the previous cards.

Future

stacles

Present Outlook

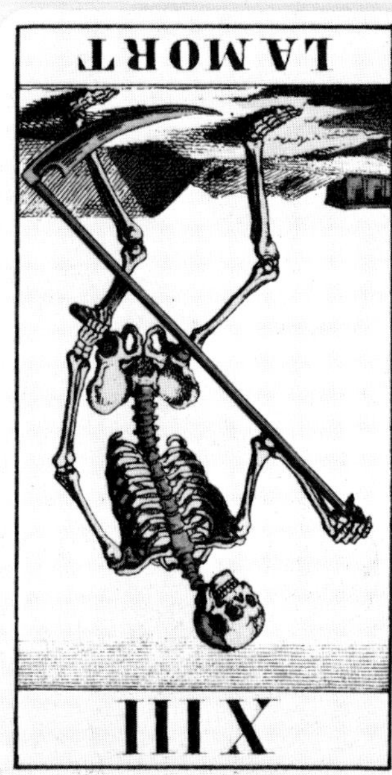

Future Influences

Ultimate Results

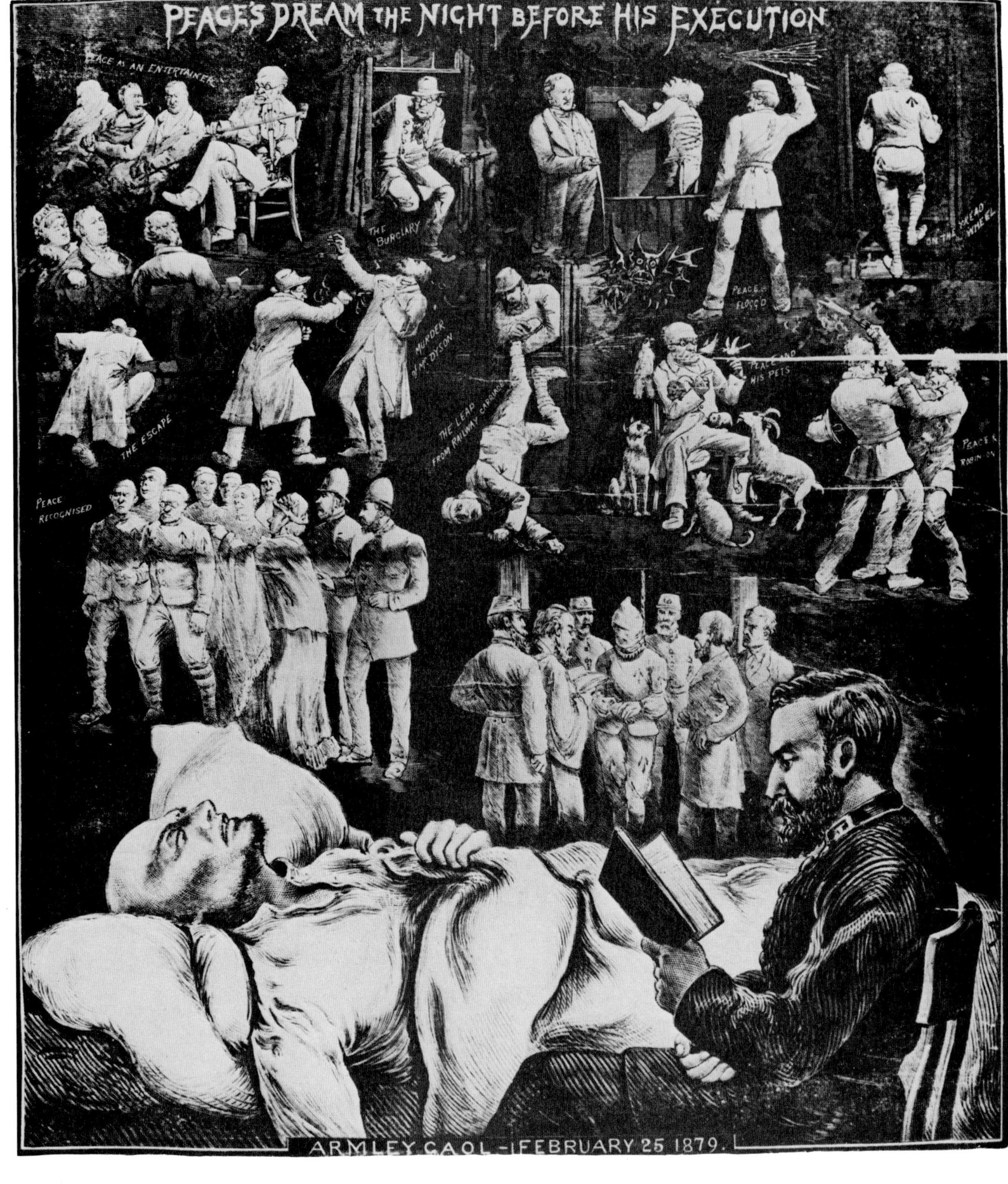
PEACE'S DREAM THE NIGHT BEFORE HIS EXECUTION
PEACE AS AN ENTERTAINER
THE BURGLARY
ON THE TREAD WHEEL
PEACE FLOGG'D
THE ESCAPE
MURDER of MR DYSON
THE LEAD FROM RAILWAY CARRIAGE
PEACE AND HIS PETS
PEACE RECOGNISED
ARMLEY GAOL – FEBRUARY 25 1879.

Chapter 6
Pictures From the Future

The traditional image of the fortune teller invariably includes a gleaming crystal ball: what do the scryers see when they stare fixedly into the mysterious globes? Where do the images of the future appear—in the crystal itself, or in the subconscious of the seer? Other pictures of events to come often appear in dreams. The sacred writings of many religions report prophetic dreams, and modern histories suggest that the future still unfolds nightly for many a restless sleeper, who—like Abraham Lincoln—may witness his own funeral in a particularly vivid dream setting. What do the psychiatrists say about these glimpses into future time?

Anyone who has been to an amusement park, a seashore resort, or a carnival, is familiar with the scene. The small, somewhat shabby tent. The painted stripes worn away by sun and bad weather. The sign—"Madame Za-Za, Fortunes Told"—tilted. The overall atmosphere more furtive than mysterious, more oppressive than welcoming. Instead of a tent at the seashore or on a fairground, the somewhat dismal scene could be a walk-up, one-room office in a town or city. Inside the tent or room sits the *scryer*—crystal gazer. Whatever country she is to be found in, she seems to fall into one of two types; she is either positive or passive. The positive prophetess is recognizable by her dark complexion, strong features and forehead, and intent stare. She uses the crystal in front of her as if it were a living thing. When she speaks her voice is deep, penetrating, forceful. The passive prophetess is pale, and usually blue-eyed. Her voice is weak and high-pitched, and she looks into the crystal almost beseechingly, as if begging the circle of quartz to show her something, anything. Sometimes the seer— whichever type she is—wears a shawl, a beaded headscarf, and earrings to suggest the gypsy or the mystic. More often nowadays she is crisply dressed, polite, and attentive—a career woman receiving you at her place of work.

You must "cross her palm with silver," of course. Originally this was done by making the sign of a cross with a coin, but today it is likely to be by handing her some folding money. The payment made, she is ready to commence the reading.

Opposite: this newspaper illustration of 1879 points up the late 19th-century English belief that murderers are haunted by their dreams. It shows the dream of a well-known thief and murderer the night before his execution. In it, he sees his shiftless life, and future end on the scaffold.

Caught by the Crystal!

Dr. Edmund Waller, an Englishman living in Paris in the early 1900s, was having a sleepless night. He wandered downstairs, and, finding the crystal his father had just bought, gazed idly into it. There, to his surprise, he saw the image of Mme. D., whom he had promised to look after during her husband's out-of-town journey.

The next day, Waller again looked into the crystal, and again saw Mme. D.—with a man. He rubbed his eyes, and looked still again. The pair remained in view, this time at a racecourse outside Paris. Agitated by all these visions, Waller went to the racecourse next day—and there met Mme. D. with a man whom he took to be the one he had seen in the crystal.

Waller continued to see Mme. D., her husband, and the other man in the crystal. One scene showed the illicit lovers in a particular Paris restaurant. On the husband's return, Waller told him about the visions. The two men went to the restaurant revealed by the crystal, and there found Mme. D. with her lover.

There was a tragic aftermath to Waller's visions: Mme. D. ended in an asylum, a broken woman after her husband had divorced her.

Her crystal—a word that comes from the Greek *krystallos* for "clear ice"—is shaded by a black velvet cloth, and placed in the center of the table. According to John Melville, the author of an extremely detailed manual on crystal gazing, the globe should be "$1\frac{1}{2}$ inches in diameter, or at least the size of a small orange." It should also be "enclosed in a frame of ivory, ebony, or boxwood, highly polished." Bending over the crystal, the prophetess spends a few minutes making passes with her right hand so that the surface becomes "magnetized." She then makes a series of similar passes with her left hand in order to increase the ball's sensitivity. In the stillness and silence that follows, clouds form over the crystal, and the prophetess can discern various pictures or visions in them.

Serious students of crystal gazing say that a good scryer is likely to have genuine psychic powers. But the amateur can make predictions based on general rules, even if he or she sees no pictures. For example, green or blue clouds mean joy; red, yellow, or orange ones indicate trouble. White mists are a good portent, but black cloudiness an evil one.

In fact, the globe may show her no more than her own distorted reflection. Its main purpose is to increase the seer's concentration so that she can "fix" in her mind the scenes that filter through from the future. Whether or not crystal gazers actually see the future in their globes, the controversial art of scrying is now flourishing in a way no fortune teller would have dared to foretell. Few cities throughout the world are without their quota of professional "Madame Za-Zas," and many are the communities that have an amateur scryer.

In the practice of scrying, the crystal should be kept immaculately clean. This entails regular washing with vinegar and water or fine soapsuds, and frequent polishing with a velvet cloth or chamois. No one else but its owner should handle the ball, and, when in use, the sphere should not be turned toward the light. The technique for making the sphere work is a simple one, and it has been estimated that about one person in every 20 is capable of either seeing vague shapes in the ball itself, or of having them imprinted in his or her mind. The room in which the sittings take place should preferably face north, and it should be discreetly lit with just enough light to be able to read by. No more than three people in all should be present, and the scryer should be at least an arm's length away from the other two. If they want to ask her any questions during the session, they should do so in a blank, monotonous voice so as not to disturb her concentration. They should never prompt or urge her because it will do no good. As the crystal experimenter Frederic Myers explains: "The visions do not seem to follow any law; they are a mixture of remembrances, dreams, telephathic or telesthetic recognitions and precognitions. In short, crystal gazing is an empirical method of arousing *cryptosthesia* (clairvoyance); the mechanism by which this comes to pass is unknown."

What the amateurs and some of the professionals do not know is that their art was condemned in earlier times as being of "satanic origin." This was the conclusion reached in 1398 by the Faculty of Theology in Paris, which could see no difference between the scryers' crystals and the then equally prevalent onyx mirrors employed by so-called witches. Of course, it was realized that the crystal was not the only medium in which the future could be glimpsed, or in which the seeker could come into contact with the universe and the "image of God." Hindus could see the shape of things to come in ink blots or in bowls of molasses. In the West, seers among the Romans, the Arabs, and the British Druids got equal results by studying fingernails, polished stones, sword blades, soap bubbles, glasses of wine, and water. In ancient Greece, it was not uncommon to learn of people's future welfare and health by "consulting the springs." The traveler and geographer Pausanias, in his *Itinerary of Greece*, described how the fortune tellers of Patrae "tie a mirror to a fine cord, and let it down so far that it shall not plunge into the spring, but merely graze the surface of the water with its rim. Then, after praying to the goddess and burning incense, they look into the mirror, and it shows them the sick person either living or dead. So truthful is this water." Occasionally, to add to the purity of the procedure, a virgin girl or boy took the place of the scryer, who supervised the event and interpreted what the youngster saw.

By the middle of the 12th century, scrying was in fashion throughout much of Europe and most of the Middle East. It won the enthusiastic support and participation of the ordinary populace—and the condemnation of the Church. In England, the philosopher and ecclesiastic John of Salisbury, spoke out against those who looked into the future by means of "objects which are polished and shining, like a kettle of good brass, glasses, cups, and different kinds of mirrors." His admonition had little effect in his day or later. In a typical case 300 years after, a Yorkshire villager named Byg confessed to scrying as a way of discovering some of his stolen property. The charge against him was of heresy. On being found guilty, he was sentenced to march through York Cathedral with a lighted torch in one hand, his "magical books" in the other, and a placard around his neck denouncing him as a *Sortilegus* (soothsayer) and *Invocator Spiritum* (invoker of spirits).

Partly because of the Church's opposition, partly because of exploits of charlatans, and partly through a general disenchantment with crystal gazing, scrying gradually gave way to other forms of fortune telling. It enjoyed a revival in the mid-19th century, however. This resurge of interest started when the novelist Lord Lytton, author of the much-admired *The Last Days of Pompeii*, boasted of the crystal ball he kept and consulted at his ancestral home. It got another boost when Andrew Lang, a writer and one-time president of the Society for Psychical Research, some years later had "an extraordinary experience which convinced me beyond all possible doubt about the efficacy of scrying."

In the winter of 1897, Lang was invited to dinner at a large house in his native Scotland. One of his fellow guests was an Englishman, who got into an argument about the genuineness of crystal gazing with the host's daughter, whom Lang called, "Miss Angus." The young lady challenged the scoffer to visualize a place or person of his acquaintance, and said that

Seeing the Future

Below: Evadne Price, who writes the horoscopes for a London woman's magazine, is also a scryer and Spiritualist. She feels that being psychic reduces her skill as an astrologer because she does not have to be a good student of the stars to tell fortunes.

Blood in the Crystal Ball!

Nell Montague was obliging a friend by reading the crystal for Mrs. H. in the home of her friend. When she had gazed into the crystal, a shock went all through her. There stood a tall balding man, nervously handling a revolver that he aimed at the door of the room from time to time. He talked on the phone several times, and then, as though tired of waiting for someone he may have been phoning, he pointed the gun at his own head. The crystal was diffused in blood. A woman came into the room and lifted the man's bloody head in her arms. That woman was Mrs. H!

Miss Montague didn't tell Mrs. H. all the details of her vision, but she did warn her of tragic widowhood to come soon. Mrs. H. simply laughed at this prediction, and Miss Montague was greatly relieved. However, as soon as she was alone, Miss Montague wrote down what she had seen exactly as she remembered it.

Three days after this event, on April 19, 1920, the London *Daily Mail* carried the story of the suicide of Mr. H. It said that he had been found at home "shot through the mouth, with a revolver in his right hand."

The picture in the crystal had come true.

Secrets of the Gypsies

Below: Derby Day in England's well-known Epsom Downs is a day that fortune tellers depend on to get many clients. Here is a young gypsy ready for trade.

she would see the same person in her globe. The Englishman conjured up a ball he had recently been to, and a beautiful girl he had danced with.

"Miss Angus," wrote Lang, "then described another room, not a ballroom, comfortably furnished, in which a girl with brown hair drawn back from her forehead, and attired in a high-necked white blouse, was reading, or writing letters, under a bright light in an unshaded glass globe." A short while later the Englishman met the girl of his scrying experiment at another formal dance, and asked her what she had been doing at about 10:30 p.m. on the night of December 21. He had never seen her other than in her ball gown, had met her only once before, and knew that she and Miss Angus were total strangers. He was staggered, therefore, when the girl told him that, at the time in question, she was indeed dressed as the scryer had stated, and had been answering letters beneath just such an unshaded gas lamp.

This example is a typical one of the scryer's powers. An even more startling, but similar, case occurred in England in 1920. Sir William Barrett, a former president of the Society for Psychical Research, reported it.

It seems that a crystal gazer named Nell St. John Montague was asked by a mutual friend, identified as Mrs. R., to give a reading to a Mrs. H.; Miss Montague, who had been paying a social visit to her friend's house, obligingly sent a servant to collect her crystal ball, making sure that the globe was wrapped in velvet so that the maid did not touch the quartz. Unlike most other scryers, Miss Montague had her client hold the crystal and concentrate on it as if in a trance. According to Sir William's write-up in the *Journal of the Society for Psychical Research*, Miss Montague's account was as follows: "When I took it from her hands," said the scryer, "I experienced a terrible shock . . . I warned her as delicately as I could that a gruesome tragedy was before her, an awful deed which would make her a widow almost immediately."

Mrs. H's reaction was to burst into laughter, which was a relief to the scryer. However, she made notes of what she had seen, in these words: "I can see a tall fair man, rather bald, pacing up and down a small room . . . close beside the desk is a telephone, he is excitedly taking up the receiver and speaking into it, he opens a drawer in the desk and holds an object taken from it in his right hand—it is a revolver." In Miss Montague's account, the man in the sphere twice more speaks into the phone, each time looking at the door with his gun at the ready. "With a sudden gesture," the notes go on, "he looks once more at the door and shakes his head as though giving up hope of it opening to admit someone for whom he seems to be waiting. He raises his right hand and staggers back, the revolver is now pointing at his own head—then I see blood everywhere gushing. A woman comes into the room, the same woman who is in the room with me now, only in the picture she wears a loose wrapper, she lifts his head—blood is everywhere."

Three days later, Mrs. H.'s husband committed suicide exactly as Miss Montague had described. However, the scryer helped save the life of a man who might have been killed by

Above: almost everyone thinks of gypsies when they think of fortune tellers. This amusement park wheel of fortune, operated by the insertion of a coin, reveals one's fortune by stopping where the gypsy's finger points.

Mr. H. This was the husband of Mrs. R., the friend who had originally introduced Mrs. H. and Miss Montague. On the day of Mr. H.'s suicide, Mr. R. visited the scryer in a great hurry. He said he had a message from his wife to go at once to see Mr. H., who "wanted to take him [Mr. R.] with him." Remembering the vision in the crystal, Miss Montague managed to delay Mr. R. for about 15 minutes. According to Mr. R., he afterward went to the H.'s home, and, as he rang the doorbell, heard a shot. Shortly after, he was told that Mr. H. had shot himself. Upon learning about Miss Montague's forecast, he realized he was the person Mr. H. seemed intent on

Dreaming the Future

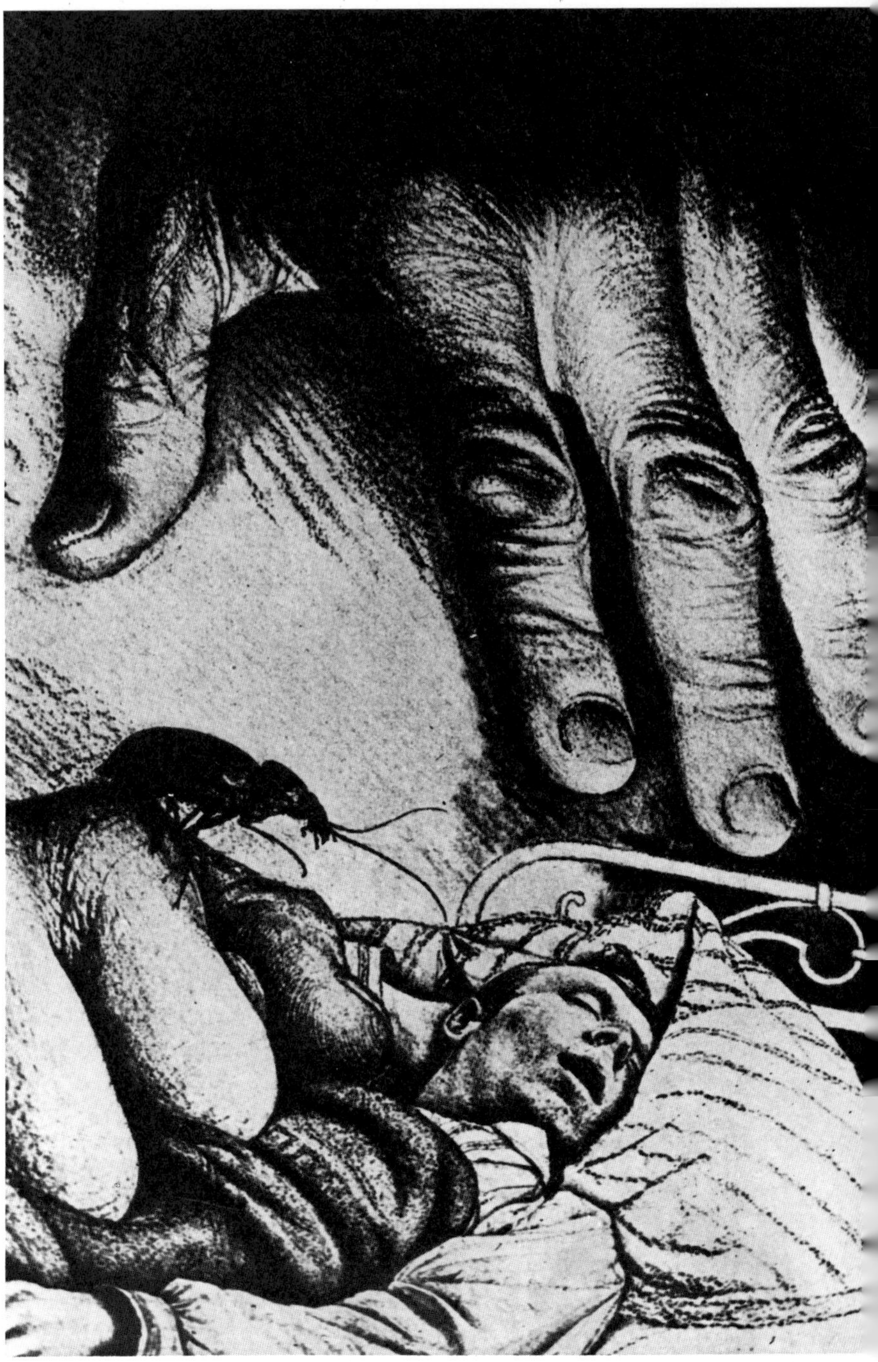

Right: this drawing graphically shows the horror of a bad dream.

Below: Freud said that dreams guard sleep. He illustrated this theory by showing the following sequence of events: 1. A child tugs at his nursemaid urgently to allow him to urinate. 2. He starts to relieve himself. 3. He continues on and on.

shooting in the vision—to take someone with him in death. "I owe my life to Miss Montague's warning," he is reported as saying.

Cases such as this restored much of its former popularity and following to scrying. A. E. Waite, the occult historian, commended it as "undoubtedly one of the most innocent, pleasing, and successful methods of minor magical practice." Attending a scrying session can be compared to going to the movies—the difference being that instead of watching a sequence of pictures about the lives of fictitious characters, you are viewing an excerpt or trailer from your own life to come. If this is so, then dreams must be our own private movies, produced for and screened each night to an audience of one—ourselves.

Not everyone appreciates this fact, and one of the most widespread fallacies about dreams is that not everybody has them. We all know the person who boasts, "Dreams? Never had one in my life. When I go to bed I sleep"! The view that dreamless sleep was possible was long accepted, despite the philosopher Immanuel Kant's statement toward the end of the 18th century that "there is no sleep without dreams," and the similar claims of modern psychologists. Then, in 1952, a scientist suddenly noticed that babies' eyes sporadically moved under their closed lids when they were asleep. This observation led to a new approach to sleep investigation, and research later showed that the movements—called REMs—take place sometime during the sleep of all humans. It was established that REMs indicate dreaming; that every man, woman, and child has from five to seven REM periods a night at hourly intervals; and that dreams take up one-third of the sleeping time of adults. These findings were also borne out by Dr. Charles Fisher of Mount Sinai Hospital, New York, who stated that: "If a sleeper is awakened in the middle of a dream, he will make up the final sequence at the next opportunity."

As dream statistics began to mount up, it was calculated that some 730 billion dreams are dreamed each year in the USA. This information added to the already impressive data compiled on dreams, which included their role in *oneiromancy* (forecasting the future from dreams), and the number of times they had signposted or warned of coming events. Among the oldest recorded prophetic dreams are those in the Bible—the most famous being that of the Egyptian Pharaoh who dreamt

4. Still there is no stopping him. 5. He has urinated a sea full. 6. His cries finally awaken the nursemaid, who has dreamed the whole episode. The dream had helped her stay asleep a little longer, according to Freud.

Symbols in Dreams

Right: the English visionary William Blake was also a painter and poet. He was fascinated with the symbolism of dreams, and was frequently inspired by them. This painting, "Queen Katherine's Dream," is typical of his fantasy.

that seven fat cows were eaten by seven lean cows, and seven ripe ears of corn were devoured by seven lean ears. Joseph, the captive slave who interpreted the dream, firmly stated that Egypt was due for seven years of plenty followed by seven years of famine. "God," he announced, "has shown Pharaoh what He is about to do."

That God was not averse to revealing His intentions in dreams, and that it was not sacrilegious to act upon His warnings, was confirmed by St. Thomas Aquinas. His writings have been called the "cornerstone of the Roman Catholic Church." In his *Summa Theologica* he acknowledged that "divination by dreams is not unlawful. It is the experience of all men that a dream contains some indication of the future. Therefore, it is vain to deny that dreams have efficacy in divination." Humans believed this as far back as 650 B.C. when King Assurbanipal of Assyria filled his library with clay tablets bearing the meanings of dreams. People still believed it in A.D. 150 when the Roman soothsayer Artemidorus of Daldis compiled his manual of dream interpretation. This manual was read and followed for the next thousand years.

By then, scholars were pondering which was the true reality—the dream state or the waking condition. This philosophical puzzle had been posed as early as the 3rd century B.C. by the Taoist mystic Chuang Tzu, who asked on waking from a dream in which he was a butterfly: "Am I Chuang Tzu who dreamed he was a butterfly, or a butterfly now dreaming I am Chuang Tzu?" His question was repeated by the 17th-century French mathematician and devotional author Blaise Pascal, who queried: "Who knows that when we think we are awake we may not be in slumber, from which slumber we awaken when we sleep?" The quandary was echoed by other philosophers, and in order to experience such fantasies and/or realities, ascetics would deliberately induce dreams of revelation by fasting, denying the appetites of the body, and making their beds in temples and sacred buildings.

They sought proof of the existence of afterlife, and declared that the symbols of dreams—no matter how obscure or mystifying—were meant to be revealing. For the less mystical person, some dreams were so clear, so vivid, so concrete that they were far more disturbing than those cluttered with symbolism. One such person was the 19th-century French dream researcher, Alfred Maury, who believed he had been taken back in time when he had a vivid dream in which the entire course of the French Revolution was paraded before him. In the dream, he was one of the participants in the uprising, and, on being accused of "crimes against the people" was sentenced to be guillotined. He was kneeling before the instrument when the bedpost suddenly broke and fell on the back of his neck.

Even more frightening than this was the dream of President Abraham Lincoln a short time before his assassination at Ford's theater in Washington, D.C. A skeptical man who dismissed the authenticity of biblical dreams, he nevertheless discussed his own "sleep premonition" with his wife and several of their friends. According to Lincoln, he had gone to bed tired one night after reading some dispatches from his generals. He soon began to dream and heard "subdued sobs, as if a number of people were weeping." In the dream he left his bed, went downstairs in the White House, and walked through a series of empty rooms until the sobbing led him into the East Room. There he met with a "sickening surprise." "Before me," he recounted, "was a catafalque, on which rested a corpse wrapped in funeral vestments. Around it were stationed soldiers who were acting as guards; and there was a throng of people, some gazing mournfully upon the corpse, whose face was covered, others weeping pitifully." Worried, Lincoln approached one of the soldiers, and demanded to know who was dead. "'The President,' was his answer, 'he was killed by an assassin!' Then came a loud burst of grief from the crowd which

Dream Books for Sale

This 18th-century engraving shows a London street peddler with her dream books for sale. People always want to know what their dreams mean, and they buy all kinds of books to help interpret them. Here are some interpretations from a dream book of 19th-century England:

Ants—a dream about ants means that you will move to a large city and have a big family of boys; it also implies wealth, but only if you are industrious.

Earwig—if this creature enters your dream, it indicates that you have an enemy working against you in secret. Beware of a small person with light brown hair!

Flying—this means that the dreamer has an aspiration he will never reach, and he had better change his course immediately or he will end up in ruin.

Ink—black ink in a dream foretells involvement in some disgraceful scheme; red ink tells of good news.

Whistling—to dream that you are whistling popular songs denotes that you can't carry even the simplest and easiest tune.

Murder Foretold!

awoke me from my dream."

A similar "death dream" featuring a head of state had come to a mining engineer in Cornwall, England on May 3, 1812. The engineer, John Williams, also related the "dreadful nightmare" to his wife, telling her that he dreamt he was in the lobby of the House of Commons in London. "A small man, dressed in a blue coat and a white waistcoat, entered, and immediately, I saw a person whom I had observed on my first entrance, dressed in a snuff-colored coat with metal buttons, take a pistol from under his coat and present it at the little man above-mentioned. The pistol was discharged, and the ball entered under the left breast of the person at whom it was directed. I saw the blood issue from the place where the ball had struck him, his countenance instantly altered, and he fell to the ground. Upon enquiry whom the sufferer might be, I was informed he was the Chancellor."

At the time the prime minister, Spencer Perceval, was also the chancellor of the exchequer, and Williams' wife and friends were convinced that it was the prime minister who had figured in his dream. So strong was their conviction that Williams debated whether or not to go to London to warn Perceval of his imminent death. However, after talking it over some more, he decided to remain at home and save himself exposure to "contempt and vexation." For the next few days he anxiously studied the newspapers as they arrived with the post. "On the evening of May 13th," he wrote later, "no account of Mr. Perceval's death was in the newspapers, but my second son, returning from Truro, [a town in Cornwall] came into the room where I was sitting and exclaimed, 'Oh father, your dream has come true! Mr. Perceval has been shot in the lobby of the House of Commons; there is an account come from London to Truro

Below: ten days before a political murder of a British military officer by Irish nationals in 1922, a friend of the murdered man foresaw his death by assassination in a dream.

written after the newspapers were printed.' The fact was that Mr. Perceval was assassinated on the evening of the 11th."

Such stories—which have been authenticated as far as is possible—fit into none of the categories or explanations offered by most men of science. To them, dreams have definite causes and occasional effects, but little or nothing to do with coming events. Sigmund Freud described dreams as "the royal road to the Unconscious," and felt that they were basically wish fulfillment. He agreed with the Latin poet Lucretius that dreams dealt with daytime interests and waking life, so that a man who was hungry might dream of food. Likewise, if the blankets were too heavy, the sleeper might dream he was being engulfed by quicksand, and if he were sexually frustrated, he would build up a sexual fantasy. Freud greatly stressed the importance of the sexual basis of dreams. He was criticized for this by his former disciple, the psychologist Alfred Adler, who believed that dreams were a "rehearsal" of man's drive for power, which renewed itself daily.

To the Swiss psychologist Carl Jung, the third outstanding figure in the new Age of Psychology, dreams had neither a sexual nor a power-seeking connotation. To him, they were a kind of receptacle or storehouse of all the memories, reflections, and impressions that had been passed on to man throughout the centuries by his earliest ancestors. Like Adler, he broke away from Freud to form his own school. This gave him a new attitude toward his patients, and a less rigid and dogmatic method of dream analysis. His aim, he explained, was to leave things to chance. As a result, his patients spontaneously reported their dreams and fantasies to him, and he merely asked, "What occurs to you in connection with that?" or, "How do you mean that?" Said Jung: "The interpretations seemed to follow of their own accord from the patients' replies and associations. I avoided all theoretical points of view, and simply helped the patients to understand the dream-images by themselves, without application to rules and theories."

Certainly as far as creative artists are concerned, it seems better to allow them to indulge in interpretation or analysis of their dreams, and to put their night visions into print. For example, dreams were in part responsible for three of the greatest horror novels in Western literature—*Frankenstein*, *The Strange Case of Dr. Jekyll and Mr. Hyde*, and *Dracula*. Frankenstein's creation led the ghoulish parade of literary monsters. The story came out of a dream by Mary Shelley in 1818. Some 70 years later, the novelist Robert Louis Stevenson had a dream that terrified his wife, but inspired him. "My husband's cries of horror caused me to arouse him," she recorded, "much to his indignation. 'I was dreaming a fine bogey tale,'" he said reproachfully. The next morning Stevenson went to his desk and started on the first draft of his nightmarish tale of Dr. Jekyll's dual personality. The following decade, in the 1890s, the author Bram Stoker went to bed after "eating generously" of cold crab meat at supper, and had a nightmare in which Count Dracula first bared his fangs to start a long and notorious career.

A contemporary writer who profited from a predictive dream

Below: the tutor of a noble had a dream in which his pupil was killed. He tried and failed to warn of possible danger. The tutor was Bishop Joseph Lanyi, and the noble was Austrian Archduke Franz Ferdinand. The assassination of the archduke thrust the world into war in 1914.

President Lincoln's Prophetic Dream

On an April night in 1865—with the trials of the Civil War still heavy on his mind—President Abraham Lincoln lay asleep and dreaming. In his dream, he was asleep in his huge bed in the White House. Suddenly he was awakened by sobbing. Getting up and following the sound of the weeping, Lincoln found himself in the East Room. There he saw people filing past a catafalque guarded by soldiers. The men and women were paying their last respects to a body laid in state.

The face of the corpse was covered from Lincoln's view, but he could see that those present were deeply affected by the person's death. Finally, he went to one of the soldiers and asked who was dead. "The President," was the answer. "He was killed by an assassin." With that horrifying reply came a loud outcry of grief from the group near the catafalque—and Lincoln woke up.

This troubling dream, which Lincoln told his wife Mary and several of their friends, turned out to be a prophetic one. In that very month, Lincoln went to the theater for a rare night away from his pressing responsibilities. Awaiting him there instead of a night of pleasure was a fatal bullet from an assassin's gun.

The Murder in the Red Barn

Below: these photographs reenact a murder committed in 19th-century England, and known as the Red Barn Mystery. It involved the killing of a girl by a farmer, who buried her under the floor of a red barn. The man then wrote regularly to the girl's parents to allay suspicion. Months later, however, the girl's mother three times dreamed of her daughter's death—just as it happened. She insisted on taking up the barn floor—and solved the mystery.

is T. E. B. Clarke, whose screenplay for *The Lavender Hill Mob* won him an Oscar in 1951. He didn't write a novel about his racing dream, but he enjoyed telling it. It happened when he was a 15-year-old schoolboy in 1922. "I was sitting in a tea-shop," he writes, "when a newsboy entered holding an evening paper with 'Derby Result' on it. I bought a paper and looked at the Stop Press. The first three were there, but on waking I could remember only the winner's name—Manna. . . . Two years later I was thrilled to see Manna among the entries for a two-year-old race. I knew then that he was destined to win the Derby the following year . . . Manna duly won the Derby at 9-to-1. The horse had probably not even been born when I had my dream."

Similar, though more serious experiences, have been recorded by leading scientists. The Nobel Prize-winning Danish physicist Niels Bohr stated that his revolutionary atomic model first came to him in a dream, and the German mathematician Karl

Gauss admitted having dreamt rather than discovered his laws of induction. The chemist Paul Ehrlich—who shared the 1908 Nobel Prize for medicine—made no secret of the fact that his side chain theory was "mainly the result of a dream." Confronted with the statements of such men, it is difficult for even the most cynical to dismiss the importance and significance of dreams.

The one thing we can be sure of is the overriding physical importance of dreams. In the words of the occult author and diplomat Benjamin Walker: "A person who is not allowed to dream while asleep will start dreaming when he is awake. The hypertense dream-psyche will burst through the waking consciousness, and he will live in a dream world, the world of the psychotic and the disoriented. Continued dream deprivation will bring mental collapse, and may eventually lead to death." Which is another way of saying that we don't live to dream, but dream to live.

Above: a contemporary engraving of the red barn in which Maria Marten was murdered in 1827.

Predictions Veritables et
Remarquables
Centures
de Michel

Chapter 7
Nostradamus and After

Is it possible that a 16th-century French physician and astrologer predicted the rise of communism, the abdication of King Edward VIII of Great Britain for love of a divorcee, and the Japanese attack on Pearl Harbor? The obscure and symbolic four-line poems of Nostradamus have been interpreted to have foreseen events all over the world since his death—and some events still to come, most notably the cataclysmic end of the world in a holocaust of flame. Other visionaries have recorded their predictions of impending global ruin. What do their visions foretell? Is there hope beyond the devastation?

It is midnight and the astrologer mounts the spiral staircase to his secret study at the top of the house. He knows that he will not be disturbed there, and that his wife will keep any unwelcome visitors away from him. He sits before a three-legged brass stool, lays down his laurel wand between its legs, and proceeds to sprinkle the hem of his robe and his feet with water. For a moment he feels frightened before the power he is about to evoke. Then his courage returns, he places a bowl of water on the stool, and peers silently into the liquid. After a while the power "speaks" to him, and he is "divinely possessed." The water becomes cloudy, and he sees therein visions of the future—pictures of war, famine, earthquake, fire, and disaster. Lighting a taper, he then goes into a trance, in which his travel into future time increases in range and detail. All the while, as the voices from space go on, and the images appear in the water, he writes down his visions in a thick vellum book. His activity lasts until dawn. Then, with the first light, he hears and sees no more. He leans back in his chair, exhausted. Downstairs, his wife will soon be preparing breakfast. In a little while he will join her, eat with her, tell her of the revelations he has seen, and rest until it is time for his labors of divination to start again the following midnight.

All this sounds somewhat like an old-fashioned melodrama, but it was serious business to the man involved in it—the French physician and astrologer Michel de Notredame, known

Opposite: the obscure rhymed predictions of the French astrologer Nostradamus have puzzled and interested the world for about 400 years. This early engraving shows him busy at his stargazing.

The Greatest of all Seers

Below: it is thought that several of the well-known Nostradamus prophecies refer to Napoleon. The following verse is one example:
"Of a name which never was held by a French king,
Never was there so fearful a thunderbolt.
Italy, Spain, and the English tremble.
He will be greatly attentive to foreign women."
The translation and interpretation of this four-line verse is the work of Erika Cheetham, English author of a recent book on the ancient prophecies. According to this author, it applies to Napoleon as follows: he was the first Bonaparte, a new name among French rulers; he was bold and powerful (a thunderbolt); all European nations came to fear him; and he was in love with three foreign women.

as Nostradamus. To him, there was nothing absurd in what he did and what he saw and heard. To him, it was the natural way —the only way—in which he could, as he put it, "leave a memorial of me after my death, to the common benefit of mankind, concerning the things which the Divine Essence has revealed to me by astronomical revelations."

Nostradamus wrote these words in a dedication to his son in the first edition of his famous *Centuries*, published in Lyons in March 1555. In his work, *centuries* do not refer to periods of a hundred years, but to a series of prophecies numbering 100 to a section. Although the prophecies came to Nostradamus with complete clarity, he did not present them clearly to his readers. Both in order not to offend the Church and to reduce the possibility of mass alarm among the general populace, he wrote his prophecies in four-line rhymes of obscure and symbolic language.

A noted scholar, Nostradamus wrote his verses in a mixture of puns, anagrams (Paris, for example, was written *Ripas*), French, Latin, and a language of his own making. "If I came to refer to that which will be in the future," he explained, "those of the realm, sect, religion, and faith would find it so poorly in accord with their petty fancies that they would come to condemn that which future ages shall know and understand to be true." In a letter to his patron, King Henry II of France—whose death, incidentally, he correctly predicted—Nostradamus added: "Some may answer that the rhyme is as easy to understand as to blow one's nose, but the sense is more difficult to grasp."

Astrology was then at one of its peaks, not to enjoy so much popularity again until the 1930s. In spite of this, Nostradamus was suspected of being in league with the Devil. A virtuous God-fearing man who had been known to burn occult books that went against the canons of the Church, the astrologer quoted the Bible in his defense, from Matthew vii. 6: "Such alone as are inspired by the divine power can predict particular events in a spirit of prophecy." His own "divine virtue and inspiration," he claimed, came directly from God the Creator, who used him as a spokesman for His own plans and intentions for the future.

Employing a blend of learning and intuition, Nostradamus concentrated mainly on *facts* about the future, rather than *dates*. He even got the date of his own death wrong, dying in July 1566 instead of November 1567, as he had predicted. However, it did not affect the success of the *Centuries*, which went from edition to edition, and which has been in print from his day to this—about 400 years running.

His nocturnal methods of divination were based largely on an ancient book called *De Mysteriis Egyptorum*, an edition of which was published in Lyons in 1547. Its author, the 4th-century Greek philosopher Iamblichus, stressed the importance of dressing in robes and using a wand and a three-legged stool. To later disciples of Nostradamus, such trappings heightened the impact of his predictions.

Here is a translation of the third verse of Nostradamus' *Century One*:

When the litters are overturned by the whirlwind and faces are covered by cloaks, the new republic will be troubled by its people. At this time the reds and the whites will rule wrongly.

This has been interpreted as a forecast of the French Revolution of 1789, and the coming of what Nostradamus called the Common Advent, or the assumption of power by the ordinary man. The "reds" and the "whites" was taken to refer to the era of Robespierre and the Terror, white being the color of the Bourbon rulers who were overthrown, and red the color of the Revolutionaries. One of his few predictions with a definite date also anticipates the French Revolution. In a letter to King Henry II on June 27, 1558, Nostradamus foretold an uprising against the Church, stating: "It shall be in the year 1792, at which time everyone will think it a renovation of the age." As it happened, the Republic of France—born and bred out of anticlerical thinking—came into being in September 1792. The year before that saw the flight of King Louis XVI and Queen Marie-Antoinette when, as the astrologer prophesied, they traveled by a "circuitous route" at night before being captured by the mob and beheaded.

Above: a drawing of the medieval seer Nostradamus holding a marble tablet on which his prophecy about the French Revolution, more than 200 years after his lifetime, is inscribed. He is showing it to a peasant woman and her child.

It seemed only natural that, as a Frenchman, some of Nostradamus' most successful prophecies should concern his own country. In verse seven of *Century One*, he speaks of "letters intercepted on their way," a prediction that could apply to the celebrated case of Captain Alfred Dreyfus 339 years later. In this case of anti-Semitism that divided the country, the innocent Dreyfus was unjustly convicted on the basis of intercepted letters said to have been sent by him to the Germans. Before getting a public pardon, Dreyfus had a review of his case by an official named Rousseau, as Nostradamus foretold. This minister was so bitterly anti-Dreyfus that he found the officer guilty a second time, even though Dreyfus was soon after fully exonerated.

These predictions were followed by a vision of the atrocities in the City of Nantes in 1793, when 1000 citizens opposed to the Revolutionaries were either guillotined or drowned naked in the river Loire—"Cries, groans at Nantes pitiful to see," were the words of Nostradamus. Napoleon comes in for a number of prophecies, including his birth ("an emperor will be born near Italy who will cost the empire dear"), his retreat from fire-torn Moscow in the winter of 1812-13 ("A mass of men will draw near . . . the Destroyer will ruin the old city"), and his defeat at Waterloo in 1815 when the Leopard (England) and the Boar (Prussia) crushed the Eagle (Napoleon).

As he said himself, however, Nostradamus had foreknowledge of more than just one country or one continent. Some of his most fascinating forecasts concern the United States, its inabitants, and its political leaders. Three times in the ten books of the *Centuries* are mentions such as "the great man . . . struck down in the day by a thunderbolt"; "the great one will fall"; "the world put into trouble by three brothers; their enemies will seize the marine city, hunger, fire, blood, plague, and all evils doubled." These references are generally taken as a warning of the assassination of President John F. Kennedy, a presentiment of the gunning down of his brother,

Overleaf: Nostradamus was one prophet of the long line that warned of the end of the world. Interpreters of his riddle-like, rhymed predictions say he foresaw the world's destruction near the year 2000. John Martin, a British artist who lived in the last century, may or may not have known about the prophetic astrologer. However, his powerful painting could almost be said to be a rendering of Nostradamus' vision of the final, horrible holocaust.

Above: the Duke and Duchess of Windsor just after their wedding. Interpreters of Nostradamus say he foresaw King Edward VIII's abdication for love of a divorcee. Erika Cheetham refers to a verse mentioning "divorce" and "king of the islands" as the prophecy.

Robert, and a hint that the troubles of Senator Edward Kennedy would be ongoing. The destruction of New York appears to be foreseen by the astrologer in three references stating the "earthshaking fire [which] will cause tremors around the New City"; "the sky will burn at 45 degrees, fire approaches the Great New City"; and the "King will want to enter the New City."

Apart from the devastation and/or invasion of New York, Nostradamus predicted that the whole of the USA would be involved in a cataclysmic third world war. This would be started by China, and would end with a sky filled with "weapons and rockets" with tremendous damage "inflicted on the left" (in this case, the Western Hemisphere). What makes this particular prophecy more chilling than most is how his verse six of *Century Two* apparently describes the atom bomb attacks on Nagasaki and Hiroshima in 1945:

> *Near the harbor and in two cities will be two scourges, the like of which have never been seen. Hunger, plague within, people thrown out by the sword will cry for help from the great immortal God.*

Predating this in time—although not in the *Centuries* them-

Below: the young Marconi looks proud and confident in this 1895 photograph of him with his first wireless transmitter. Evidence that Nostradamus predicted radio and electricity is given by Erika Cheetham from this prophecy:

"When the animal tamed by man
Begins to speak after great efforts and difficulty,
The lightning so harmful to the rod
Will be taken from the earth and suspended in the air."

selves, which are not chronological—is his line about "fire in the ruined ships of the West." This has been interpreted as the blazing American vessels and battleships during the Japanese attack on Pearl Harbor in December 1941. As for England, in *Century Ten* the astrologer anticipated the abdication of King Edward VIII, who gave up his throne to marry the twice-divorced American woman, Wallis Simpson. "The young born to the realm of Britain, which his dying father had commended to him . . . London will dispute with him, and the kingdom will be demanded back from the son."

By the time of his death, Nostradamus had predicted such unrelated and varied events as the victory of General Charles de Gaulle to gain the leadership of France, the Hungarian Revolution of 1956, the death of Hitler in his Berlin bunker, the collapse of the French Maginot Line in World War II, and the influenza epidemic that swept through the world in 1918–19—"the pestilence" following the "dreadful war."

Wide Range of Predictions

The work of Nostradamus was not formally condemned by a Papal Court until 1781, when it was put on the Index of prohibited books. By then, the visionary's influence and example had built up a following among both the clerical and the secular. One of the most remarkable of the prophets who came after Nostradamus was the 18th-century poet Jacques Cazotte, whose pleasant manners and modest talents were enough to gain him a place in French high society of the day. His most famous recorded prophecy took place on a summer's evening in 1788, toward the end of a garden party given by the Duchess de Gramont. As a protégé of his hostess, Cazotte's

Below: the Great Fire of London in 1666 seems to be clearly predicted by Nostradamus in these first two lines of one of his rhymes, as translated and interpreted by Erika Cheetham: "The blood of the just will be demanded of London Burnt by fire in three times twenty plus six."

An Age of Revolution

Above: the rise of Oliver Cromwell, shown here, meant the fall of Charles I after the English Civil War. The prophetic rhyme supposed to foretell this event talks of a man who was "born of obscure rank" in England, and who was to "gain empire through force." Cromwell was of a humble family, and became the English ruler after the Civil War.

principal purpose at such gatherings was to read his latest sonnets or odes. This he usually did in mild, gentle tones. On this particular occasion, however, the poet showed the sharp side of his nature and talent. It came when Guillaume des Malesherbes, one of Louis XVI's ministers, proposed a toast to "the day when reason shall triumph in the affairs of men—even though I shall not live to see that day."

Cazotte swung round on him, and his party mask dropped. "On the contrary, sir," he exclaimed. "You *will* live to see the day— to your cost! It shall come in five years time with a great French Revolution!"

While the guests stood open-mouthed around him, Cazotte turned to several other highly placed politicians and courtiers, and told them what their fates would be. The King's favorite, Chamfort, would join his friend Malesherbes on the guillotine, he predicted; the Marquis de Condorcet would "cheat the executioner" by taking poison; as for the Duchess herself, she would "ride to the scaffold in a woodcutter's cart." As the shock gradually wore off, the aristocrats began to snigger self-defensively among themselves. Then one of the company—an atheist named Jean La Harpe, who later wrote an account of the evening—stepped forward.

"What of me, Monsieur Cazotte?" he asked mockingly. "Don't tell me that I, of all people, am not destined for the guillotine!"

Cazotte smiled at him. "You are not, sir," he replied, "but only so that you can undergo an even more horrible fate. For you, Monsieur Atheist, are to become a devout and happy Christian!"

The laughter at this was even louder. But Cazotte had the final, I-told-you-so laugh. Everything came about as he had said it would, and La Harpe—whose conversion to Christianity was one of the sensations of the day—bequeathed his manuscript about Cazotte and his "ridiculous predictions" to the monastery in which he had become a man of God.

The prediction of the violent end of Louis XVI remained the outstanding example of predictive powers in the world until the morning of May 13, 1917. On that day, three small children were quietly herding sheep in the hills near the village of Fatima in central Portugal. Ten-year-old Lucia dos Santos and her cousins Jacinta, aged seven, and Francisco, nine, suddenly saw two dazzling flashes of light. The illumination came from a stubby oak tree nearby. Suspended in the center of the "ball of light" was the figure of a beautiful woman. As the youngsters stiffened and gazed at her, she told them not to be afraid. "I will not harm you," she said as she became indistinct and gradually faded away.

Her last words were to ask the children to return to the spot on the 13th of each month until October, at which time a great and dreadful secret would be revealed to them. Despite a beating they received from their parents for "telling lies," Lucia and her cousins—together with some 50 inquisitive villagers—were back on the hill at noon on June 13. The children knelt and said their rosaries, and the beautiful lady radiated into view from the east, like a "glowing messenger from God." This time her message was not so encouraging. She asserted that Jacinto

Above: this somewhat allegorical view of the execution of King Charles I of England in 1649 was done by an artist of the period. The Nostradamus rhyme put forward as a prophecy of this event speaks of a fortress near the Thames River, a king locked up inside, and the death of the king.

and Francisco would soon be "called to Heaven," and that Lucia would live only in order to spread the Madonna's message. At this, the belief grew that the luminous visitor was the Virgin Mary.

The Virgin Mary's next appearance was on July 13. Before an audience of more than 5000 people—of whom only Lucia, Jacinta, and Francisco could actually see her—she warned of a coming catastrophe that would be even greater than World War I, and that would destroy the world. The first sign of the disaster would be seen in the heavens—"a bright, unknown light which will be God's sign that he is about to punish the people of the world for their crimes." Once again the three children were beaten—and even imprisoned. The charge was taking God's name in vain—as well as scaring the souls out of the adults in the village.

However, the children's persistence impressed everyone. In addition, the story of a similar vision that had appeared to two little shepherdesses in La Salette, France in 1846, created more interest and a tendency to belief. Therefore, some 80,000 spectators converged on Fatima on October 13 to watch Lucia receive her briefing on humanity's fate. Like the Madonna of La Salette, the Fatima Virgin spoke of "vast destruction by

Above: an illustration of a horoscope cast for King Louis XVI and Queen Marie-Antoinette by the 18th-century English astrologer Ebenezer Silby. He foresaw their doom. The revolution that led to their execution was said to have been predicted by Nostradamus in this verse: "When the litters are overturned by the whirlwind and faces are covered by cloaks, the new republic will be troubled by its people. At this time the reds and the whites will rule wrongly."

disease and fire . . . Nature will protest at the evil done by men and earthquakes will occur in protest." As she spoke—again only to Lucia and her companions—the sky was streaked and spattered with color like a giant palette. The sun nose-dived toward earth, then flattened out and rose again. Vivid shadows flitted over the ground. The onlookers prostrated themselves in terror, crying out to God to spare them. But the children remained calm and in command of themselves.

Not long afterward, Jacinta and Francisco died in the post-World War I flu epidemic said to have been forecast by Nostradamus. As a result of her experiences—and to escape from the publicity that was turning her into a sideshow freak—Lucia decided to become a nun. She entered a convent school and became a novice in the fall of 1926. Adopting the name of Sister Marie das Dores, (Sister Mary of the Sorrows), she prepared to receive future warnings from on high. In 1927, she claimed that Christ himself had visited her, and that he had asked her to be ready for "the Lady's" final and most momentous message of all—which would be imparted to her some time in the year 1960.

Before that date arrived, something happened that seemed to be a fulfillment of Lucia's earlier visions. On the night of January 25, 1938, the Aurora Borealis, or Northern Lights, was visible throughout western Europe. The bright streams of green, violet, yellow, and flaming red that forked like lightning in the sky made many people think of the words of the Madonna 21 years earlier, when she spoke to Lucia of the "bright light by night." In 1960—the year Lucia said she would get the

Virgin's final message—she was cloistered in the Portuguese convent of Coimbra. Thousands of Catholics throughout the world demanded to know what the Madonna had said to her. But Lucia now aged 53, was not talking. She did not reveal her secret until 1967, and then only to Pope Paul VI.

It is still not known what she said to the Pope—whether she confessed that her story had been a fake all along, or whether he felt that her prophecy was too frightening, too extreme to be made known to mankind. Whatever it was that she whispered to the Pope, it was said that he turned white and swung away from her.

The Sleeping Prophet

Had the message concerned the inevitability of World War III—which is a possibility—it coincided not only with the major predictions of Nostradamus, but also with those of the renowned American clairvoyant Edgar Cayce (pronounced Casey). Called the "sleeping prophet," Cayce was best-known as a faith healer. Born on a Kentucky farm in March 1877, he was also a visionary, much in the manner of William Blake or the Swedish theologian Emanuel Swedenborg. Cayce first spoke to his "vision visitors" at the age of six. By his death in 1945, he had predicted such things as laser beams, the discovery of the Dead Sea Scrolls, the Wall Street crash of 1929, and the earthquakes, hurricanes, and tidal waves that struck California, Japan, and the Philippines respectively in 1926.

Like Nostradamus, Cayce was deeply religious. A daily reader of the Bible, he believed that he was merely an instrument through which the Almighty channeled his cosmic information. Of the 8000 trancelike readings that he gave over a period of 43 years, none had more influence or significance than his prophecies about a third world war, due to start around 1999, and the end of civilization as we know it shortly after A.D. 2000. He saw the end of the world in a dream in which he was reborn in 2100 in Nebraska, and flew over a desolated United States in an odd-shaped metal aircraft. He also foresaw the total destruction of Los Angeles and San Francisco along with much of the western part of the country.

His vision of the future—as gloomy as any in the doom-laden history of divination—took place in 1936. It dealt with more than just the usual devastation coming out of the sky—the "darts in the sky" that Nostradamus wrote of when prophesying the final war between East and West. To Cayce, there was also danger from below. It came from the submerged and mythical continent of Atlantis, which is allegedly been lying beneath the waters of the Atlantic as a lost civilization for some 12,000 years.

According to Cayce, Atlantis was the original Eden, the first place on Earth in which "man changed his spiritual for his physical form." Because of man's self-destructive inhumanity, went Cayce's prediction, he has been sentenced to extinction by the reemergence of Atlantis, whose inhabitants were the first possessors of death rays, atomic bombs, and machine-minds. Before this comes about, however, Communism will have been destroyed. Again like Nostradamus, Cayce feared the growth and increasing power of Marxism. (In *Century Nine*, Nostradamus warns that "the anti-Czar will exterminate

Below: miracle healer and clairvoyant, Edgar Cayce was one of the most famous psychic figures of recent times. According to his own records, he diagnosed and treated some 30,000 patients. He worked while in a trance state, and, sometimes, from hundreds of miles away. In 1936, Cayce had a prophetic dream about vast upheaval in the world, in which much of the United States was destroyed.

Where Once was New York City

Edgar Cayce, one of the best-known seers and faith healers of this century, had a cosmic vision in 1936. In it, he was reborn in the year 2100 with the knowledge that he had been Edgar Cayce from 1877 to 1945. With the scientists who were investigating his story, he flew across North America in an odd-shaped aircraft at fantastic speed. They landed among the ruins of a huge city, which was in the process of being rebuilt, and asked what the name of it was. "New York City," came the startling reply.

Along with the vision of a devasted New York, Cayce foresaw violent changes in all of the United States and the world. Nebraska had become the west coast after earthquakes had shattered the rest of the west—including Los Angeles and San Francisco—and Alabama was partly under water. Much of Japan, too, was submerged, and northern Europe had been completely altered by chaotic upheavals. During the cataclysmic changes, new lands had appeared from beneath both the Atlantic and Pacific oceans.

With this vision, Cayce joined the prophets who have foretold of vast destruction throughout the world around the year 2000.

everyone.") Cayce, however, believed that the attempt to "level not only the economic life but also the mental and spiritual welfare as well, will not last very long." He adds: "When one forgets to love one's neighbor, the Lord cannot have clemency, and such a situation cannot continue."

While time sped toward the day of reckoning set by Cayce for 2000, a simple old Italian woman, Mamma Rosa, was being honored by the latest visitations from the Virgin. In the two years between 1965 and 1967, Mamma Rosa had been informed that "the world is in mud . . . the world is being lost little by little . . . the world is on the threshold of terrible tribulations." In June 1967, she was asked by her vision to "do everything to console the minds as the hour of terrible punishment has struck . . . the warning has sounded. . . . We are already 130 years after La Salette and 50 years after Fatima . . . carry only love and peace in the heart. Then when the terrible moments of darkness come you will have Jesus . . . and you will be strong." In December 1967, Mamma Rose was told by the Madonna that she had been chosen as Christ's messenger because "of all people you are the most ignorant."

Do the seers never foresee a rosy future? There does not seem to be much hope and light in most of the prophets'

Below: Edgar Cayce shown in court with his wife and secretary after being charged with telling fortunes. His case was dismissed by a New York magistrate on a technicality.

visions. However, gloomy as he was for the most part, Nostradamus had a sincere and often-stated belief in a Golden Age that was to succeed the holocaust.

This gleam of optimism in the *Centuries* was seized upon by the Nazis during World War II (another event foreseen by the astrologer), and was perverted to their own use. This came about when Goebbels, the Minister of Propaganda, was introduced to Nostradamus' work by his wife, who chose the rhymes nightly as bedtime reading. Goebbels found the verses to his occult taste, and, together with the Gestapo chief, twisted their meanings to announce predictions of a total German victory. In May 1940, the Germans dropped copies of the altered *Centuries* by air over France to demoralize the populace. The Allies later retaliated by scattering their own version of the rhymes for propaganda purposes over the towns and cities of Germany.

Because Nostradamus deliberately obscured his meanings, his verses lend themselves to greatly different interpretations. His disciples have been accused of something worse than differing interpretations, however. They have been indicted for fitting prophecies to known facts. Many also regard the prophecies themselves as falling within the Theory of Probabilities, which states that if forecasts are sufficient in range and number, some of them must inevitably come true. Whether or not this theory is accepted, Nostradamus' account of the third world war tells of the appearance of Lucifer in the shape of a man, the collapse of the papacy, and the dominance of Communism.

With the razing of Rome, Paris, New York, and London, there will be 27 years of pain and bloodshed while the "King of Horror" deploys his aerial forces to eliminate his "enemies," according to details of the prediction. The red flag will flutter over the ruins of the Vatican, and the hemisphere-to-hemisphere firing of atomic warheads and weapons will ensure that "the universal conflagration shall be preceded by many great inundations, so that there shall scarce be any land that shall not be covered with water. . . . Before and after these inundations in many countries there shall be such scarcity of rain, and such a great deal of fire, and burning stones shall fall from Heaven, that nothing unconsumed shall be left. All this shall happen before the great conflagration."

However, there is a silver lining in the cloud: all the death, anguish, and havoc is for the ultimate good of mankind. Nostradamus stresses that the diasters and tribulations at the end of the 20th century are necessary in order to prepare the ground for building the ideal world—rather in the way that filthy and decaying slums are demolished to make way for sound new housing. Nostradamus dedicated *Centures* to his young son, whose "years are too few and months incapable to receive into thy weak understanding what I am forced to define of futurity." In this dedication, the astrologer closes on a note of cheer and optimism with a prediction that the best of all possible worlds will follow the worst.

"After this [the man-made and natural disasters] has lasted a certain time, there will be renewed another reign of Saturn, a truly great and golden age."

"A Truly Great and Golden Age"

Below: Lenin, the great leader of the 1917 Russian Revolution, here is shown addressing a crowd. Did Nostradamus foretell the communist victory when he talked about the "Great Red One?" Medievalist Cheetham interprets it so.

Chapter 8
The Modern Seers

Do seers and visionaries live among us now? What messages do they have to give us of events which have yet to come? The American clairvoyant Jeane Dixon has an extraordinary record of prophecies that have come true, the most memorable being her prevision of the assassination of President John F. Kennedy 11 years before it happened, in the very church in which his funeral was held. How does she look into the future—and having once seen a picture of future events, is it possible for those events to be averted or changed? Other of her predictions have yet to be fulfilled—what lies ahead for mankind?

As she entered St. Matthew's Cathedral in Washington D.C. on a drizzly morning in the fall of 1952, Jeane Dixon felt no immediate premonition of evil. A deeply religious woman, she was, in fact, glowing with anticipation—a feeling that had possessed her for several days. "It was a feeling of expectancy," she explained, "as if something momentous was going to happen, and I would be involved." She moved forward to start her devotions, and stood reverentially before the statue of the Virgin Mary. Then something happened that was to haunt her for the next decade and more. ". . . Suddenly the White House appeared before me in dazzling brightness. Coming out of a haze, the numerals 1-9-6-0 formed above the roof. An ominous dark cloud appeared, covering the numbers, and dripped slowly onto the White House . . . Then I looked down and saw a young man, tall and blue-eyed, crowned with a shock of thick brown hair, quietly standing in front of the main door.

"I was still staring at him when a voice came out of nowhere, telling me softly that this young man, a Democrat, to be seated as President in 1960, would be assassinated while in office. The vision faded into the wall—into the distance as softly as it had come, but it stayed with me until that day in Dallas when it was fulfilled." That day in Dallas came 11 years later with the assassination of President John F. Kennedy. His funeral mass was said in the very church in which Jeane Dixon had had her vision.

In 1952, Jeane Dixon was 34 years old. At the age of eight in

Opposite: President Kennedy won the affection and respect of most of his countrymen in the brief period he held office before an assassin's bullet cut him down.

The Greatest Living Seer

Below: Jeane Dixon, America's most famous living clairvoyant, sees things to come through telepathy, revelation, meditation, and dreams. Her prediction of President Kennedy's untimely and violent end made her name a household word from coast to coast.

California, she had been taken by her mother to see a gypsy fortune teller. The gypsy lived in a canvas wagon, which she shared with a brood of chickens, and was used to being approached by the local people from Santa Rosa. When she took Jeane's hands in hers and turned them over, however, she dropped her customary mask of impassivity. "This little girl is going to be world famous," she gasped. "She will be able to foresee worldwide changes, because she is blessed with the gift for prophecy. Never have I seen such palm lines!" Several marks on Jeane's hand excited the gypsy, who told Jeane's mother of their significance. "They mean that this child will grow mightily in wisdom," she said seriously. "The lines in the left hand are the blueprint of one's dreams and potential. Those in the right hand signify what you do with what God has given you. She is already developing fast." Later, a Hindu mystic said that markings like Jeane's occurred no more than once in a thousand years.

As Jeane grew up, she discovered that her Extra Sensory Perception (ESP) was far in excess of that of most people. Tests showed that her ability was somewhere between 90 and 97 percent, while others were lucky to have a rating of between 3 and 7 percent. Jeane learned astrology from a Jesuit priest at Loyola University in Los Angeles, and though she preferred to give personal readings by means of a crystal ball, she believed it possible to help people through reading the stars. Her popular column, "Jeane Dixon's Horoscope," began to appear in more than 300 newspapers throughout the United States, where it has been estimated that some six million newspaper readers follow the stars each day. She attracted attention at highest social and political levels by her obvious sincerity and desire to do good.

Mrs. Dixon recounts that President Franklin D. Roosevelt summoned her to the White House at the height of World War II late in 1944. He wanted to know how much time he had left in which to complete his "mission for mankind." Mrs. Dixon looked solemnly at the aging President, and asked him if he really wanted to know the truth. He affirmed that he did, and her answer was abrupt. "You have no more than six months," she told him. He died suddenly on April 12, 1945.

By then, Jeane Dixon had taken her place among the leading seers of the mid-20th century, and she went on to demonstrate that—for her at least—the present and the future were one. She accurately predicted the partition of India, which she saw in her crystal in 1945. At that time, she told an Indian military attaché at a Washington reception that his country would be divided on June 2, 1947. At a party in Washington early in 1945, she told Winston Churchill that he would lose the coming election. He protested crossly that "the people of England will never let me down"; but he was defeated and replaced as prime minister that July. She foresaw the deaths of UN Secretary Dag Hammarskjold and Mahatma Gandhi; the suicide of Marilyn Monroe; the launching of the Soviet space capsule Sputnik 1; and the "uncontrollable blaze" that killed three young astronauts and destroyed an Apollo rocket at Cape Kennedy in 1967.

Like Mother Shipton—the 16th-century English oracle who predicted that the world would end in 1881—Mrs. Dixon has

Left: deeply devout, Jeane Dixon goes to church early every morning. Here she is shown lighting devotional candles in St. Matthew's, the very church in which she had the vision of John Kennedy's assassination, and in which his funeral mass was said.

Below: the bereaved widow and brothers of President John Kennedy march in his funeral procession. Later, Jeane Dixon made a prediction that Robert Kennedy too would be assassinated in the Ambassador Hotel in Los Angeles. Ironically, Mrs. Dixon made her accurate forecast in the very same hotel that was the scene of the killing.

made her mistakes. She was wrong, for instance, when she forecast that China would cause a world war in 1958. She explains this error by the fact that she is a "mere channel of communication," and, although she was shown the correct symbols, she failed to interpret them correctly.

Refusing money except for her writings, Mrs. Dixon makes a habit of giving predictions before sizeable gatherings of people. At a lunch on the roof of the Washington Hotel in 1968, she told her immediate neighbor at the table not to fret about Martin Luther King and his thousands of followers marching on Washington. "Don't you worry about that," she said, with an unexpected sadness in her voice. "Martin Luther King will not get to Washington . . . he will be shot before he

Above left: Mrs. Dixon told an ill-looking President Roosevelt that he had only six more months to live in late 1944. "I could sense that he had felt a premonition of his own death," she later said.

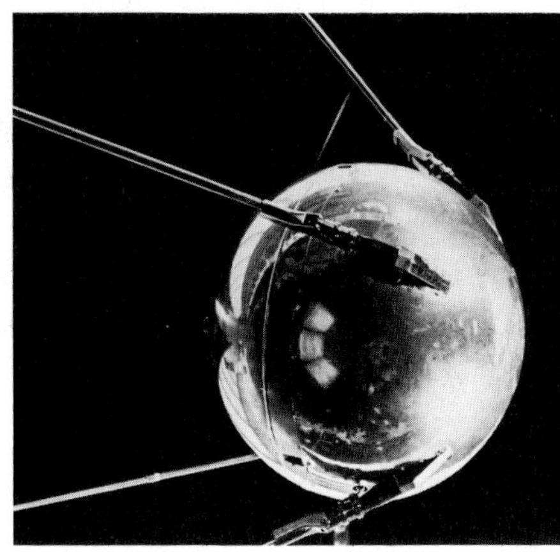

Above: Sputnik I, the world's first satellite, was successfully launched by the Soviet Union on October 4, 1957. Four years earlier, on a television program, Jeane Dixon had gazed into her crystal, and had described a vision of "a silver ball" going into space.

can get here. He will be shot in the neck . . . He will be shot first . . . and Robert Kennedy will be next!"

A few days later, the first part of her prophecy came true with the killing of Martin Luther King. On May 28, 1968, Mrs. Dixon felt sure that death was "finally and irrevocably" closing in on Senator Kennedy. She was addressing a convention in the Grand Ballroom of the Ambassador Hotel in Los Angeles, and invited questions from the floor. One woman asked her whether Robert Kennedy would become president, and everyone in the room waited eagerly for the reply. "The answer came to me with a fierce, unrelenting finality," Jeane wrote later. "It came in the form of a black curtain that descended between the audience and me . . . It dropped down like lightning, and did not stop until it had reached the floor. It was black . . . and swift . . . it was final! . . . 'No, he will not. He will never be president of the United States,' I answered calmly, 'because of a tragedy right here in this hotel.'"

The next week Robert Kennedy was due to speak at the Ambassador Hotel, and Mrs. Dixon repeated her warning to an American Legion official and to the mother-in-law of the lieutenant governor of Florida. The official advised her not to upset anyone. The woman, however, made a serious effort to contact the senator's mother about the warning from the "Prophetess of Washington." Her telephone calls were not returned. Early on the morning of June 5, a bullet fired by an assassin ended Robert Kennedy's life at the Ambassador Hotel.

Could the senseless killings of the Kennedy brothers have been averted through Mrs. Dixon's prophetic warnings? Mrs.

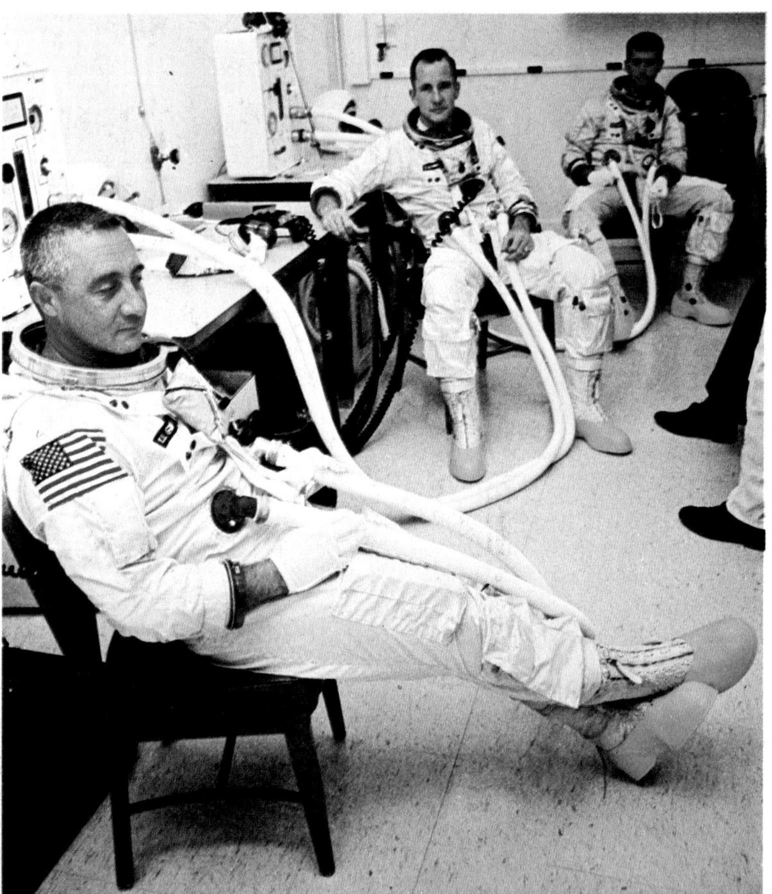

Right: astronauts Grissom, White, and Chaffee were the first fatalities of the US space program, killed in a fire that destroyed Apollo 4 on January 27, 1967. A month earlier—during what should have been a happy holiday meeting with a friend—Jeane Dixon had foreseen the tragedy with terrible and exact clarity.

Visions of Untimely Death

Dixon herself feels that the younger brother's might have been, but not the president's. She explains this by making a difference between what she learns of the future by "revelation," and what she foresees by "telepathy." In the case of revelation, no power on earth can stop the event revealed. Revelations come rarely to Mrs. Dixon, but her vision of President Kennedy's assassination was one of them. In the case of telepathy, which is an almost continuous part of Mrs. Dixon's daily existence, the outcome can be altered by altering the situation. Because her foreglimpse of Robert Kennedy's killing was by telepathy, it might have been avoided on her warning—perhaps by a change of time or place of the speech.

Although Jeane Dixon's early vision of President John Kennedy's death was particularly detailed, it was not the only precognition of the tragedy. Many people throughout the world—some of them professional seers, most of them average citizens—felt that John Kennedy's doomed future had been revealed to them. One of the warnings came from an Englishman. He wrote to President Kennedy on October 25, 1963, less than a month before the President's death. In his letter, he quoted this passage from an article of his own previously published in *Fate Annual*: "The President may make powerful enemies among his own people, and I would not rule out the possibility of an attempted assassination or worse if he is caught off his guard. There may be a strange turning of the Wheel of Fate, for it is just a century ago since the American Civil War was raging with unabated fury. President Lincoln was shot by a madman in 1865 . . ." He then added directly:

Below: a photograph of the ruined space capsule in which three young astronauts had lost their lives revealed a tool entangled in a mass of wires. Mrs. Dixon had predicted that the capsule had faulty wires, and that some kind of tool would be found "at the trouble site."

The Warning that Failed

"I am deeply concerned for your personal safety, and would respectfully urge you to strengthen your bodyguard, especially when you are in the street and other public places."

If the visions of Jeane Dixon were not always taken seriously in America, seers like her were believed at the highest level in Burma. When the Burmese gained their independence from Great Britain in 1948, their leaders called in astrologers to advise them. Based on the astral calculations they were given, politicians chose the seemingly eccentric hour of 4:20 a.m. on January 4 to launch the new nation. Nine years later, and acting on similar advice, nearby Nepal began its new national life at 4:50 a.m. on June 30. In 1950, the Burmese cabinet resigned because of information they got from astrologers. The new ministers were sworn in less than 24 hours later exactly between 9:15 and 9:20 a.m. "It is then," the fortune tellers told Prime Minister Thakin Nu, "that the stars and planets will most favor our country and bless all that we do."

Another modern clairvoyant whose forecasts received much publicity was Elisabeth Steen. In 1964 she started to have precognitive flashes about the destruction of San Francisco, where she then lived. She had previously predicted the horror of the flood that devastated much of her native Holland in 1952, and had also foreseen the death of Martin Luther King—although she was wrong on the date by two days. On the strength of these successes, newspapers reported her every psychic utterance, the late pop singer Mama Cass made a record called "California Earthquake," and the Steen family moved from San Francisco to the state of Washington. According to Elisabeth, the disaster would strike toward the end of March 1969. While thousands of San Franciscans prayed for deliverance at that period—and hundreds of others made a point of being out of town—nothing happened to the city. There was one victim, however, although she no longer lived in California. On March 28, Elisabeth Steen died suddenly in Spokane.

Opposite top: like some dreadful remake of a film, family members gather at the grave of Senator Robert Kennedy, the second brother to fall from an assassin's bullet. Both events had been foreseen by Mrs. Dixon through psychic powers.

The way in which Mrs. Steen had projected knowledge of her own impending doom onto that of an entire community is not untypical of some of those who get glimpses of our tomorrows today. In the case of a beautiful young actress at the Comédie Française in Paris, however, her intimations of disaster were limited strictly to herself. Mademoiselle Irene Muza frightened her colleagues and friends when, in an hypnotic trance, she wrote down what the future held for her. "My career will be short," she stated. "I dare not say what my end will be: it will be terrible." Before Mlle. Muza came out of her trance, her friends destroyed her written words and swore not to tell her what she had foreseen.

A few months passed. Then one day the actress went to the hairdresser and met her self-predicted terrible end! An assistant accidentally dropped some antiseptic lotion on a lighted stove, and Irene Muza was like a "blazing doll" within seconds. She was rushed to the hospital, but died within hours of severe burns that had left her without skin or hair.

Opposite bottom: no warning vibrations came to Jeane Dixon on Martin Luther King's first great march on Washington in 1957. In 1968, however, she forecast that he would be shot before reaching the capital city.

Time and again in recent history, scientists and nonscientists have come up with theories and possible evidence suggesting that, while our memory dwells on the past, part of

Above: San Francisco was devastated by the big 1906 earthquake. If Elizabeth Steen's vision of a 1969 catastrophe had come true, the more built-up modern city might have suffered even more.

our thinking and reasoning exist simultaneously in the present and future. The distinguished English astronomer and physicist, Sir Arthur Eddington, spent much of his career studying the mysteries of time and space. He concluded that it was not time which moved, but we ourselves. "This division into past and future is closely associated with our ideal of causation and freewill," he wrote. "In a perfectly determinate scheme, the past and future may be regarded as lying mapped out—as much available to present exploration as the distant parts of space. Events do not happen, they are just there, and we come across them." He also realized how much humanity was subject to the pull of the universe in all that it thought and did. This belief was echoed by Giorgio Piccardi, head of the Institute for Physical Chemistry at the University of Florence, who declared: "To be subjected to cosmic effects, man does not have to be shot into space; he does not even have to leave his home. Man is always surrounded by the universe, since the universe is everywhere."

At the moment, no modern prophets seem to be able to see a future much beyond the year 2000. Like Nostradamus, many of them feel that the world will have just barely survived and be recovering from a global holocaust at that time. However, on the material level, scientists do not bear out such forebodings. Dr. Herman Kahn, director of the Hudson Institute, has predicted the 100 technical innovations that will have been invented by the year 2000—and they will include "programmed dreams."

Although Jeane Dixon asserts that the years just before 1999 will hold great struggles for humanity, she also believes that we will win through to a better life for all. She bases this belief on the "most significant and soul-stirring" vision of her life, which took place shortly before sunup on February 5, 1962. At 7:17 a.m. on that day, she rose and gazed out of her window in Washington. Her eyes did not meet "the bare-limbed trees of the city," but beheld an "endless desert scene, broiled by a relentless sun." When the sun's rays parted, Mrs. Dixon saw Queen Nefertiti of ancient Egypt hand in hand with her Pharaoh. In her free arm, the Queen cradled a baby in soiled and ragged clothing. The infant was in "stark contrast to the magnificently arrayed royal couple." In her biography of Jeane Dixon, *A Gift of Prophecy*, Ruth Montgomery recounts Mrs. Dixon's interpretation of her dream as follows:

"A child born somewhere in the Middle East shortly after 7 a.m. (EST) on February 5, 1962, will revolutionize the world. Before the close of the century he will bring together all mankind in one all-embracing faith. This will be the foundation of a new Christianity, with every sect and creed united through this man, who will walk among the people to spread the wisdom of the Almighty Power. This person, though born of humble peasant origin, is a descendant of Queen Nefertiti . . . There was nothing kingly about his coming—no kings or shepherds to do homage to this newborn baby—but he is the answer to the prayers of a troubled world. Mankind will begin to feel the great force of this man in the early 1980s, and during the subsequent 10 years, the world as we know it will be reshaped and revamped into one without wars or suffering. His power will grow until 1999, at which time, the peoples of this earth will probably discover the full meaning of the vision."

Asked how she felt at the time of her vision, Jeane Dixon answered: "I felt suspended and enfolded, as if I were surrounded by whipped cream. For the first time I understood the full meaning of the Biblical phrase, 'My cup runneth over.' I loved all mankind. I felt that I would never again need food or sleep, because I had experienced perfect peace."

Like her prophetic forerunners, Jeane Dixon has not broken through the time barrier into the 21st century. For that vision—be it of Jeane Dixon's perfect peace, of Nostradamus' golden age after the holocaust, or of an entirely different picture—we must await a new prophet for whom the future is now.

Mysteries of Time and Space

Below: this orange grove in California was pushed out of line by the San Andreas fault, which also affects San Francisco.

Below left: the mild shock that hit San Francisco in 1966 left rubble like this behind. Perhaps this minor quake helped people believe in Mrs. Steen's prediction of a calamity in 1969.

New Hope for the World

It was a wintry February day in Washington, D.C. in 1962. Jeane Dixon—called "the Prophetess of Washington"—awoke just before sunup, and moved toward her bedroom window facing east. There, instead of the city streets lined with bare trees, she saw a vivid desert scene. Out of the rays of a sun that glowed like a golden ball stepped Queen Nefertiti of ancient Egypt, hand-in-hand with her Pharaoh. She carried a newborn baby, whose ragged clothing jarred the eye compared to the gorgeous raiment of the royal couple. A few minutes later, the baby had grown to manhood. He was surrounded by worshipers of every color, race, and creed—and Jeane Dixon felt herself to be inside the very center of the vision with the adoring crowds.

This, then, was "the most significant and soul-stirring" vision ever experienced by the modern seer, Jeane Dixon. She interprets it as the promise of a great "new Christianity" that will unite all the world as one in peace. The leader will be the baby of her vision. "His power will grow greatly until 1999," she says, "at which time the . . . earth will probably discover the full meaning of the vision."

Chapter 9
The Queen of Sciences

Today virtually every newspaper makes a special feature of its horoscope, and practically everyone can say under which astrological sign he was born. Behind this popular interest, deeper questions stand: is there truly a relationship between the heavenly bodies and human beings? How can that relationship be explained? Does the planetary position at the moment of birth influence the personality and destiny of the newborn throughout their whole life? How did the curious art of astrology develop, and how long have we been guided by its interpretations? How has it changed over the centuries? What is the position of astrology now?

On February 24, 1975, members of royal families and leading statesmen from all over the world gathered in Nepal to attend the coronation of the country's new king. It was an elaborate and glittering ceremony, filmed for millions of television viewers across the globe. In accordance with Eastern custom, the date of the coronation had been chosen by Nepal's astrologers. King, government, and country had awaited their choice of a favorable date.

Opposite: a Dutch painting of 1663 of an astrologer in the gloom of his study, surrounded by the trappings of his ancient art.

The leaders of Nepal are by no means the only Asian rulers of modern times to adhere to traditional oriental astrology. In both Burma and Sri Lanka, formerly Ceylon, new governments take office at the exact times worked out as propitious by official astrologers. In Sikkim, a province of northern India, the then Crown Prince married his American bride in March 1963 after waiting a year for astrologers to choose their wedding day. Pandit Jawaharlal Nehru, one of the founders of modern India and his country's prime minister for 14 years, was a firm believer in astrology. When his first grandson was born in 1944, he at once suggested to the child's mother that a horoscope be made for the baby. In Malaysia too, high-ranking members of the administration take careful note of the times of their children's birth so that an accurate horoscope may be drawn up for them.

No one could regard these eminent believers in astrology as ignorant people who happen to have attained high office. They are men and women of intellectual sophistication, capable of meeting other world leaders on a basis of perfect equality.

"Never Been More Popular"

Below: the many commercial astrologers of New York vie for business. Here one advertises by means of a sandwich man.

Interestingly enough, their belief in "the celestial science" is sometimes in contradiction to their political ideology. Thus the government of Sri Lanka, a coalition of Marxist groups that officially regard astrology as an outmoded superstition, have followed the advice of their country's Buddhist astrologers just as devoutly as their more conservative predecessors.

Many Western countries have also come under the influence of astrology at various times in their history, and astrology today claims many followers among the educated and the sophisticated in the West as in the East. Astrological forecasts appear in almost every popular magazine and newspaper in the Western world, and are eagerly read by millions. Whether they believe in astrology or not, most people would probably admit to sneaking at least an occasional glance at articles on astrology. The signs of the zodiac have become household words, and almost everyone knows whether he or she is a Piscean or Leo or Virgo.

Astrology—the subject that was once regarded as "the Queen of the Sciences"—has never been more popular. In both the United States and Europe every community of any size has dozens, sometimes hundred, of professional astrologers, and thousands of amateur ones. Millions of horoscopes are cast every year in the United States alone. There are numerous magazines devoted exclusively to astrology, and other popular occult magazines are crammed with astrological advertisements. Although a good deal of criticism can be—and is—leveled at astrology, most people would probably like to believe that there could be something in it. But something in what exactly? What is the strange body of beliefs we call astrology?

Astrology is based on the belief that there is a relationship between the heavenly bodies and human beings, and that this relationship can be interpreted. More specifically, astrologers claim that the position of the Sun, Moon, and planets at the time and over the place of a person's birth has an important bearing on the kind of individual that person is and on the future course of his or her life. Astrologers believe that the planets are somehow bound up with the rhythms of human life, and that everyone and everything on Earth is affected by the cosmic conditions that prevailed at the time of a person's birth. Thus the planetary patterns at that moment are thought to indicate the pattern of a newborn's personality and destiny throughout the rest of life.

Astrologers study these patterns by means of a horoscope or natal chart. This is a map of the zodiac—the band of sky within which the Sun, Moon, and planets appear to move—showing the exact positions of all the planets at the time a person was born. Astrologers divide the zodiac into 12 zones represented by 12 different signs. The planets are thought to influence a person's life according to the signs they were in at the moment of birth, their distance from each other, and their exact location in the natal chart.

When astrologers began to write forecasts for magazines and newspapers they obviously could not publish a separate horoscope for each of their readers. They therefore devised a system of "Sun Signs" based simply on the date, rather than the precise time, of birth. So today when someone says "I'm a Leo," he means that he was born sometime between July 23 and August

Left: the coronation of Birendra Bir Bikram Shah Dev as king of Nepal and reincarnation of the Hindu god Vishnu in early 1975. The exact moment for his crowning by the high priest of the Court was determined by the Court astrologers, and the king had waited, uncrowned, for the most astrologically propitious day.

Left: a wax gypsy presides over a booth selling computer-produced horoscopes. Astrology has never been more broadly popular, and computer technology offers an obvious link-up, providing cheap individual horoscopes. But the need for mystery lives on—in spite of the convenience of science—and exotic, jewelry-laden Esmeraldas still have their part to play.

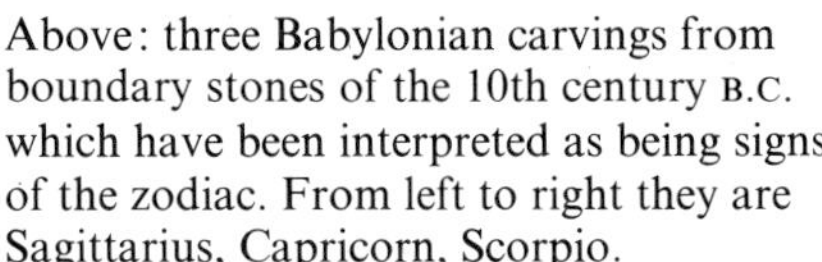

Above: three Babylonian carvings from boundary stones of the 10th century B.C. which have been interpreted as being signs of the zodiac. From left to right they are Sagittarius, Capricorn, Scorpio.

Right: Maharaja Jai Singh II of India, a renowned mathematician, had this great observatory built in his new city of Jaipur to follow the track of the constellations of the zodiac across the sky during his reign in the 18th century.

Roots Deep in Human History

23 when the Sun is located in the zone of the zodiac known as Leo. It was this use of Sun Signs that made astrology accessible to millions of ordinary people, and marked a new era in the long and sometimes star-crossed history of astrology.

The origins of astrology probably go back almost as far as humankind itself. Archeologists have recently unearthed a bone over 30,000 years old bearing marks that appear to refer to the phases of the Moon. Monuments like the great stone circle at Stonehenge in Britain are believed to have been sophisticated astronomical observatories, and to testify to prehistoric peoples' interest in the heavens. In the early cultures of Asia, Europe, and America, people constructed giant watchtowers and observatories so that their priests could search the night sky for the key to human destiny.

Left: an Aztec priest from a 16th-century Spanish history with pictures by Indian artists, shown observing a comet from a temple. The Aztecs were greatly concerned with all aspects of astrology and astronomy, and regarded comets in particular as evil portents. A year before Hernando Cortes and the conquering Spaniards arrived, a series of comets were sighted. Montezuma, the Aztec ruler, correctly interpreted them as a sign that his empire would fall.

It was in the dry and cloudless climate of Mesopotamia, however, that astrology first emerged in something resembling its modern form. Five thousand years ago the priest-magicians of Babylon were already studying and naming the stars. By about 700 B.C. they had discovered the extent of the zodiac and had invented the 12 signs of the zodiac that we now know so well. They had attributed good and bad qualities to the planets and had begun to interpret *aspects*—the supposedly significant angles between one planet and another.

Astrology spread from Babylonia to Egypt and Greece. Some of the Egyptian pharaohs decorated their tombs with astrological symbols, but Egypt does not appear to have become enthusiastic about astrology until long after the golden age of the pharaohs and it was in Greece that astrology as we know it developed.

The Greeks identified the Sun, Moon, and planets with their own gods and goddesses. The planet Venus, for example, was

Above: the Egyptian sky goddess Nut, surrounded by the signs of the zodiac, from a mummy case dating from the 2nd century A.D.

Below: this Roman coin minted in Spain depicts Capricorn, the zodiacal sign of Emperor Augustus.

identified with Aphrodite, goddess of love, and Jupiter with Zeus, the king of the gods. The Babylonians had judged the effect of a planet according to its appearance, believing that Jupiter had a favorable influence if it shone white and an unfavorable influence if it were red. The Greeks gave no importance to appearance. Instead they regarded planets as consistently favorable, a "benefic" or unfavorable, a "malefic." Zeus' planet Jupiter was a benefic while Mars, identified with Ares, the bloody god of war, was a malefic. The Greeks also turned the planets into personalities, and combined the practical techniques of the Babylonian astrologers with the philosophies of their own great thinkers to add a moral significance to astrology.

The Greeks made personal horoscopes fashionable. They enabled a Babylonian astrologer to set up a school of astrology on the Greek island of Cos in 280 B.C., and from about 200 B.C. onward a number of widely circulated manuals were published on the subject. The most important of these was the *Tetrabiblos*, written in the second century A.D. by the Alexandrian Claudius Ptolemy, the greatest astronomer of ancient times.

Ptolemy's catalogs and atlases of the stars and planets were unmatched for accuracy until the 17th century, and his was probably the most influential book on astrology ever written. Ptolemy gathered together most of the astrological teachings of his own and preceding centuries in his book, which contained all the essentials that have gone to make up modern astrology, and included full details of how to calculate an individual horoscope.

By the time of Ptolemy, astrology had already captured the imagination of the Roman Empire. Rich man and poor, freeman and slave acknowledged its importance and accepted its doctrines. The great Augustus, first of the Roman Emperors, believed in it fully, perhaps partly because at the time of his birth the astrologer Nigidius had prophesied that he would become "master of the world." Augustus even stamped the sign of Capricorn—his birth sign—on some of the coinage he issued.

The main opponents of astrology in the ancient world were the early Christians. They saw astrology as being basically pagan and fatalistic, teaching that man has a fixed and unalterable future instead of being able to change and redeem himself through baptism and the other sacraments of the Church. At first such opposition had little effect, for the early Church was a small and despised sect whose members were themselves the subject of harsh attack. In fact, many of the Christian denouncements of astrology were replies to those who condemned Christ as a magician, and accused his followers of crimes such as cannibalism and incest. However, with the growth of Christianity and its acceptance in the 4th century A.D. as the official religion of the Roman Empire, astrology gradually fell into disrepute, and its practitioners were regarded as little better than demon worshippers. By the time Rome fell to the barbarians in A.D. 410 there were few, if any, practicing astrologers left in the western half of the Empire, and within a few more decades the art had been largely forgotten.

In the Byzantine Empire of the East, however, astrological writings and techniques survived, and were passed on to the

Astrology: the Pagan Art

Arabs. Arab scholars made a serious study of astrology side by side with astronomy. They added to the work of their Greek predecessors, particularly in attaching importance to the motion and positions of the Moon in the calculation of horoscopes.

It was through Latin translations of Arabic astrological texts that 12th-century European scholars rediscovered astrology. By the 16th century astrology had again become an acknowledged part of the cultural outlook of all men of learning. The great astronomers of the 16th and early 17th centuries, such as Johannes Kepler, were also practicing astrologers and regularly cast horoscopes as part of their work. Every king and prince had his Court Astrologer to advise him on matters of state. Astrology had by then become the true Queen of the Sciences.

One of the best known of the 16th-century astrologers who acted as advisers to royalty was Dr. John Dee. This man was no mere stargazer, but a key figure in the intellectual life of his time. Born in 1527 of Welsh parents who had settled in London, Dee was a precocious child. He entered Cambridge University when he was only 15 years old, and throughout his time there he spent no less than 18 hours a day studying subjects that ranged from Greek to mechanics.

Dee continued his studies in the city of Louvain, now in Belgium, where he met and favorably impressed some of the greatest scientists of his age. All this time Dee was perfecting his knowledge of astrology and astronomy, and becoming adept at astrological calculation and interpretation.

Like many other scientists of his day, Dee was more attracted to the new Protestant interpretations of Christianity than to traditional Catholicism. He returned to England in the 1550s

Below left: a medieval miniature of the Greek Ptolemy, who lived in the 2nd century A.D. His great work *Tetrabiblos* gathered most of the astrological lore of the preceding centuries. He was concerned not only with movements of the stars as portents of the future, but for their own sake. His astronomy became the basis of all medieval study until his geocentric view was challenged by Copernicus in the 15th century.

Below: the Greeks incorporated much of their mythology into their astrology by identifying gods with constellations. For example, the Gemini twins became Castor and Pollux, as shown in this 18th-century illustration in an atlas.

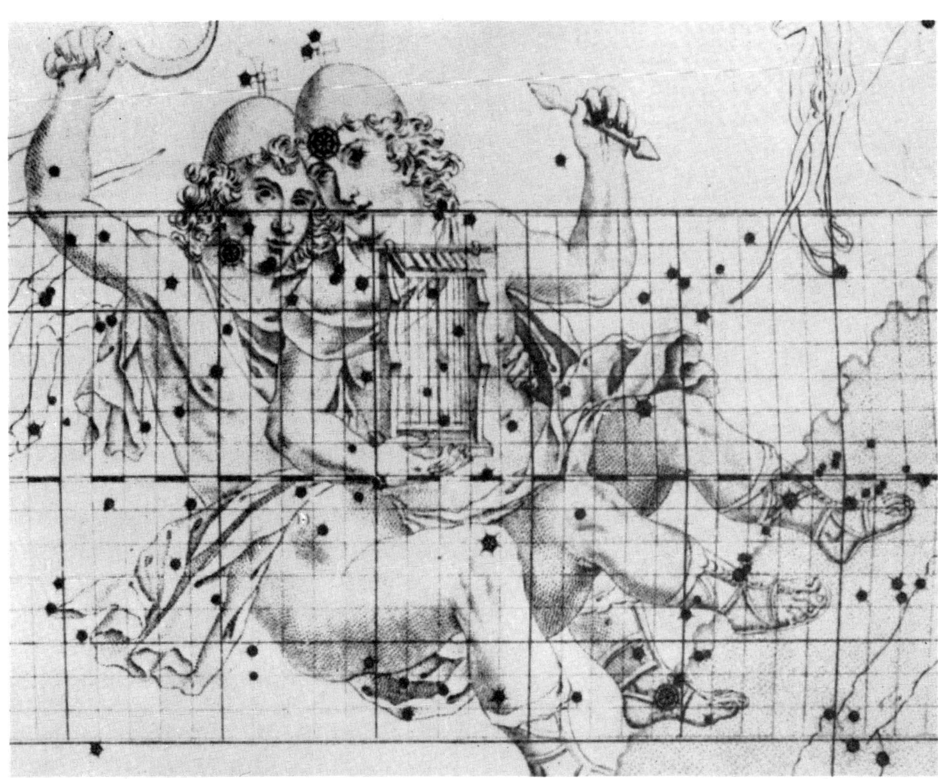

Right: after astrology in the West was gradually discarded, and the last traces buried by the barbarian influx, the Arabs kept the writings and techniques alive. In this illustration from a 17th-century Muslim design, an astrologer takes a reading of the position of a star. Near him is a model of the zodiac showing the 12 signs.

when the Catholic Queen Mary was persecuting the Protestants, and his religious views put his life at risk. At this time, Queen Mary's young half-sister, the future Queen Elizabeth I, who was known to have Protestant sympathies, was being kept a prisoner at Woodstock near Oxford. Queen Mary was under pressure from some of her Catholic advisers to get rid of her half-sister by whatever means possible, so Elizabeth was in fear of assassination throughout her imprisonment. She knew she was in danger of being executed on a trumped-up charge of treason, or even of being killed by poison—a standby of 16th-century monarchs who wanted to dispose of dangerous rivals.

It is hardly surprising that Elizabeth was anxious to know what the future held in store for her, and she decided to consult an astrologer. It so happened that Blanche Parry, Elizabeth's confidential maid-in-waiting, was a cousin of John Dee, and on her recommendation Elizabeth turned to Dee for advice. Dee prepared an astrological forecast for Elizabeth, and also showed her horoscopes he had calculated for Queen Mary and her husband Philip of Spain. Elizabeth's horoscope survives in the British Museum, and Dee's interpretation of it appears to have been accurate as well as optimistic. In letters secretly delivered to Elizabeth at Woodstock, Dee is thought to have told her that, although her situation was perilous, her life was in no danger. She was destined to rise to an outstanding position—perhaps to the throne itself—and would probably live to a ripe old age.

Dee's prophecies no doubt pleased and comforted Elizabeth, but the relationship between the two was soon discovered by Mary's secret agents. Dee was thrown into prison, accused not only of having unorthodox religious opinions, but also of showing a confidential document—Mary's horoscope—to Elizabeth and of practicing black magic. He was suspected of attempting to kill Queen Mary by sorcery so that Elizabeth could inherit the throne.

The Arab Astrologers

Left: in this miniature from India, dating from about 1600, the casting of a birth chart for the newborn baby of the ruler is shown as a natural part of the celebrations. The astrologer's work goes on at the same time as the rejoicing.

John Dee: Seer to the Queen

Dee was eventually acquitted on all the charges for lack of evidence, but he spent some months languishing in jail. Even after his release he was forced to live in seclusion until Elizabeth came to the throne on Mary's death in 1558.

The new queen remembered Dee's services and regularly consulted him on astrological matters. Dee even decided the date of her coronation using a technique known as *electional astrology*—a method like that still used in many Eastern countries to determine the most favorable time for undertaking some new and important enterprise.

In spite of Queen Elizabeth's friendly regard for Dee she did not display favor too openly. Probably she felt that she could not afford to be publicly associated with a man who had twice been accused of sorcery and might be so again. However, she employed Dee as a secret agent in Europe, where he was believed to be one of her most trusted spies. Dee seems to have gathered some of his intelligence by conventional means—16th century equivalents of the techniques used today by the CIA and the Soviet Union's KGB—but most of the time he used astrology and other occult methods to predict the plans of England's enemies. He also made maps for the Queen and helped to draw up plans for naval defense.

Dee died in 1608 at the age of 81. Forty years after his death the science of the stars was still an influence in politics, and astrologers were playing an important role in the English Civil War—the struggle between Roundheads and Cavaliers to decide whether Parliament or King should rule the country. These astrologers were the psychological warfare experts of the time, producing predictions designed to keep up the morale of the partisans of each side. In London the astrologer William Lilly produced almanacs at more or less regular intervals. In them he prophesied the success of Parliament and the downfall of the Royalists. From Oxford, the headquarters of King Charles, Royalist astrologers published almanacs asserting exactly the opposite.

Not surprisingly these distortions of astrology for political ends tended to bring the art into disrepute. Thinking people concluded that if astrologers could produce diametrically opposite findings from identical sets of data—the positions of the Sun, Moon, and planets in the zodiac—their subject could hardly be considered a science. The same conclusions were reached in Europe where astrology was used as a psychological weapon during the Thirty Years' War fought in central Europe from 1618 to 1648.

When their political opinions were not involved, however, certain 17th-century astrologers seem to have made some amazingly accurate predictions. Thus William Lilly, the astrologer who foresaw the Parliamentary victory, prophesied the 1665 outbreak of plague in London and the Great Fire of 1666 that followed it more than 10 years before these events took place. He expressed these predictions in the form of symbolic drawings, published as woodcuts in the early 1650s. Their meaning was so plain that Lilly was suspected of being involved in a plot to start the Great Fire deliberately, and he was called before a parliamentary committee to explain how he had known

Below: the astronomer Johannes Kepler, born in 1571. Part of his job as court mathematician to Emperor Rudolf II in Prague was to draw up horoscopes for the emperor and other dignitaries.

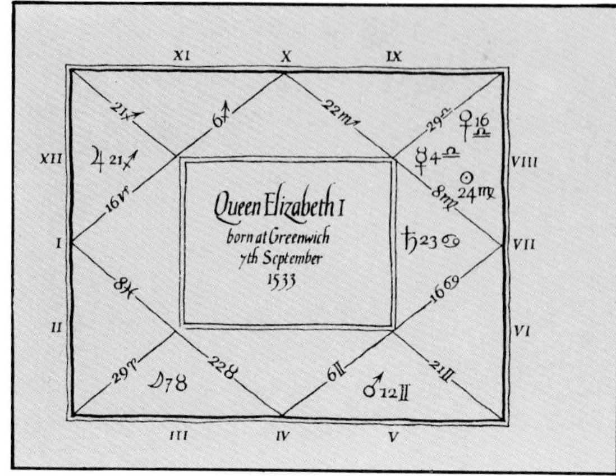

Above: Elizabeth I's birth chart. Born under Virgo, she had Saturn in Cancer in the Seventh House, the house of partners, which might be expected to indicate a delay in marriage. In fact, she died as she was crowned, a spinster queen.

Left: Queen Elizabeth I dressed in her coronation robes. She was crowned on January 15, 1559, the date selected by John Dee (who had earlier cast her horoscope) as astrologically favorable for the beginning of a fortunate reign.

about the fire in advance. Fortunately for the astrologer, he was able to convince the Members of Parliament who interrogated him that his predictions had been made on a purely astrological basis.

Successes such as those of Lilly kept the belief in astrology alive, but could not stop its decline. With few exceptions only the most old-fashioned scholars still regarded astrology as a science or discipline by the turn of the century. One exception

He Predicted the Fire of London

"Having found, Sir, that the City of London should be sadly afflicted with a great plague, and not long after with an exorbitant fire, I framed these two hieroglyphics . . . which in effect have proved very true." So spoke William Lilly, a 17th-century astrologer, suspected of intrigue in the Great Fire of London by a government inquiry committee in 1666. One of the astrologer's "hieroglyphics" of prophecy is shown below. It is a drawing of Gemini, the sign of the City of London, falling into flames, and it was done 15 years before the fire that destroyed most of London. According to Lilly's report about the Parliamentary committee, he was released with "great civility."

was Sir Isaac Newton, the great philosopher and mathematician who defined the law of gravitation in the 1680s. He originally took up mathematics in order to practice astrology. Another was John Flamsteed, England's first Astronomer Royal. He took the subject so seriously that he used electional astrology to choose August 10, 1675 as the date for laying the foundation stone of the Royal Observatory at Greenwich.

As the 18th century wore on the practice of astrology almost completely died out in mainland Europe, and in England it was largely confined to the producers of yearly almanacs. These books were published shortly before the beginning of each new year. They included some astrological and astronomical information as well as lists of public holidays, farming hints, and other practical information. Their readers were mostly small farmers, and few of them probably had much faith in astrology to judge from the contents of some almanacs. The publisher of *Poor Robin's Almanac*, for instance, poked fun at astrology with jokes like, "Mars inclining to Venus ensureth that maids who walk out with soldiers on May morning will have big bellies by Christmas."

In the years 1780 to 1830, however, astrology enjoyed a small but significant revival in England. Perhaps because of an interest in the past that marked this period, old textbooks on the subject were reprinted. Some new texts were also written, and two astrological magazines were published. Once again it was possible to find professional as well as amateur astrologers.

These astrologers were a new breed—no longer men of learning, but occultists. These men and women combined their astrology with subjects such as alchemy—the supposed art of turning lead and other base metals into gold—fortune telling by the use of playing cards, and even the manufacture of talismans and other good luck charms.

The astrologers of this period also showed an excessive and gloomy preoccupation with the prediction of death. One of them, John Worsdale, published his analysis of 30 horoscopes in which he sought the dates of his clients' deaths, and he appears to have gained great satisfaction from telling these people of their impending doom. When a young girl named Mary Dickson approached him in August 1822 and asked him to predict the date of her marriage, Worsdale told her with apparent relish that "something of an awful nature would occur, before the Month of March, then next ensuing, which would destroy Life." Mary "laughed immoderately," but was sufficiently interested to ask Worsdale what would be the exact cause of her death. "I told her," reported the astute astrologer, "that it appeared to me that Drowning would be the cause of her Dissolution."

On the following January 7 Worsdale's prediction was fulfilled to the letter when Mary Dickson, who was traveling in a river boat, fell overboard and "when taken out life was found to be extinct."

The English astrological revival never completely receded. Throughout the 19th century astrology continued to attract people in Britain and the United States who were interested in the occult. After 1890 American and British astrology received a considerable boost from the occult revival launched by Madame

"The Ancient Wisdom..."

H. P. Blavatsky and her Theosophical Society—founded in 1875 but not really important until the 1890s—and a host of lesser known occult societies that derived their astrological knowledge from India. These groups saw astrology as part of "the Ancient Wisdom"—traditional lore which, they believed, had been wrongly rejected by modern science—and they placed added emphasis on the occult aspects of the art.

Thus in the early 20th century Alan Leo, a British member of

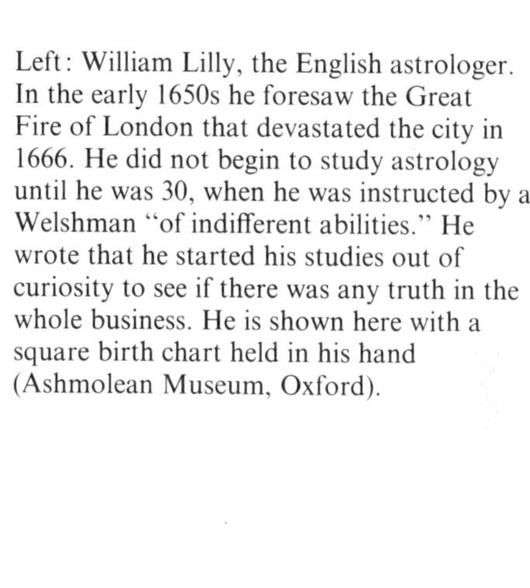

Left: William Lilly, the English astrologer. In the early 1650s he foresaw the Great Fire of London that devastated the city in 1666. He did not begin to study astrology until he was 30, when he was instructed by a Welshman "of indifferent abilities." He wrote that he started his studies out of curiosity to see if there was any truth in the whole business. He is shown here with a square birth chart held in his hand (Ashmolean Museum, Oxford).

Above: a caricature of a fortune teller by Thomas Rowlandson in 1815 when astrology was in decline in Britain. The poem that accompanies the drawing tells us that the astrologer meets his death when his chair collapses—but he failed to predict it.

the Theosophical Society, wrote a whole series of influential astrological textbooks from the occult point of view. Leo was a highly successful astrologer who claimed that "every human being belongs to a Father Star in Heaven or a Star Angel as did Jesus Christ according to our scripture." (Even some of the early Christians who had clung to a belief in astrology saw the Star of Bethlehem as evidence of astrological truth, but most astrologers before Leo had denied that Christ was actually influenced by the Star of the Nativity.)

Leo's books were often written in obscure and confusing occult jargon, but he had skill in simplifying the techniques. He believed that "the problem of the inequalities of the human race can only be successfully solved by a knowledge of astrology," and much of his writing outlined astrological techniques in a clear way so that the ordinary reader could apply them for himself. With another astrologer, Leo also edited *The Astrologer's Magazine*—later renamed *Modern Astrologer*—whose first issue included the horoscopes of Jesus Christ, of Britain's Prince of Wales (later to become King Edward VII), and of the explorer Henry Morton Stanley.

Leo's magazine was aimed at the general public, and his do-it-yourself books helped to transform 20th-century astrology. Until his writings simplified the subject, astrology required years of painstaking study and the mastery of comparatively advanced mathematics. With his books it became possible for anybody of reasonable intelligence to become a fairly competent astrologer after only a year or two of part-time study.

Revival in the Modern Age

The result was explosive. As Leo's books were reprinted in the United States and published in German translation, and as others imitated his approach, a host of new astrologers—some amateur and some professional—joined the ranks of the old guard. By 1930 most Americans, Britons, and Germans who were at all interested in the world of the occult knew at least one person capable of casting and interpreting a horoscope.

Probably the most famous of the astrologers who learned their art from Leo's books was Evangeline Adams. Born in 1865, she was a descendant of John Quincy Adams, sixth president of the United States, and she seems to have inherited his determination and sense of purpose. Believing in her own reading of her stars, she made a move to New York City from her hometown of Boston in 1899. She created an immediate sensation. On her first night in the hotel she had booked into, she read the horoscope of the proprietor and warned him of a dreadful disaster. The next day the hotel burned down—and the proprietor's report of her warning to the newspapers put her name in the headlines. Evangeline Adams so gained the kind of publicity that more than offset the loss of much of her belongings in the fire. She set up a business as a reader of horoscopes, and was soon on the way to becoming America's most popular astrologer.

In spite of—or perhaps because of—her success, Evangeline

Below: the Royal Observatory, Greenwich, designed by Christopher Wren. John Flamsteed, England's first Astronomer Royal, selected the date for laying its foundation stone by using electional astrology. It was duly laid August 10, 1675.

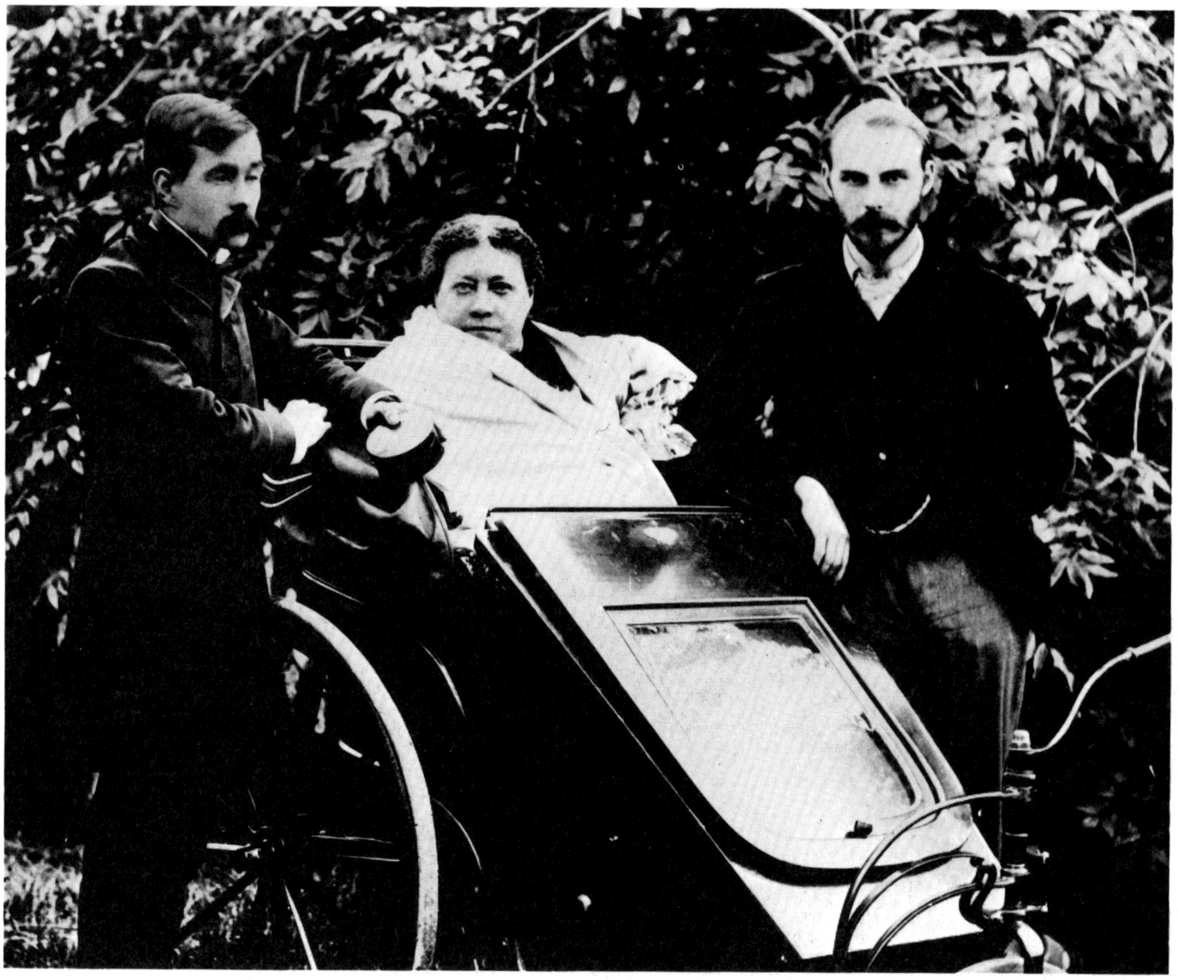

Above: Madame Blavatsky, founder of the Theosophical Society, with two of her colleagues in 1875. Her society appears to have mainly encountered astrology through its enthusiasm with the wisdom of India, in which astrology played a long-standing and very important role.

Right: Alan Leo, one of the first modern popularizers of astrology, shown in his own horoscope. After Leo's death in 1917, people wrote to his widow that he was still teaching astrology and theosophy to them "on the astral plane." On a more earthly level, his books had a tremendous impact, educating a new generation of astrologers.

Adams was arrested for fortune telling in 1914. Although she could have elected to pay a fine and go free, she decided to stand trial and argue her own defense. Armed with a pile of reference books, she told the court precisely how she made her analyses and predictions. To prove her point, she offered to make a reading from the birth date of someone she had never met, without even knowing who that person was. The person chosen was the judge's son, and this judge was so impressed with her reading that he concluded, "The defendant raises astrology to the dignity of an exact science." Evangeline Adams was acquitted, and in New York at least astrology was no longer regarded as fortune telling.

Evangeline Adams' triumph had struck an important blow for the respectability of astrology. She proceeded to open a studio in Carnegie Hall in New York City, where she was consulted by politicians, Hollywood stars, royalty, and Wall Street tycoons. Her clients included the Duke of Windsor, Mary Pickford, Caruso, and the financier J. P. Morgan for whom she provided regular forecasts concerning politics and the stock market. There is evidence that many of her clients took her advice seriously, using it as the basis for major decisions regarding their careers, investments, and political activities. Certainly they paid her substantial fees, and by the 1920s she was a wealthy woman.

In 1930 Evangeline Adams began a series of regular radio broadcasts on astrology, and within a year she was receiving 4000 requests a day from listeners who wanted her to cast their horoscope. Her book *Astrology: Your Place Among the Stars* became a best seller, and a number of present-day astrologers first became acquainted with the subject through it. Nevertheless, Evangeline Adams did not escape attacks on her character. It was said that she was not the true author of most of her book. Aleister Crowley, the notorious British magician and a keen amateur astrologer, claimed that he had written the book for Evangeline Adams in return for a fee—a fee that Crowley maintained he had never received. Many of the horoscopes analyzed in the book were for people whom Crowley particularly admired, such as the 19th-century explorer Sir Richard Burton.

Such attacks did nothing to cloud Evangeline Adams' reputation, however. Throughout 1931 her radio show continued to bring her masses of mail from fans who regarded her as a kindly adviser and friend. In that year, Evangeline Adams prophesied that the United States would be at war in 1942, and the following year she is said to have forecast her own death. She explained that she would be unable to undertake a lecture tour for late 1932, and in November of that year she died.

Such was Evangeline Adams' popularity that the public flocked to the Carnegie Hall studio where her body lay in state. Crowds of fans attended her funeral, and there were thousands of telegrams of condolence. No one before Evangeline Adams had done so much to bring astrology to the attention of the general public. By the time of her death, she had become the most popular and successful astrologer of our century—and possibly of all time.

By comparison, the career of another well-known woman astrologer was played out in a more muted key. Elsbeth Ebertin

"A Glimpse into the Future"

Below: Evangeline Adams, who helped make astrology respectable as well as popular. A woman of courage and determination, she has been quoted as saying, "I have Mars conjunct my natal Sun in the 12th house. I will always triumph over my enemies!" In fact she was immensely successful, and from about 1914 to 1932 her clients included the great and the wealthy.

Above: the German astrologer Elsbeth Ebertin. She was a gifted journalist with the ability to write about astrology in a simple and interesting fashion. When sent Hitler's birth date in 1923 from one of his many enthusiastic women supporters in Munich, she published a prediction that "a man of action" born that day was "destined to play a 'Führer-role' in future battles." Although her prediction was uncannily accurate, she was wrong about his Sun being in Aries—because her correspondent had not sent Hitler's birth hour. He was born at 6:30 p.m. by which time the Sun had passed into Taurus.

was an honest, competent, and totally unaffected German astrologer, who was born in 1880 and commenced her professional life as a *graphologist*—an interpreter of character from the study of a person's handwriting.

In 1910 Elsbeth Ebertin met a woman who also claimed to be a graphologist, and who was able to give accurate delineations of character. Yet in talking to her, Elsbeth Ebertin discovered that this woman did not even know the basic principles of graphology. It turned out that she was really an astrologer, but preferred not to admit this to her clients because few of them had even heard of astrology.

Impressed by this woman's ability, Elsbeth Ebertin decided to become a professional astrologer herself. She started to study textbooks issued by a small publishing house called the Astrological Library. These included German translations of Alan Leo's writings and books by Karl Brandler-Pracht, an occultist who was busily engaged in reviving German astrology. By 1918 Elsbeth Ebertin had become a competent astrological practitioner, publicist, and writer. She had a sizeable private clientele, gave lectures on astrology, and published at regular intervals an almanac called *A Glimpse Into the Future*, containing predictions of the future of Germany and the world.

The first issue of *A Glimpse Into the Future* was published in 1917, and the almanac then and later was often impressively accurate in its forecasts. One of Elsbeth Ebertin's most famous predictions was contained in the July 1923 edition. It read: "A man of action born on April 20, 1889, with Sun in the 29th degree of Aries at the time of his birth, can expose himself to personal danger by excessively rash action and could very likely trigger off an uncontrollable crisis. His constellations show that this man is to be taken very seriously indeed. He is destined to play a 'Führer-role' in future battles . . . The man I have in mind, with this strong Aries influence, is destined to sacrifice himself for the German nation, and also to face up to all circumstances with audacity and courage, even when it is a matter of *life and death*, and to give an impulse, which will burst forth quite suddenly . . . But I will not anticipate destiny. Time will show . . ."

In fact Elsbeth Ebertin's forecast anticipated destiny rather well. The "man of action born on April 20, 1889" was none other than Adolf Hitler. In November 1923, four months after Elsbeth Ebertin's prediction, he launched an "excessively rash action"—the unsuccessful Munich *Putsch*. This was the attempt by Hitler, then a relatively obscure political adventurer, to overthrow the legally constituted German government by force. It resulted in the killing of a number of his followers—members of the infant Nazi party. Hitler himself dislocated his shoulder during the fighting and served a term of imprisonment for treason.

As for the rest of Elsbeth Ebertin's prediction, that too was fulfilled. Hitler did indeed play a "'Führer-role' in future battles." In spite of his destructive nature it could be said that he "faced up to all circumstances with audacity and courage," and at the end of his life, in the burning ruins of Berlin, he committed suicide—or, as he himself expressed it to his intimates in the very words of the famous astrologer, "sacrificed himself for the German people."

The Führer and the Astrologers

Elsbeth Ebertin continued publishing her almanac until 1937, when she was apparently forced to close it down as a result of pressure from the Gestapo. Possibly some of her past prophecies came too close to the truth for comfort, and the outspoken nature of her predictions may have made the Nazis fear that publications like hers could exert a political influence not to their taste.

Nevertheless, Elsbeth Ebertin kept up her private practice until her death in an air raid in November 1944. According to her son Reinhold, a distinguished German astrologer of the present day, his mother foresaw the bomb that killed her, but felt she should not move to possible safety out of regard for her neighbors. They took comfort from her continued presence among them, saying "As long as Frau Ebertin is here nothing very much can happen to us."

Since the end of World War II astrology has had a boom. All over the world institutes now exist for the serious study of astrology, and in 1960 Harvard University accepted a thesis on astrology for the B.A. degree. The American Federation of Astrologers and the British Faculty of Astrological Studies have thousands of members who pass examinations for a diploma in their subject, and subscribe to a code of ethics. Interest in

Below: Adolf Hitler surrounded by some of his many women admirers. In this case they are Austrian girls he met during the May Day celebrations in Berlin in 1939.

Astrology in the Computer Age

Opposite: today the signs of the zodiac are familiar to people in all walks of life. One executive in the entertainment world even has a zodiac in his Hollywood pool.

Below: the current enthusiasm for astrology, like other fads, finds avid fans in Hollywood. There an interior decorator designs rooms for homes and offices that harmonize with the astrological character readings of the occupants.

astrology has never been greater. But can we really believe in horoscopes today?

The successful career of Carroll Righter might indicate that many people still do. At the age of 75 years, Righter is the dean of American astrologers—not just in age, but also in status. He might be said to have taken the mantle from Evangeline Adams, whom he met when he was only 14 years old. As a friend of the family she cast his horoscope and found him likely to be a skillful interpreter of the stars. She urged him to become an astrologer. Some 25 years went by before he finally followed her advice, but when he did, he fast became a leader in the field. Based in Hollywood, he has counted among his clients such past and present stellar names as Tyrone Power, Susan Hayward, Marlene Dietrich, and Ronald Colman. It is thought that he might be a millionaire with earnings from numerous newspaper and magazine columns, day-by-day astrological forecasts, and books on how astrology can help in business and finance, and in marriage and family relationships.

Before he became a professional astrologer in 1939, Righter had been in law practice and had also worked on civic projects. During the Depression he began to use astrology to help the unemployed. He found that he could help direct people to jobs by showing them what their horoscopes said they were best suited for. This made many of them look for work that they might never have considered otherwise.

Another astrologer whose career seems to show that there is a place for astrology in modern life is Katina Theodossiou. This well-known British practitioner is one of the world's foremost business astrologers. She is consultant to more than 50 companies in the United States and Europe, giving advice on such matters as mergers, takeovers, staffing, and investment. Many a company has even been born at the time and on the date that she has suggested by the guidance of the stars.

Katina Theodossiou has also helped bring astrology into the computer age. In one assignment for a New York firm, she programmed a computer in order to produce computerized horoscopes for sale. It was a notable success. She worked on the project for 15 months during which time she fed 40,000 separate items of astrological information into the machine.

Astrologers themselves are divided on the subject of computer horoscopes, but few if any would call Katina Theodossiou to account for insincerity or incompetence.

Astrology has never lacked its critics, however, and there are many people today who would not hesitate to dismiss the subject as a ridiculous and outmoded set of doctrines appealing only to the naive and superstitious. Serious astrologers are the first to admit that their art contains a number of inconsistencies and vague assumptions that are difficult to verify. Still they are convinced that astrology is based on truth, and that it can play a valuable role in helping human beings understand more about themselves and their place in the Universe. Today some orthodox scientists are coming to share their point of view. The very people who have long been most skeptical of astrology are now providing evidence to suggest that the ancient art of astrology may be founded on fact.

Chapter 10
Astrology is For Real!

Is there a scientific basis to astrology? Long dismissed by orthodox scientists as pure superstition, astrology is receiving new attention as researchers discover evidence that suggests that the relationship astrology claims between humans and the stars may truly exist. Experiments into shortwave radio reception, the biological cycles of creatures as diverse as flies and oysters, and the variations in electrical charges given off by the human body suggest that all life moves to a regular rhythm which might be linked with the shifting pattern in the heavens. Will astrology once again be accepted as a science, as it was centuries ago?

In March 1951 John H. Nelson, an American electronic and radio engineer, published a sensational article. There was nothing sensation about the journal in which the article appeared, however. That was the straightforward *RCA Review*, a technical journal published by the Radio Corporation of America and devoted to all aspects of radio, television, and electronics. Nelson's article was an equally serious account of his research into factors affecting radio reception. But his report was to shatter orthodox views about humans and the Universe, for his findings appeared to confirm the basic belief of astrology—that the planets can and do influence our lives. The story behind Nelson's article began when RCA scientists noticed an apparent connection between the difficulty or ease of shortwave radio communication and the varying positions of the Earth's planetary neighbors. Was this link pure coincidence, RCA wanted to know, or was it the result of some hitherto unknown cosmic influence?

The first step in answering this question was to set up a basic statistical investigation of the phenomenon. RCA asked several astronomers to undertake this task, but all refused. In their opinion the idea that planetary positions could affect radio waves was so ridiculous that it was not worth investigating. However, RCA was unwilling to abandon the inquiry, and assigned Nelson, an experienced radio engineer, to investigate.

As Nelson checked records of radio disturbance dating back

Opposite: a 15th-century illustration of Saturn with the signs of the zodiac and the professions which that planet is supposed to govern. This link between the planetary position at the time of birth and the profession that a person follows is an aspect of astrology which has been supported by statistics.

Scientific Support

to the 1920s he made a series of exciting discoveries. He found that magnetic storms—the cause of radio disturbance—occur when two or more planets, viewed from the Earth, are very close together at right angles to one another or 180° apart. The position of the planets did appear to influence radio reception, and in a way that came as no surprise to the astrologers. These particular relationships—the aspects—between the planets have been important in astrology since ancient times, and none of them is regarded as favorable. The *conjunction*—when the planets are very close together on the same side of the Sun—is considered neutral, being good or bad according to certain factors modifying it. When the planets are in *square*—at right angles to one another—it is seen as disharmonious, difficult, and even evil. The same applies when planets are in *opposition*—180° apart on opposite sides of the Sun.

Nelson's subsequent discoveries also tied in with traditional astrological beliefs. He discovered that magnetic disturbances were notably absent, and that shortwave reception was therefore good, when two or more planets were 60° or 120° apart. These are precisely the aspects that astrology regards as harmonious, easy, and good. Further, Nelson found that aspects of 150° and 135° also had an effect on radio reception—a discovery of particular interest since these aspects were not used by astrologers of the ancient world, but are used by many present-day ones.

The test of a scientific theory is whether it enables the accurate prediction of future events. While Nelson had discovered a number of fascinating correlations between planetary positions and radio reception, they just might have been the result of chance. The real question was whether Nelson could use his findings to predict future magnetic disturbances.

He tried—and his predictions were 80 percent accurate. Later, by refining his methods to include details of all the planets, he increased his success rate to an amazing 93 percent. Nelson had provided the first piece of scientific evidence to show that life on Earth could be influenced by the planets, and the claims of the astrologers—for long regarded as totally irrational—were seen to have some justification.

Nelson's discovery was not an isolated one. Other work carried out by scientists in recent years had also tended to back up astrology's basic beliefs about the influence of the Sun, Moon, and planets on earthly events and on people themselves.

For example, the late Dr. Rudolf Tomaschek, an academic physicist and chairman of the World Geophysical Council, made a statistical analysis of 134 large earthquakes. He found that planetary positions in relationship to the place and time these earthquakes occurred were highly significant. The "earthquake aspects" almost always included one or more of the planets Jupiter, Uranus, and Neptune, and the stronger the earthquake the more likely these planets were to be involved—usually in traditionally sinister aspects such as the square.

Dr. Tomaschek believed in astrology so that, in spite of his academic qualifications, some people were skeptical of his findings. The same criticism could not be leveled at the work of Dr. A. K. Podshibyakin, a Soviet physician who discovered a remarkable connection between physical events on the Sun and

Opposite: this diagram shows the kind of planetary grouping that would coincide with magnetic storms and poor radio reception on Earth, according to a theory developed by Nelson for predicting periods of radio disturbance. In this configuration foretelling trouble in the way of a magnetic storm (X), Mercury (A) is in *square* or 90° to Venus (B) and Mars (C); Saturn (D) is in *opposition* or 180° to Earth; and Jupiter (E) is in *square* to both Earth and Saturn.

Below: John H. Nelson, an electronic and radio engineer who did research on the relationship between the position of the planets and the quality of radio reception. He found that certain planetary positions can make reception poor.

D
90°
C
B
90°
A
E
X

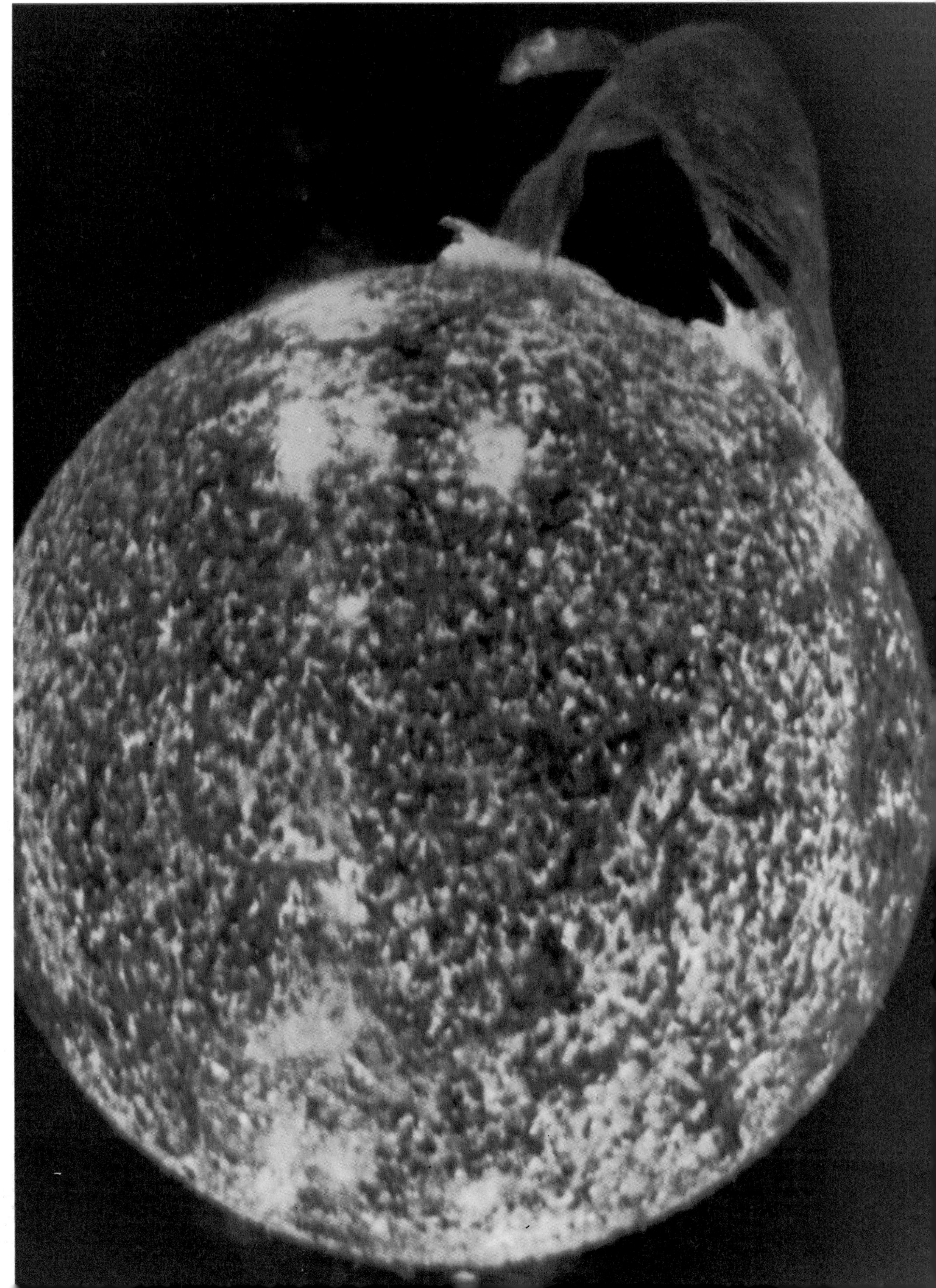

the incidence of road accidents in the Soviet Union.

Dr. Podshibyakin's findings, published in 1967, were based on statistics compiled over a number of years at Tomsk Medical College. These studies showed that the day after a solar flare—a magnetic storm on the surface of the Sun—there was a marked increase in road accidents, sometimes to as much as four times the daily average. Dr. Podshibyakin pointed out that this link between solar flares and road accidents was not confined to the Soviet Union, but had also been observed by researchers in West Germany. He gave a possible explanation of the phenomenon, based on the known fact that a solar flare produces a tremendous amount of ultraviolet radiation, which causes changes in the Earth's atmosphere. Dr. Podshibyakin suggested that this radiation affects the human body, slowing it down.

No such explanation can be provided for even stranger influences produced by the Sun and Moon on earthly life—influences that have astonished and puzzled the scientists who have observed them. One such scientist is Dr. Frank A. Brown, Professor of Biology at Northwestern University.

For the last 25 years Brown and his team have been conducting research into "biological clocks"—the natural rhythms shown by all life on Earth. These clocks manifest themselves in many ways, from the regular sleeping and waking patterns of human beings to the small movements made by certain plants during the night. There have been many efforts to explain the nature of these life rhythms, varying from the idea that they are the response of living beings to air ionization, to the suggestion that each separate organism possesses its own internal timing mechanism—a biological clock in the strict meaning of the term.

None of these explanations satisfied Dr. Brown. He found it impossible, for example, to trace any mechanism by which air ionization could trigger off the purposeful and meaningful activities of life rhythms. Equally, he was unable to find any physical organ in living beings that could serve as a mechanical clock.

Over a 10-year period Brown and his associates ran experiments on a variety of phenomena. These included the movement of bean plants in the night, the amount of running performed by caged rats during successive days, the sleep pattern of flies, the opening and closing of oyster shells, and changes in the color of fiddler crabs.

What emerged was astonishing. All these phenomena followed rhythmical cycles, and those cycles were triggered not by some internal clock, but by cosmic influences—notably those connected with the Sun and the Moon. Thus, for example, rats living under controlled conditions in darkened cages were found to be twice as active when the Moon was above the horizon as when it was below it. They seemed to know instinctively when the Moon was up and responded to it, although they had no way of seeing it.

Equally surprising was the behavior of oysters. When they are in their natural habitat, oysters open and close their shells according to the rhythm of the tides. At high tide they open their shells to feed, and at low tide they close them as a protection against drying out. While the tides are, of course, produced by the gravitational pull of the Moon and Sun, it had always been assumed that the movement of the tides alone caused the opening

Solar Flares and Earthquakes

Opposite: a satellite photograph of an immense solar flare (in the upper left) spanning more than 367,000 miles across the solar surface. The Soviet physician Dr. A. K. Podshibyakin discovered a statistical connection between solar flares and road accidents.

Below: debris left after the 1970 earthquake in Peru. Dr. Rudolf Tomaschek, a respected physicist, made an analysis of earthquakes, finding certain planets often to be in traditionally sinister aspects.

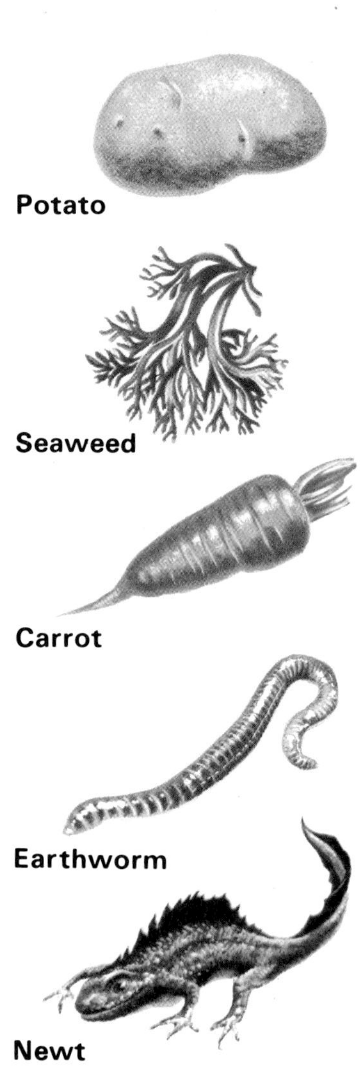

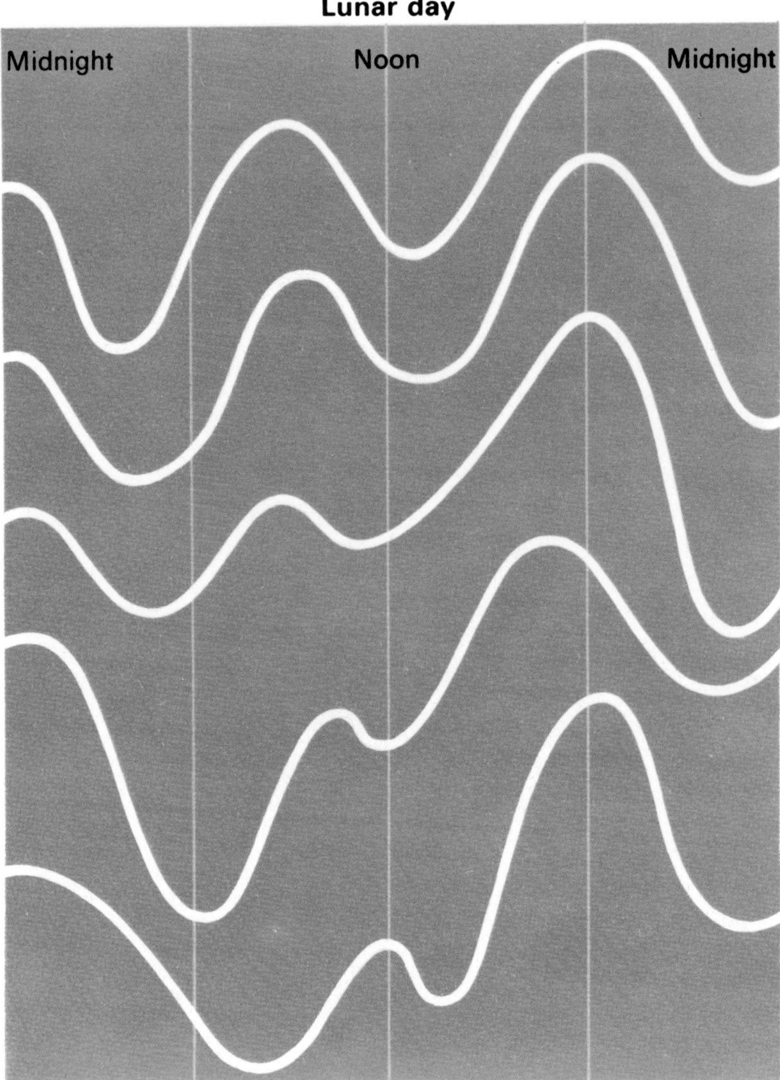

Above: the metabolic rate of various plants and animals, shown by the curved lines in this diagram, all follow a similar pattern of change during the lunar day. Dr. Frank A. Brown of Northwestern University explains that some external stimulus, which is common to all these living organisms, also follows a lunar-day pattern.

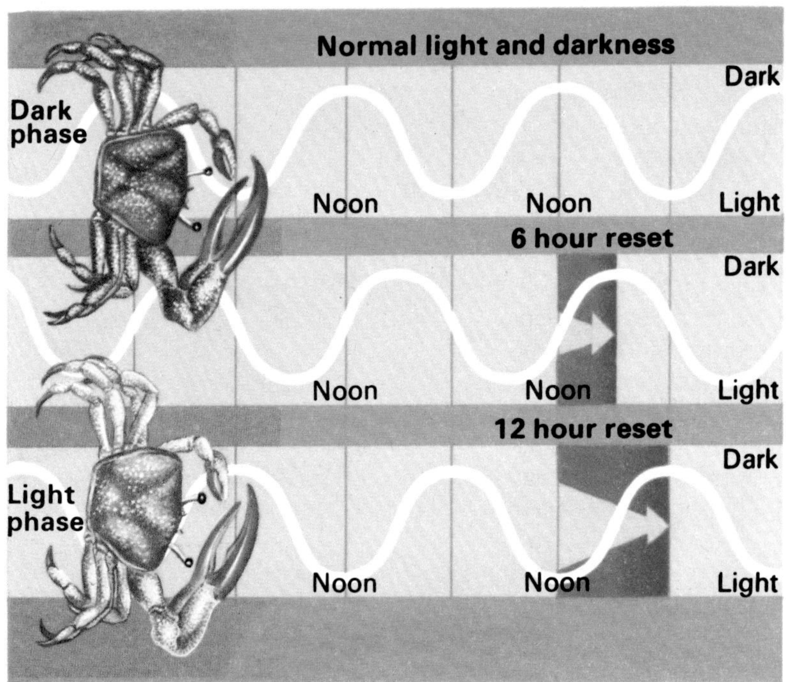

Right: normally fiddler crabs change from a dark color during the day to a light color at night. If kept in constant darkness they will continue to change color in the way normal to them. But if they are subjected to a new 24-hour cycle of light and dark, they reset their biological clock and change color according to the new time. Then if once again returned to constant darkness, the crabs go by the new time cycle.

and closing of the oysters' shells. No one had ever been bold enough to suggest that the oysters were responding directly to the Moon and Sun. Yet Brown discovered that they were apparently doing just that.

What Dr. Brown had done was to remove some oysters from the Atlantic seaboard of the United States, and place them in darkened containers so that no sunlight or moonlight could reach them. He had then taken them to his laboratory in Evanston, Illinois, a thousand miles from the sea. Within a fortnight the oysters had lost the pattern of opening and closing that they had displayed in their old home in the Atlantic, and were following the rhythm of what the tides would have been in Evanston had that town been on the sea. In other words, the oysters were not directly influenced by the tides, but by some other signals apparently related to the Moon and Sun.

What about people? Do the Sun, Moon, and planets really affect us, as astrologers claim? A study published in 1960 by another American scientist, Dr. Leonard Ravitz of Duke University, has shown a direct link between the behavior of human beings and the Moon. His findings coincide with the age-old belief that there is a connection between the Moon and madness.

Over a long period Ravitz plotted the variations in the small electric charges that are continually given off by the human body. He worked with both the mentally ill and a control group of healthy people. He found that the body's electrical potential underwent regular changes in all the people tested, and that these changes coincided with the phases of the Moon. The most marked changes occurred when the Moon was full, and the more disturbed the patient, the greater was the extent of the change.

Dr. Ravitz was therefore able to predict emotional changes in his mental patients, and to confirm that the full Moon does tend to provoke crises in people whose mental balance is already disturbed. "Whatever else we may be we are all electric machines," says Ravitz. "Thus energy reserves may be mobilized by periodic universal factors, such as the forces behind the Moon, which tend to aggravate maladjustments and conflicts already present."

The rhythms of the Moon may also have some effect on the patterns of human birth. Not enough research has been done on this subject to come to any definite conclusions, but it is interesting to note that in 1938 a Japanese scientist made a study of the cosmic factors in 33,000 live births. He found that high numbers of births occurred at the full and New Moons and low numbers one or two days before the Moon's first and last quarters. According to a report published in 1967 an American gynecologist has confirmed these findings from a study of no less than half a million births. This evidence at least supports the theory.

The date of a person's birth depends of course on the time of conception, and this in turn depends on the time of ovulation—the release of an egg from the ovary. Psychiatrist Eugen Jonas of Czechoslovakia has discovered a clear connection between the time of ovulation and the Moon. His studies have shown that a woman tends to ovulate during the particular phase of the Moon that prevailed when she was born. Jonas has even used his findings to provide women in Eastern Europe with a new and entirely natural method of contraception. His charts, drawn up

How the Moon Affects Life

Below: Dr. Eugen Jonas. His research convinced him he had discovered a clear connection between the time of ovulation and the Moon, which provided him with a method of natural contraception. Some claim a 98 percent success rate.

Scientists Who Accept Astrology

Below: John Addey, British philosopher, statistician, and astrologer. By means of statistics he studied the relationship between long life and the position of the planets at the time of birth. He found a significant connection.

to show the days on which a woman can conceive, have proved 98 percent effective—as efficient as the contraceptive pill.

It has long been believed that a woman's menstrual cycle, with its average of 28 days or the length of time between two full Moon is in some way connected with the rhythms of the Moon, and there is some scientific evidence to support this view. At the beginning of this century, Swiss chemist Dr. Svante Arrhenius made a study of 11,000 women. He found that the onset of menstruation reached a peak at the new Moon. In the 1960s two German researchers, who had kept records of the onset of menstruation in 10,000 women over a period of 14 years, came to a similar conclusion.

There is certainly evidence of a connection between bleeding in general and the phases of the Moon. The American physician Dr. Edson Andrews found, for example, that in 1000 cases of unusually heavy bleeding following tonsillectomies, 82 percent of the bleeding crises occurred between the Moon's first and third quarters. "These data have been so conclusive," said Dr. Andrews, ". . . that I threaten to become a witch doctor and operate on dark nights only."

These are only a fraction of the discoveries scientists have made concerning the influence of cosmic events on life on Earth. Many other experiments also make it clear that the Sun, Moon, and planets seem to exert a profound effect on us and our environment, and that the basic belief of the astrologers is in no way unscientific. Has this led any scientists to a belief in astrology?

Some—but not very many. Nevertheless, the scientists who have come to accept the fundamental claims of astrology have often been outstanding in their fields. The late Carl G. Jung, whom many consider to have been the greatest psychologist of the 20th century, was outspoken in his admiration for this traditional art. He claimed that astrology would eventually have to be recognized as a science. "The cultural philistines," he said, "believed until recently that astrology had been disposed of long since and today could safely be laughed at, but today, arising out of the social deeps, it knocks at the doors of the universities from which it was banished some 300 years ago."

Jung believed so profoundly in astrology that in later life he insisted on having a horoscope for each of his patients. He maintained that the horoscope provided an excellent guide to character and psychological disposition. He also carried out some elementary observations to test the ancient astrological belief that there are significant interactions between the planetary positions in the horoscopes of married couples.

Jung's experimental work was by no means complete, but he did find significant Sun-Moon interrelationships in the horoscopes of the 483 married couples he studied. In pairing off the horoscopes of husband and wife Jung found, for example, that the woman's Moon was frequently in conjunction with the man's Sun—the aspect that astrologers claim most favors marriage.

In recent years Jung's approach to astrological research has found favor with a number of investigators, among them the British philosopher John M. Addey, a dedicated astrologer who is also a competent statistician. Surprisingly enough, Addey's

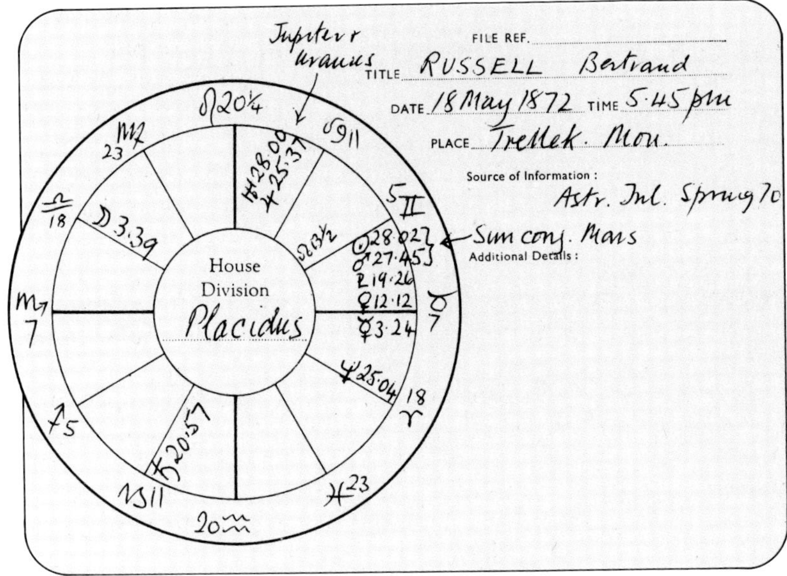

Left: Bertrand Russell's birth chart, as worked out by Addey. The Sun position, just separating from conjunction with Mars and a sextile with Jupiter, is typical of the planetary aspects found in charts of the 970 notable people of 90 years of age or over whom Addey took as his sample group.

Below: Bertrand Russell, the British philosopher who became world-renowned for his vigorous defense of individual liberty. He was an avowed pacifist, and his views on sexual morality made him a controversial figure. He was not exactly the relaxed and passive individual that might be indicated by his horoscope. However, he did live to the ripe old age of 98.

work sprang originally from a feeling that there was a good deal wrong with astrology in its traditional form. "So far as the practical rules . . . are concerned there are a host of uncertainties," he said, ". . . intractable problems which can only be solved by careful, persistent work; . . . our records are scattered and contain many errors . . . The chief obstacle is the opposition of the scientific fraternity, and to silence or check their criticism would seem to be the first step in presenting our case to a wider public . . ."

Addey's first attempt to "silence or check" continuing scientific objections to astrology involved 970 people over 90 years of age whose names appeared in the British *Who's Who*—a biographical directory of the eminent in all walks of life. A horoscope was prepared for each of these long-lived people, and all the horoscopes were compared to see if they had any factors in common.

Addey first checked to see if there was any truth in the ancient astrological tradition that people born under certain Sun Signs are more likely to be long lived than others. No such connection was found. The traditionally long-lived Capricornians, for instance, were no better represented among the 90-year-olds than the traditionally short-lived Pisceans. Addey did, however, discover one remarkable link in the horoscopes of his long-lived subjects. This concerned aspects—the relationships between two or more planets standing at significant angles to one another. Astrologers have always divided aspects into two types: *applying*—when a fast-moving planet is moving *into* a significant angle with a slow-moving planet; and *separating*—when a fast-moving planet is moving *away* from such a position. Addey found that the horoscopes of his 90-year-olds showed a preponderance of separating aspects.

This is precisely what one would expect if there is any truth in astrology, for astrologers have always held that separating aspects indicate the conservation of physical and mental energy, relaxation, and passivity—just the characteristics likely to be

Above: a 16th-century woodcut of Mars as the patron of certain occupations, mainly military. These traditional ideas were long dismissed as purely superstitious until the French scientist Michel Gauquelin produced statistical results suggesting that a person's choice of profession had a definite relationship to the positions of planets at his or her birth.

found in people who manage to live into their nineties.

Was this result merely a fluke? Addey decided to investigate another group of people with characteristics as opposite those of the 90-year-olds as possible—people who would be likely to expend their energies, be tense, nervous, and active. If the preponderance of separating aspects in the horoscopes of the 90-year-olds was more than a coincidence, then the opposite group should show an equivalent preponderance of applying aspects.

The group that Addey selected for his investigation was one to which he himself belonged—people who had been physically handicapped to some extent following an attack of polio. He chose this group because it is generally accepted by physicians that most polio victims who suffer long-term damage from the disease are of a particular physical and mental type. They tend to be athletically active rather than sedentary, alert rather than sluggish and plodding, and outgoing rather than introspective. When the horoscopes of the polio group were analyzed they completely fulfilled Addey's expectations. Their case was exactly the opposite of the long-lived sample—it showed a significant preponderance of applying aspects.

Addey was, of course, predisposed to a belief in astrology. Other statistical investigations have been carried out by researchers with a far more skeptical approach to the subject. The most outstanding work of this kind has been produced by the French scientist and statistician Michel Gauquelin, who began his research in 1950 with the object of *disproving* astrology.

Gauquelin's first step was to examine the sets of supposed statistical evidence in favor of astrology which had been produced earlier in the century by the astrological writers Paul Choisnard, Karl Krafft, and Leon Lasson. Using advanced statistical techniques Gauquelin had no difficulty in showing that all the evidence produced by Choisnard and Krafft rested on too small test groups or faulty mathematical methods. There remained the work of Lasson, who had investigated planetary positions in relation to people's professions, and had produced some surprising results. Lasson had found that, in an exceptionally high number of cases, Mars figures prominently in the horoscopes of medical men, Venus in the horoscopes of artists, and Mercury in those of actors and writers.

Gauquelin concluded that Lasson's test groups had probably been too small and decided to run an analysis of his own, using the horoscopes of 576 medical academics. To his amazement, he found that an unusually high percentage of these men had been born when Mars or Saturn was either coming over the horizon or passing its highest point in the sky. Gauquelin then checked his findings with a new test group of 508 eminent physicians. Mars and Saturn were prominent in exactly the same way. Taking the two test groups together, the odds against these planetary positions being due to chance were ten million to one.

Gauquelin's results received widespread and favorable coverage in the French press. Their reception by Gauquelin's fellow statisticians and scientists was less favorable. Some claimed that Gauquelin's test groups must have been insufficient; others said that he had merely discovered a national peculiarity, since all his subjects were French. "Your conclusions are nothing but pulp romances . . ." the Belgian scientist Marcell Boll told Gauquelin. "If you undertook the same enquiry in Great Britain, Germany, the United States and Russia you would come out with nothing but other national idiosyncracies."

Undaunted by his critics, Gauquelin tested 25,000 Dutch, German, Italian, and Belgian horoscopes. The results backed up the French ones, and experiments with new professional groups produced further confirmation. In the horoscopes of 3142 military men either Mars or Jupiter was in a significant position. Politicians and athletes were also linked with Mars, scientists with Saturn, and actors with Jupiter. The odds against these links occurring simply by chance ranged from between one million and 50 million to one. From doctors to artists, every one of the test groups showed that planetary positions were related to profession—and in just the way astrology had always claimed. Statisticians were finally forced to take Gauquelin's results seriously.

Counter-experiments were performed in which Gauquelin's methods were applied to random groups of men and women who did not have a profession in common. In every case these random groups produced results in accordance with the laws of chance. This so impressed a number of Gauquelin's opponents that they withdrew their criticism of his work.

Gauquelin has carried out more than 20 years of statistical research in astrology, but his results should not be overestimated. He has neither proved the truth of every astrological doctrine, nor found that astrological predictions can be completely trusted. What he has shown is that there is a definite relationship between the positions of planets at the moment of birth and the

Statistical Studies on Zodiac Types

Below: the planetary correlation to vocational success as worked out by Gauquelin. He chose for his sample subjects eminent members of each profession since, if the astrological theory were valid, the planetary position would favor success in the chosen field.

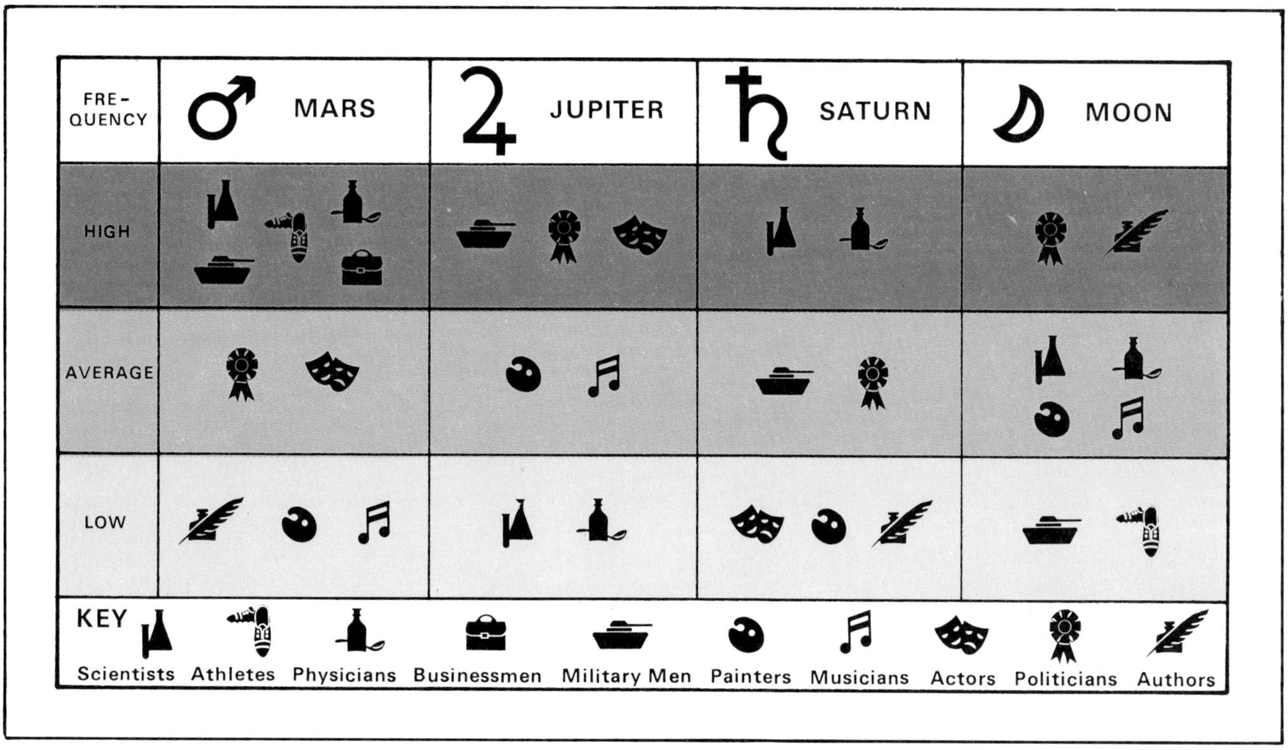

FRE-QUENCY	♂ MARS	♃ JUPITER	♄ SATURN	☽ MOON
HIGH	Scientists, Athletes, Physicians, Military Men, Businessmen	Military Men, Politicians, Actors	Scientists, Physicians	Politicians, Authors
AVERAGE	Politicians, Actors	Painters, Musicians	Military Men, Politicians	Scientists, Physicians, Painters, Musicians
LOW	Authors, Painters, Musicians	Scientists, Physicians	Actors, Painters, Authors	Military Men, Athletes

KEY: Scientists, Athletes, Physicians, Businessmen, Military Men, Painters, Musicians, Actors, Politicians, Authors

Testing Accuracy of Horoscopes

Below: Thomas Ring, well-known German astrologer. He worked with Prof. Hans Bender on a series of tests in which he predicted the life and character of a subject of whom he knew nothing except the birth facts on a horoscope.

Below right: Ernst Meier, Swiss astrologer. He is working with German psychologist Hans Bender at the Institute for the Study of Borderland Areas of Psychology and Mental Health in further attempts to provide some scientific information on the validity of astrological theory.

profession a person chooses to follow. This is, of course, in complete accord with traditional astrological beliefs.

What about all the other details that an experienced astrologer claims to be able to detect from a person's horoscope? Has any serious research been carried out on the accuracy of horoscopes as a whole? Not enough, by any means, but sufficient to provide a strong case for further investigation.

Hans Bender, Professor of Psychology at the German University of Freiburg, has been one of the few academics to carry out scientific research in this field. As early as 1937 Professor Bender began to make experiments in "blind diagnosis," in which an astrologer is given an anonymous horoscope with no other information about the person to whom it belongs. The professor then compared the astrologer's findings with known facts about the life and character of the individual concerned. The results of these early tests were inconclusive, and in 1944–45 Bender made more extensive experiments with the astrologer

and psychologist Thomas Ring. Their findings were promising and, when World War II had ended, Bender decided to continue the tests on an even larger scale.

Bender tested more than 100 astrologers, using blind diagnosis and another procedure known as "matching." For the matching tests each astrologer was given detailed notes on the lives, personalities, and appearance of up to half a dozen unidentified individuals and an equal number of horoscopes. Their task was to match up the horoscopes with the right individuals.

Results from the matching tests were confusing and unsatisfactory. The findings from blind diagnosis were more rewarding. A large number of the astrologers made statements about the individuals whose horoscopes they had examined which were true, but would be true of almost anybody. A smaller number, however, produced specific statements that were impressively and minutely accurate. Interestingly enough, these astrologers were able to justify each of their statements in terms of the astrological tradition. This made it less likely that their success was due to clairvoyance or to some other psychic gift rather than skill in their art.

Bender continued his investigations with this smaller group. He found that one particular astrologer, Walter Boer, excelled in one type of matching test as well as blind diagnosis. The particular matching test involved written records about two groups of people—one psychologically maladjusted and one normal. The records were locked in a safe to which Boer had no access, and he was given no details about the people concerned except the dates, times, and places of their birth. In a high number of cases he was able to match the psychological conclusions about these people with their horoscopes.

In 1960 American psychologist Vernon Clark carried out even more rigorous tests of this kind. Clark first selected the horoscopes of 10 people, five men and five women, each of them of a different profession. They were a musician, an accountant, a herpetologist (an expert on snakes), a veterinary surgeon, a teacher, an art critic, a puppeteer, a pediatrician, a librarian, and a prostitute. Clark then gave the horoscopes and a separate list of the professions to 20 astrologers and asked them to match up the two. As a control, he gave the same information to a group of 20 psychologists and social workers. The control group came out with the number of correct answers that could be expected to be obtained by chance. The astrologers produced far better results—a hundred to one against them being the result of chance.

Clark remembered, however, that 100 to one shots sometimes romp home, as anyone who plays the horses knows. He also realized that he had to make sure that the results were not due to the astrologers being psychics, unconsciously practicing some form of ESP.

The next series of tests was therefore designed to reduce the possibility of ESP to a minimum. Each of 23 astrologers was given 20 horoscopes divided into 10 pairs. With these were 10 sets of biographical data, one for each of the 10 pairs. The astrologers were told that *one* of each pair of horoscopes corresponded to the biographical data given for that pair. The

Above: Karsten Kroenke, German astrologer who specializes in astrological predictions on a commercial basis and works for industry and business. For many astrologers' clients, scientific research is interesting but not strictly relevant. What keeps most of them paying astrologers' fees is that the service seems to work.

Jung and Astrology

Above: Carl G. Jung, the Swiss psychologist who developed a theory on how astrology works. He suggested that cosmic influences synchronize, or coincide, with events in a person's life. This means that planetary aspects do not *cause* behavioral patterns or happenings, but *coincide* with the birth of people who will behave in a certain way and who will have certain experiences.

other horoscope of each pair, they were assured, pertained to someone of the same sex and approximate age, but with a different personal history. In fact these second horoscopes were fakes, prepared for imaginary people. This was the course taken to diminish as much as possible the chances of ESP being involved.

The task of the astrologers was to fit each set of biographical data to the correct one of each of the pairs of horoscopes. Once again the results were good—100 to one against them being the result of chance. This result seemed to prove the possibility of astrological prediction. For if Clark's test astrologers could successfully decide on the basis of a horoscope which person had suffered, say, a broken leg, they could in theory have predicted that broken leg by looking at the same horoscope before the accident happened.

Clark undertook a third test, which again involved the astrologers being given pairs of horoscopes. This time one of each pair pertained to someone who had cerebral palsy. The other, a similar chart, referred to a highly gifted individual. The astrologers had to decide which of these horoscopes belonged to which of the two individuals.

Once more the results were impressive, and the odds were again 100 to one against them being the result of chance. The odds against the figures for the three experiments together being the result of chance were over a million to one. Clark's experimental findings were examined by statisticians, who found his mathematical techniques to be faultless.

What was Clark's own conclusion? "Never again," he said, "will it be possible to dismiss the astrological technique as a vague, spooky, and mystical business—or as the plaything of undisciplined psychics—or as merely the profitable device of unscrupulous quacks. Those who, out of prejudice, wish to do so will have to remain silent or repeat these experiments for themselves."

So there is evidence that astrology works. But if so, how? There have been many attempts to give a scientific answer to this question. The best known of these is the theory suggested by the psychologist Carl G. Jung.

Jung believed in what he called "synchronicity," or the meaningful coincidence. Synchronicity, said Jung, is the other side of cause and effect. In other words, if two events happen at the same time, or shortly after one another, they may be related because one event caused the other. Alternatively neither event may have caused the other, yet the two may still be linked in a meaningful way.

In the case of astrology this would mean that the Sun, Moon, and other cosmic influences do not cause particular events, but they synchronize, or coincide meaningfully with those events. According to Jung's theory, it is not the particular planetary aspects at birth that *cause* an individual to be, say, short-lived. It is merely that these aspects *coincide* with the birth of short-lived people.

An imaginary example may help to make this concept clearer. A man feels hungry and eats a meal at the same time every evening. Each evening as he begins to feel hungry the hands of the electric clock in his apartment always indicate that the time is 7 p.m. But it is not the position of the clock hands that produces the hunger, nor the hunger that affects the clock hands. There is no causal relationship between the two. But there is a synchronistic relationship—both the hunger and the clock time reflect the 24-hour period of the Earth's rotation.

Applying this example to astrology, the planetary positions are the "hands of the clock," and the inborn characteristics and destiny of a person born under those positions are the "feelings of hunger." Neither is the cause of the other, but both reflect some vast cosmic cycle of which we know nothing.

Curiously enough, the theory of synchronicity is almost as ancient as astrology itself, although Jung thought he had invented it. Sophisticated astrologers have adhered to it for centuries, although they have expressed it differently. The way they put it is that "the planets and the signs of the zodiac are symbols of cosmic forces, and the patterns they form synchronize with events on Earth."

Totally different theories have, however, been put forward by some modern scientists to explain the results they have obtained when studying cosmic influences. Dr. Frank A. Brown, famous for his experiments on biological clocks, has suggested that a "trigger mechanism" may account for the rhythms found in the opening of oyster shells and the activity of rats. The Moon and the Sun, Brown suggests, supply an extremely minute amount of some unknown energy to each living organism. In spite of its smallness, this energy is enough to pull a biological trigger within the organism, setting off a chain reaction that ultimately leads to the organism expending a large amount of energy.

Brown's theory is, of course, thoroughly scientific, being expressed in terms of cause and effect. However, there is no more evidence for the existence of either the trigger or the energy that supposedly sets it off than there is for the existence of the "internal clocks" that Brown had previously rejected.

Another explanation of planetary influences has been put forward by Michel Gauquelin, who worked on the relationship between horoscopes and professions. His latest theory arose from a five-year study of 30,000 parents and children during which he discovered that children tend to be born under the same, or similar, planetary positions as their parents were. We inherit our horoscopes, Gauquelin suggests, in the same way that we inherit other genetic factors. Some element in our genetic makeup is sensitive to a certain set of cosmic influences, helping to determine when we are born and affecting the future course of our lives, including our probable choice of the profession we will follow.

Of the prevailing theories, synchronicity—the idea that the positions of the planets do not cause things to happen but merely coincide with those happenings—is still the most popular explanation of how astrology works, and the one to which most astrologers adhere.

In a sense all such theories take second place to two important facts. Cosmic influences have been shown to exist, and astrology—the art of interpreting those influences—can be made to work. This even extends to predicting future events.

Below: Al Morrison, past president of the Astrologers' Guild of America. He was one of seven New York astrologers consulted by a reporter for an article exploring the consistency of astrological interpretation. The article showed that stargazers often differ in what they see in a horoscope.

Chapter 11 The Power of Prediction

Did astrology play an important role in the decisions made by the Nazi leaders of Germany's Third Reich? To what extent was Hitler himself influenced by the predictions of astrologers and the general enthusiasm for the occult of his close associate Heinrich Himmler? Himmler's trust in unorthodox methods to foresee and control the future became well-known in the German high command, and his British opponents relied on that faith in setting up an elaborate counterespionage ploy, using astrological predictions for propaganda purposes. How far in fact did astrology influence the leaders in World War II?

It was the evening of November 8, 1939. The main speaker and some of his close associates had left the Munich meeting hall unexpectedly early, but the platform was still crowded with minor dignitaries. In the body of the hall the audience smoked, drank beer, chatted, and laughed. Suddenly there was an ear-splitting roar as the shock wave from an explosion swept through the rooms. For a while all was confusion. The smoke- and dust-laden air masked the cries of the wounded, and the failure of the lights hampered the efforts of their would-be rescuers. When lights were finally brought and some sort of order restored, the extent of the damage became apparent. The speaker's platform, where the explosion had occurred, was completely wrecked. Although the rest of the hall had suffered lightly, seven men lay dead and more than another 60 were injured, some of them severely.

The meeting that ended with such fatal suddenness on that November evening had been held to celebrate the 16th anniversary of Hitler's *Putsch*—his attempt to overthrow the German government—in 1923. That had also taken place in Munich. And the man who had escaped almost certain death by leaving early was none other than Adolf Hitler himself.

By 1939 Hitler and the Nazis had been in power for six years. Throughout the years of their rule the memory of the unsuccessful *Putsch* was kept alive. Hitler's followers who had fallen in 1923 were given the status of political martyrs, and on each anniversary

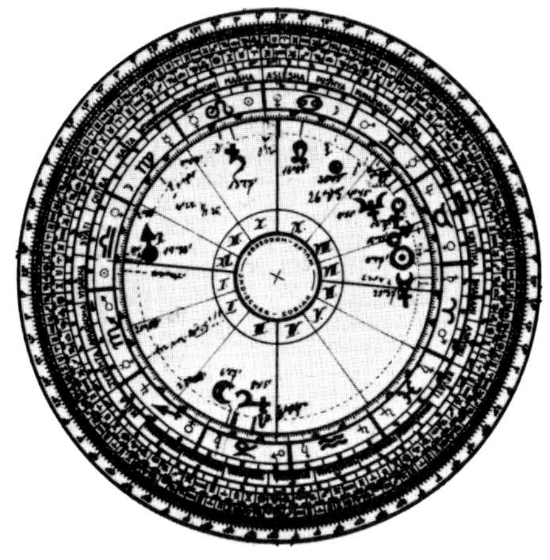

Above: Hitler's birth chart, drawn up by Himmler's personal astrologer Wilhelm Wulff. In an analysis long after World War II, Wulff pointed out that Hitler's horoscope—with a Libra ascendant and Uranus rising—suggests unrest and catastrophe. Another configuration of Venus, Gemini, and Taurus shows Hitler's end in suicide with his woman friend. Opposite: a portrait of Adolf Hitler in honor of his 50th birthday in 1939, which was a crucial year.

Astrology and the Third Reich

of their death the Nazi "old fighters" gathered in beer halls all over Germany. Officially their purpose was to mourn their fallen comrades, but in reality they drank, gossiped over old times, and listened to speeches from their leaders.

The most notable of these annual meetings took place in Munich itself at the Bürgerbräu Beer Cellar on November 8, 1939. It was well known that Hitler would head the celebration, and the would-be assassin had placed his bomb carefully on a pillar right behind the speaker's platform. Was it just chance that caused Hitler to leave before the bomb exploded, or did he have some foreknowledge of the assassination attempt?

It has been suggested that this attempt on Hitler's life was a put-up job. The man who constructed and installed the bomb was Georg Elser. He was arrested and later died in a concentration camp. However, some people allege that Elser was the tool of a group of Gestapo men who were anxious to rid themselves of rivals in the Nazi party. It is said that Hitler himself was a party to the plot, and that he left the gathering earlier than expected in order to avoid the explosion he knew was coming.

Such a scheme would certainly have been in keeping with Hitler's known ruthlessness. However, all the evidence indicates that Hitler genuinely believed Elser to be the agent of a group of conspirators, probably inspired by British intelligence agents.

Below: the ruins of the Munich meeting hall after the bombing on November 8, 1939, in an apparent assassination attempt on Hitler.

Hitler was backed up in this view by Heinrich Himmler, sinister chief of the Nazi secret police—and for a most extraordinary reason. Himmler was a devotee of the occult, and had sought the advice of a psychic in trying to find the person responsible for the bombing. He went to a *psychometrist*—a type of medium who is alleged to sense events associated with particular objects simply by touching or being near them. Himmler gave the psychometrist some fragments of the bomb mechanism to examine. She held these to her head, went into a trance, and claimed to see visions of the individuals behind the explosion. These were a group of men talking to someone named Otto. Himmler believed that this Otto could be none other than Otto Strasser, an old associate of Hitler's. He had broken with the Führer in 1930 and become leader of an underground anti-Nazi group called the Black Front.

Hitler was not unduly impressed by this medium's revelations, but he does seem to have been surprised and alarmed by a prediction of the explosion made some days before the event by the astrologer Karl Ernst Krafft.

Krafft was a Swiss astrologer who had moved to Germany shortly before the outbreak of war in September 1939. Some say he was pro-Nazi and others that he was not. In any case he had personal contacts with a number of officials of Himmler's intelligence service. It was to one of these, Dr. Heinrich Fesel, that Krafft sent his prediction on November 2, 1939. He reported that Hitler's horoscope indicated that he would be in great danger in the period November 7 to 10, and that there was the "possibility of an assassination by the use of explosive material."

As soon as Krafft heard of the fulfillment of his prophecy he sent a telegram to Rudolf Hess, Hitler's deputy, drawing attention to his prediction. This telegram, Krafft was to write later, "exploded like a second bomb in Berlin." Dr. Fesel was ordered to hand over Krafft's original report, and by the morning of November 9 it was in the hands of Hitler. He was apparently impressed by its amazing accuracy.

The following day Krafft was brought to Berlin for interrogation by the Gestapo in the belief that his foreknowledge of the bomb must mean that he had been involved in the plot against Hitler's life. However, in demonstrating the exact astrological rules that had led him to his conclusions, Krafft managed to convince the Gestapo that astrology enabled its practitioners to make accurate forecasts of future events.

As a result, Krafft was employed to carry out astrological work of a political nature for the SS (Hitler's special police), the Nazi Propaganda Ministry, and even the Foreign Office. As in the 17th century, astrology was once again to be used as a means of psychological warfare, aimed at boosting the morale of the home country and demoralizing the enemy. During World War II both sides used the prophecies of the 16th-century French astrologer and seer Nostradamus to predict the defeat of the other. Krafft did some detailed research on the prophecies of Nostradamus, and this work was used by the Propaganda Ministry for their ends. He also prepared leaflets based on other ancient occult documents that could be interpreted to prophesy a German victory. In addition, he regularly cast horoscopes of the leading enemies of Nazism, such as Britain's Winston Churchill.

In the course of his work for the government Krafft made contact with a number of leading Nazis whom he converted to a belief in astrology. Among them were Robert Ley, leader of the Labor Front—the Nazi equivalent of the AFL-CIO—and Dr. Hans Frank, "the butcher of Warsaw," Hitler's brutal governor

Below left: Himmler's birth chart by Wilhelm Wulff. Unlike Swiss astrologer Karl Krafft, who at least originally found his contact with high Nazi leaders exhilarating, Wulff was most wary of his involvement. He had the additional worry of seeing in his calculations a future that would in no way please his Nazi masters. He interpreted the chart after the war as showing that Himmler would be a commanding officer. He concluded this from the fact that Mars is in the Sixth House. The exact opposition of Saturn and Neptune foreshadowed a violent death. The favorable aspects of Jupiter could only indicate the high position he would achieve in life—it could not change the end.

Below: Himmler in Vienna in 1938. Head of the SS, he was always fascinated with unorthodox theories. There was supposed to have been a joke that one general was "worried about the stars on his epaulette and [Himmler] about the stars in his horoscope."

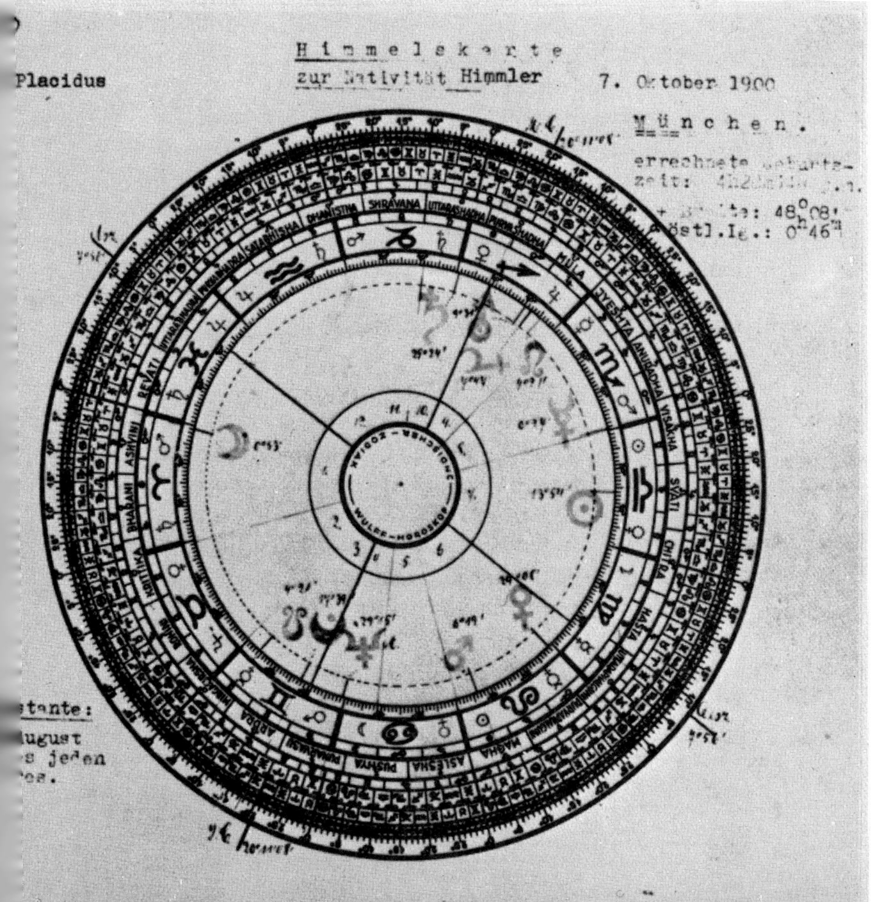

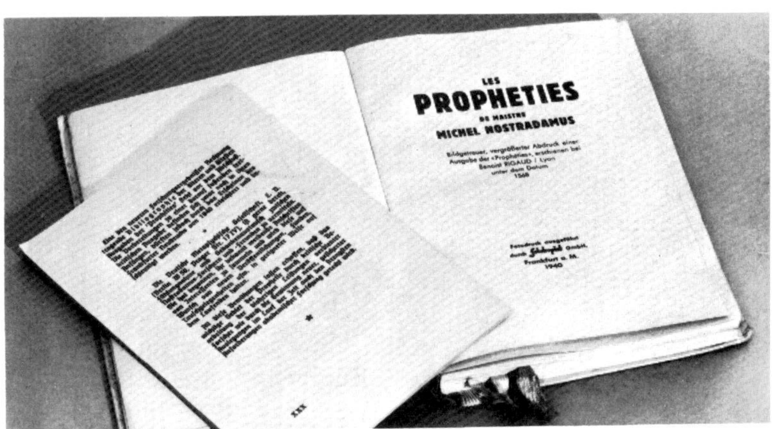

Above: Karl Ernst Krafft, the Swiss astrologer who early in November 1939 reported to Himmler's intelligence service that Hitler would be in particular danger between the 7th and 10th of that month. When his prophecy was spectacularly proved true, he came to the attention of the Third Reich leaders, including Hitler himself, and was brought in for questioning by the Gestapo. He managed to convince them that his eerie preknowledge had been acquired solely through traditional astrological methods.

Above right: Krafft's facsimile edition of the prophecies of Nostradamus which he produced for Joseph Goebbels' propaganda ministry. In it Krafft assembled a few of the ambiguous quatrains with interpretations that pointed to imminent and complete Nazi victory over all opponents.

of occupied Poland. It was to these men that Krafft made another surprisingly accurate prediction in the spring of 1940. Far from continuing to forecast German victory as his Nazi masters might have wished, Krafft foretold serious trouble. He produced a *dynogram*—an astrological forecast expressed in the form of a graph—which showed a pessimistic view of Germany's future. The dynogram indicated that Germany would meet with one military success after another until the winter of 1942–43. After that, said Krafft, the astrological indications became decidedly unfavorable, and Germany would be well advised to make peace before the end of 1942. Frank assured Krafft that the war would be over long before then.

In fact, of course, it wasn't—and in January 1943 the German armies met with the military disaster of Stalingrad, which was a turning point of the war.

Unpopular though Krafft's forecast was with the Germans, it was a demonstration once again that astrological techniques could produce accurate predictions of future events. Indeed, before his involvement with the Nazis, Krafft had come up with some even more surprising prophecies. They were made as a result of an experiment in blind diagnosis which he undertook early in 1938. Krafft had been asked to forecast the future of two individuals simply on the basis of the planetary positions at the time of their birth, without knowing who these people were or any other information about them.

Krafft declared that the first of these two people had a schizoid personality, that he was partly Jewish, and that he was unlikely to be alive after November 1938.

The second person, he said, occupied a position of authority and eminence, but would be unlikely to retain it after September 1940.

Krafft's predictions proved perfectly correct. The subject of the first blind diagnosis was Cornelius Codreanu, the half-Jewish leader of a Rumanian political movement called the Iron Guard. He was shot dead on November 30, 1938. The second person was Rumania's King Carol, who was forced to abdicate in favor of his son on September 6, 1940.

In spite of his undoubted abilities as an astrologer Krafft fell from favor with the Nazi leadership in the spring of 1941. Along with many other German astrologers, he was arrested and im-

Krafft: Astrologer to the Nazis

prisoned. This seemingly abrupt change in the Nazi attitude toward astrology arose from a most unusual incident. In May 1941 Rudolf Hess, deputy leader of the Nazi Party, took a fighter plane, flew it to Scotland, and attempted to open peace negotiations with the British. Hess, who was generally believed to be under the influence of astrologers, had an astrologer on his staff. It was thought that astrological charts indicating that he was destined to make peace between Germany and Britain had persuaded him to undertake his extraordinary action. Whether or not this was true—and Hess's astrologer, naturally enough, denied it—fears had been growing for some time that astrology was exerting undue political influence in Germany. The Hess incident gave the Gestapo the ideal opportunity to move against the astrologers. It also provided a scapegoat to blame for Hess's action.

The British interned Hess. They made little use of his flight for propaganda purposes, but the incident had seriously alarmed Hitler and the other Nazi leaders. They rounded up amateur and professional astrologers, banned the public practice of astrology, suppressed all astrological magazines, and strictly forbade all astrological speculation about the future course of the war.

Nevertheless, the Nazis continued to make use of the astrologers they were so busily persecuting. So it was that after a year in solitary confinement, Karl Krafft was transferred to a Propaganda Ministry building. He was forced to produce an astrological analysis slanted against President Franklin Roosevelt and designed for political warfare purposes. In it Krafft distorted astrological principles in an attempt to prove that the president and his wife were no more than puppets of Wall Street and "international Jewry." Krafft had evidently been promised that if his work met with the approval of his Nazi masters, he would earn his release. However, it soon became apparent that the

Left: one of Krafft's most remarkably accurate predictions came as a result of an experiment in which he was given samples of handwriting and birth data of two men, but no further details. He predicted that one of them enjoyed a position of considerable authority, but would experience a disastrous reversal of fortune in or about September of 1940. The subject was King Carol of Rumania, pictured with his son on a state visit. He was forced to abdicate on September 6, 1940.

The Enigma of Rudolf Hess

promise would not be kept, and after a few months Krafft refused to collaborate any further with his jailers. He was then interned in a concentration camp for two years. He was due to be transferred to the notorious camp at Buchenwald when he died in January 1945.

Meanwhile the authorities in Britain were also endeavoring to use astrology to aid the war effort. Britain's military leaders had not been converted to a belief in the "science of the stars," but they had come to believe that Hitler employed an astrologer to advise him, and that he might be making at least some of his political and military moves in accordance with astrological indications.

This idea had first been suggested by Virgil Tilea, the Rumanian Ambassador to London. Tilea had once met Krafft in Switzerland, and had been impressed by the astrologer's skills as a prophet. During 1940, well before Krafft was arrested, Tilea wrote to him and asked him to make a forecast of coming events. Krafft showed the letter to Dr. Fesel, his contact in the intelligence service, and asked him how he could get a reply through to London. Fesel immediately saw the possibility of using Krafft's forecast as a political weapon. He and the other security chiefs promised to get a letter to London provided they could dictate its contents. Krafft tried to drop the affair, even attempting to resign his post, but a forecast was nevertheless prepared and despatched to Virgil Tilea.

Below: Rudolf Hess. In 1941 he was deputy Führer, although he had slid into the background of the Nazi leadership since 1939. He was certainly neurotic, and passionately attached to Hitler. He was found guilty at his trial in Nürnberg, and sentenced to life imprionsment. Now nearly 80 years old, he is the last Nazi leader still imprisoned—the only inmate of Berlin's Spandau prison.

The fact that the forecast came from Berlin and seemed such an obvious piece of political propaganda convinced Tilea that Krafft was in the pay of the Nazis—perhaps even of Hitler himself—and he alerted the British authorities accordingly. If Hitler was employing an astrologer, he argued, it would be only wise for Britain to do the same. Then their astrologer could "predict the predictions" of his Nazi counterpart, and possibly anticipate Hitler's moves.

The first problem for the British was to find an astrologer sufficiently well acquainted with the techniques used by the Nazi astrologers, particularly Krafft. This was essential if the Nazi forecasts were to be anticipated correctly. Sir Orme Sargent, a high official of Britain's Foreign Office, approached a number of British astrologers. None of them, however, felt sure of using the same procedures as those employed in Berlin. It was Virgil Tilea who finally found a willing astrologer capable of doing the job. He was Hungarian-born Louis de Wohl, a partly Jewish refugee from Nazi persecution who had lived in London since 1935.

Within a short time de Wohl was head of the newly created Psychological Research Bureau, an organization which, in spite of its all-embracing title, was concerned exclusively with astrology. Throughout 1940 and the first half of 1941 the Bureau produced a stream of reports for the British Admiralty and the War Office. These included astrological analyses of the course of the war, of Hitler's probable political and military moves, and of the future careers of Nazi leaders and their allies. They were often amazingly accurate. In 1941, for example, de Wohl examined the horoscope of the Italian dictator Benito Mussolini and correctly predicted his "violent and sudden end" in 1945 at the hands of

Above: the crashed remains of the Messerschmitt 110 in which Rudolf Hess flew to Scotland in a bizarre peace mission in 1941. He hoped to persuade Britain to give Germany a free hand against the Soviet Union in exchange for a peace settlement between them. It was suggested that this idea came from an astrologer whom Hess had on his personal staff, and the Gestapo took the opportunity of the fiasco to suppress astrology in Germany by burning most of the books and imprisoning astrologers.

the partisans.

At this stage of the war, however, Britain's position seemed desperate. Almost all of Europe was either under German occupation or ruled by pro-Nazi governments. Hitler's armies were gaining victory after victory over the Soviet Union. The United States was still neutral and seemed likely to remain so. To many Americans, including Joseph Kennedy, father of the future president, it seemed that a German victory was inevitable.

The Nazi propaganda machine did everything in its power to convince American public opinion that this was indeed the case. No channel of communication was neglected—not even American astrological magazines. Through German agents and native-born Americans who sympathized with the Nazis, astrological forecasts prophesying a speedy German victory were planted in many American occult publications.

De Wohl's task was to ensure the publication of counter-propaganda predictions with a pro-allied content. He drew up astrological analyses that appeared in magazines from Los Angeles to Lagos, Nigeria. At a later stage of the war de Wohl also prepared "black propaganda"—information based on astrology that did not openly come from an allied source but appeared to originate from inside Germany itself. Under Sefton

Right: astrologer Louis de Wohl was on the payroll of the British government during World War II. He was hired to check on what advice might be given the Germans by their official astrologers.

Delmer, head of British "black" political warfare, de Wohl wrote articles for fake issues of *Zenit*, a well-known prewar German astrological magazine. These were printed by skilled British forgers in a brilliant imitation of a German typeface, and smuggled into Germany from Sweden.

Despite the Nazi ban on astrological publications, these issues of the phony *Zenit* achieved a surprisingly widespread circulation inside Germany. They played a part in sapping the morale of both the civilian population and members of the armed forces. The submariners who went to sea in Germany's U-boats, for

Right: a cover of *Der Zenit*, a fake German astrological magazine which de Wohl edited in London in 1943. It was then infiltrated into Germany. The timing of printing was carefully planned so that the pessimistic predictions of U-boat disasters might appear to have been fulfilled: it was done when British intelligence received reports of the sinkings. There was an authentic *Zenit* published before the war, and great pains were taken to make the fake appear authentic.

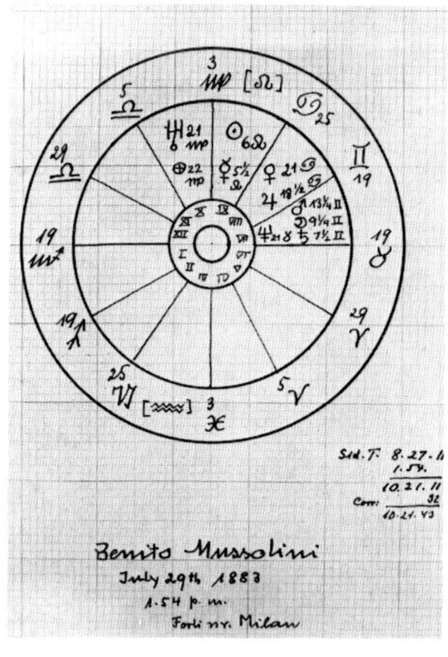

Far right: this is Mussolini's horoscope as cast by de Wohl in 1941. De Wohl rightly predicted that the Italian dictator would meet "a violent and sudden end."

example, were hardly cheered by the predictions contained in the April 1943 issue of the false *Zenit*. Typical forecasts were: "April 4, Advisable not to go to sea if the Captain's horoscope is unfavorable; April 20, Very bad for U-boats."

Even more gloomy reading for patriotic Germans was an article in the same issue forecasting that Heinrich Himmler and other SS leaders would one day betray Hitler.

Interestingly enough, this prediction was accurately fulfilled toward the end of the war when Himmler, Schellenberg, and other trusted SS men tried to abandon the Führer and make independent arrangements with the Allies.

Himmler was himself a convinced believer in astrology—as he was in almost every form of the occult. In the later stages of the war he hardly ever made a move without consulting his favorite astrologer, Wilhelm Wulff. Far from enjoying the influence this gave him over the powerful SS chief, Wulff found his position an extremely difficult one. His astrological calculations convinced him that Germany was bound to lose the war, and that both Himmler and Hitler were destined for early and unpleasant deaths. Because he was too honest an astrologer to conceal these conclusions entirely, he consequently ran the constant risk of being thrown into a concentration camp as a "defeatist."

Astrology as Propaganda

Below: Sefton Delmer, head of the British "black" warfare department, making a radio broadcast during World War II. Black warfare was the name given to propaganda prepared in Britain but presented as though it originated within Germany itself. De Wohl worked for Delmer's department.

DEUTSCHLAND
ERWACHE

Nazi Occultism

Heinrich Himmler, the notorious head of the SS and one of the most powerful men in Nazi Germany, was a fanatical occultist. To pursue his interests fully and undisturbed, he obtained a ruined castle in Westphalia and made it the center of his own cult. This was a kind of paganism based on the most way-out aspects of occult subjects.

Himmler renovated the castle in handsome style, and the great banqueting hall became the center for important rites and conferences. Around a gigantic table in the hall were throne-like wooden chairs upholstered richly in pigskin. Each chair had the name of its regular occupant inscribed on a silver plate at the top. There were never more than 12 others besides Himmler, and each was a favorite of his.

Why precisely 13 around the table? Some say it was a parody of the Last Supper, others that it represented Himmler as the Sun surrounded by the zodiacal 12 signs.

Whatever the significance of the number, the 13 SS men would sit at the table both for meetings about SS business and for group meditation. In meditating they would sit in silence for many hours. Their purpose? To become more closely identified with the Aryan "race soul."

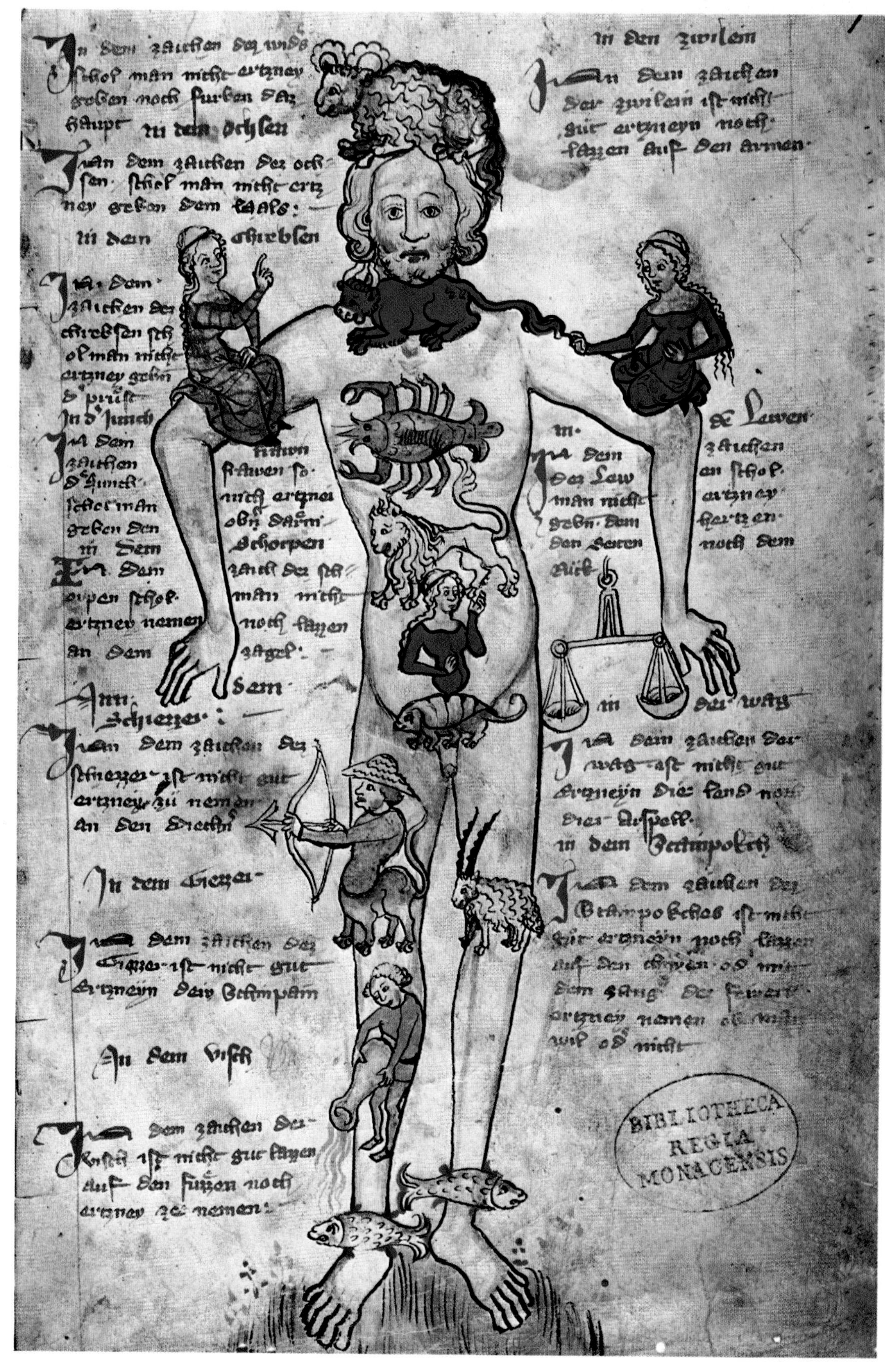
in den zwilein
BIBLIOTHECA
REGIA
MONACENSIS

Chapter 12
The Zodiac and You

What are the various systems used in astrology to cast and interpret a horoscope? How can the novice astrologer best begin to master his art? Traditional astrology is based on the use of the zodiac. What exactly is the zodiac? Can it be seen in the heavens today? What is a Sun Sign, and how should it be interpreted? What can we learn about ourselves from knowing the characteristics of our individual Signs, and—equally important—what further information do we need to define our characters more accurately? Here we are given the basic qualities and some personality types of the 12 Sun Signs.

As the Russian shells whined overhead and crashed to earth with a deafening roar, Alfred Witte hugged the half-frozen mud that formed the floor of his dugout and swore. Two minutes before, the quarter-mile corridor of snow-covered Polish landscape which separated the Russian and German armies on that clear cold day of January 1916 had been peaceful enough. Now it was a hell of exploding shell and mortar bombs, a strip of death swept by rifle and machine gun fire. Far from alarming him, however, this sudden barrage both annoyed and puzzled Witte, an enthusiastic peacetime astrologer from Hamburg who had been conscripted into the German army at the beginning of World War I.

The cause of his annoyance was simple enough—he had just finished a spell of guard duty and had been hoping to get some sleep. His puzzlement had a deeper source. He simply could not understand where his astrological calculations had gone wrong. For some months past Witte had kept a careful record of the occurrences of major Russian artillery barrages, and had checked them against the astrological conditions prevailing at the time. He had acquired such a knowledge of the planetary and zodiacal positions associated with previous Russian artillery assaults that he felt confident he could accurately predict the times and dates of future ones. But somehow an error had crept into his calculations. Witte had been sure that no barrage was due—but here he was, right in the middle of one.

Opposite: an illustration showing the correlation of the signs of the zodiac with parts of the human body, from a German manuscript on astrology of the 14th century.

Right: Alfred Witte, the founder of the Hamburg School, a method of astrological prediction based on the assumption that other planets, so far undiscovered, pass through the zodiac, and thus produce new planetary relationships.

Far right: Percival Lowell, the American astronomer who first suspected the existence of Pluto. Lowell died in 1916, and it was not until 1930 that his theory was finally confirmed by the photographs of the new planet.

Over the next few months he and a colleague who had worked with him on developing an astrological technique of bombardment forecasting puzzled over the matter. After much consideration and study the two men came to a surprising conclusion. They decided that there was another planet, unknown to either astronomers or astrologers, whose movements through the zodiac were throwing out their calculations. Witte called this hypothetical planet *Cupido.* He believed that it was situated beyond the orbit of Neptune. On the basis of the failures of his prediction technique, he worked out what he thought Cupido's movements were. Using these hypothetical movements in his horoscopes he claimed to be able to forecast artillery barrages with considerably greater—although not complete—accuracy.

In fact, at the time that Witte came to believe in the existence of Cupido there *was* an unknown planet beyond Neptune. It was not discovered until 1930, when it was named Pluto. The hypothetical orbit of Cupido was so different from that of Pluto, however, that Witte cannot be hailed as an astronomer ahead of his time. Nor is there the slightest evidence for the existence of seven further planets that Witte and his fellow astrologer Sieggrun claimed to discover beyond the orbit of Cupido. Nevertheless, Witte and Sieggrun worked out a detailed account of the movements of these alleged planets. They published these movements in tabular form, and they have resulted in some amazingly accurate astrological forecasts.

By the late 1920s the tables had become widely available. Astrologers who wished to do so could incorporate the positions of the so-called new planets of Cupido, Hades, Zeus, Chronos, Apollo, Admetos, Vulcan, and Poseidon in the horoscopes that they drew up. The few who chose to do so created the Hamburg School of astrology, as it was called.

Today the Hamburg School draws its supporters largely from Germany and Austria, but its adherents include one or two American and British astrologers. These astrologers calculate enormously complicated horoscopes with the aid of *The Rule Book for Planetary Pictures*—a textbook of Witte's system

Witte and the Hamburg School

originally published in 1928—and a dial-like apparatus which all members of the School learn to operate.

Practitioners of the Hamburg School affirm that their system is capable of infallibly predicting the future, and of revealing the exact nature of past events. Thus in the late 1950s Ludwig Stuiber, a Viennese engineer and a devotee of Witte's theories, published a series of short pamphlets entitled *Convincing Astrological Experiments*. These gave details of how Hamburg School techniques had been successfully used to answer even the most improbable questions. In one example Stuiber told how one Hamburg School astrologer had been given the time, date, and place of birth of a woman whose identity was completely unknown to him, and was asked, "What happened to this woman in Vienna at 4 p.m. on March 4, 1954?" After consulting his dial and rule book, the astrologer answered correctly: she had been shot in the back.

Herr Stuiber was a convinced believer in the theories of Alfred

Left and below left: these two historic photos, taken at a three-day interval, show how the changing position of the planet Pluto (marked by arrows) confirmed its existence. Although, like Witte's hypothetical planet Cupido, its position is beyond Neptune, the orbit of Pluto as now observed and the orbit of Cupido as calculated by Witte are entirely different—and so far there is no evidence for the further seven planets Witte's system assumes.

Above: Reinhold Ebertin, the son of Elsbeth Ebertin who analyzed Hitler's horoscope with such spectacular accuracy. Her son considers himself an astrological pioneer, a "cosmobiologist." His astrological methods are decidedly antitraditional. He ignores such basic "normal" horoscope data as division into houses, and even pays little attention to the zodiac. However, his astrological texts are read with great interest by serious-minded astrologers not only in Germany but all over the world.

Witte and the Hamburg School, so it would be easy enough to believe that he had exaggerated or even invented stories of the system's infallibility. Curiously enough, however, astrologers who were skeptical of Witte's "new planets" and their use in astrology have sometimes found his system effective when they have lightheartedly experimented with it.

Odder still is the case of Ellic Howe, a distingGished historian of astrology. He does not believe in astrology himself, but he has learned to use its techniques in the course of his research. In his book *Urania's Children*, Howe tells how he was approached by Arthur Gauntlett, a professional British astrologer. Gauntlett challenged Howe to try to tell him what had happened to him on two specific days in the past. Although he expected nothing to come of his attempt, Howe applied Witte's system. To his own amazement he came up with answers which, according to Gauntlett, "were so extraordinarily close to the actual events that, had I not known otherwise, prior knowledge might have been suspected."

Such remarkable successes are perhaps coincidental, but the Hamburg School would seem to be worthy of further investigation. For although such planets as the hypothetical Cupido are almost certainly nonexistent, it is just possible—if extremely unlikely—that Witte had identified certain points in the solar system which, like the angles that form the aspects in a horoscope, have some unexplained astrological importance.

Whether or not this is so, the very existence of the Hamburg School is a reminder that, while we talk in general terms of "astrology" and "astrological methods," there are in reality a number of astrological systems. Most of these agree with one another except in points of detail, but some of them have almost completely abandoned the astrological traditions that have grown up over the centuries.

Apart from the members of the Hamburg School with their eight new planets, some of the most revolutionary modern astrologers are the German "cosmobiologists" associated with Reinhold Ebertin. Despite the success of his mother Elsbeth Ebertin—who always used traditional methods and who forecast Hitler's future with such accuracy—Reinhold Ebertin has thrown overboard what he calls "astrology's medieval ballast." He and his fellow cosmobiologists concentrate on complexes of planets situated on a common axis. They pay little attention to the signs of the zodiac.

The overwhelming majority of Western astrologers, however, do not believe that it is necessary or desirable to go so far. They admit that there are some out-of-date elements in their tradition, some absurd superstitions, and a few crude suppositions, but they feel that the traditional system is basically sound. They hold that the use of the zodiac is a key—perhaps *the* key—to astrology.

The zodiac is a circular band of sky extending about eight degrees on either side of the *ecliptic*—the apparent path of the Sun through the sky. The zodiac band is called the "racetrack of the planets." As we look into the heavens from Earth, we see the planets always within this belt of sky. Although the Earth and the other planets revolve around the Sun, from Earth it appears that the Sun, Moon, and planets are moving around the

Cosmobiology

Earth, tracking their circular pathway within the zodiac band.

As almost everyone knows, there are 12 signs of the zodiac: Aries, Taurus, Gemini, Cancer, Leo, Virgo, Libra, Scorpio, Saggitarius, Capricorn, Aquarius, and Pisces. It was the Babylonians who first divided the zodiac into 12. They noticed that the zodiac contained 12 major constellations, and they named each section of the zodiac after the constellation that lay within it.

However, the 12 signs of the zodiac as we know them today no longer correspond with the constellations that bear the same names. For example, if you were born between September 24 and October 23, it is said that your Sun Sign is Libra—meaning that the Sun was in that particular sign on the date of your birth. (During the year the Sun takes to pass through the zodiac, it appears to stay in each sign for 30 days.) Today this does not mean that you were born under the *group of stars* called Libra, however. That might have been true two or three thousand years ago, when the Sun did appear to be among the Libra group of stars during that period of the year. But today the constellation of Libra is many degrees away from the sign of the same name. This is because the Earth's axis has a slight wobble, and the zones of the zodiac as we see them from Earth are no longer in line with the constellations that gave them their names. This slow shift in the sky pattern as we on Earth view it takes 25,800 years to come full circle. At the end of that period, therefore, the constellations and the signs once more coincide; but they immediately start to diverge again.

Modern astrologers are not concerned with the constellations as such, but only with the signs. They divide the zodiac circle of

MENSCH IM ALL

KOSMOBIOLOGIE

Mitteilungsblatt des „Arbeitskreises für kosmobiologische Forschung" und der „Kosmobiologischen Akademie Aalen, Arbeitsgemeinschaft e.V."

30. Jahrgang 1 Januar 1963

AUS DEM INHALT:

Zum Beginn des 30. Jahrgangs

Möglichkeiten und Grenzen kosmischer Thematik

Die persönlichen Punkte im Kosmogramm

Médium coeli = Ichbewußtsein

Abnormitäten

u.a.

Left: Ebertin's *Kosmobiologie*, the most reputable German magazine devoted to astrology. Reinhold Ebertin founded it originally in 1928, and then resumed publication after World War II in Aalen, where he has now also established an annual astrological conference.

Zodiacal Signs Remain the Key

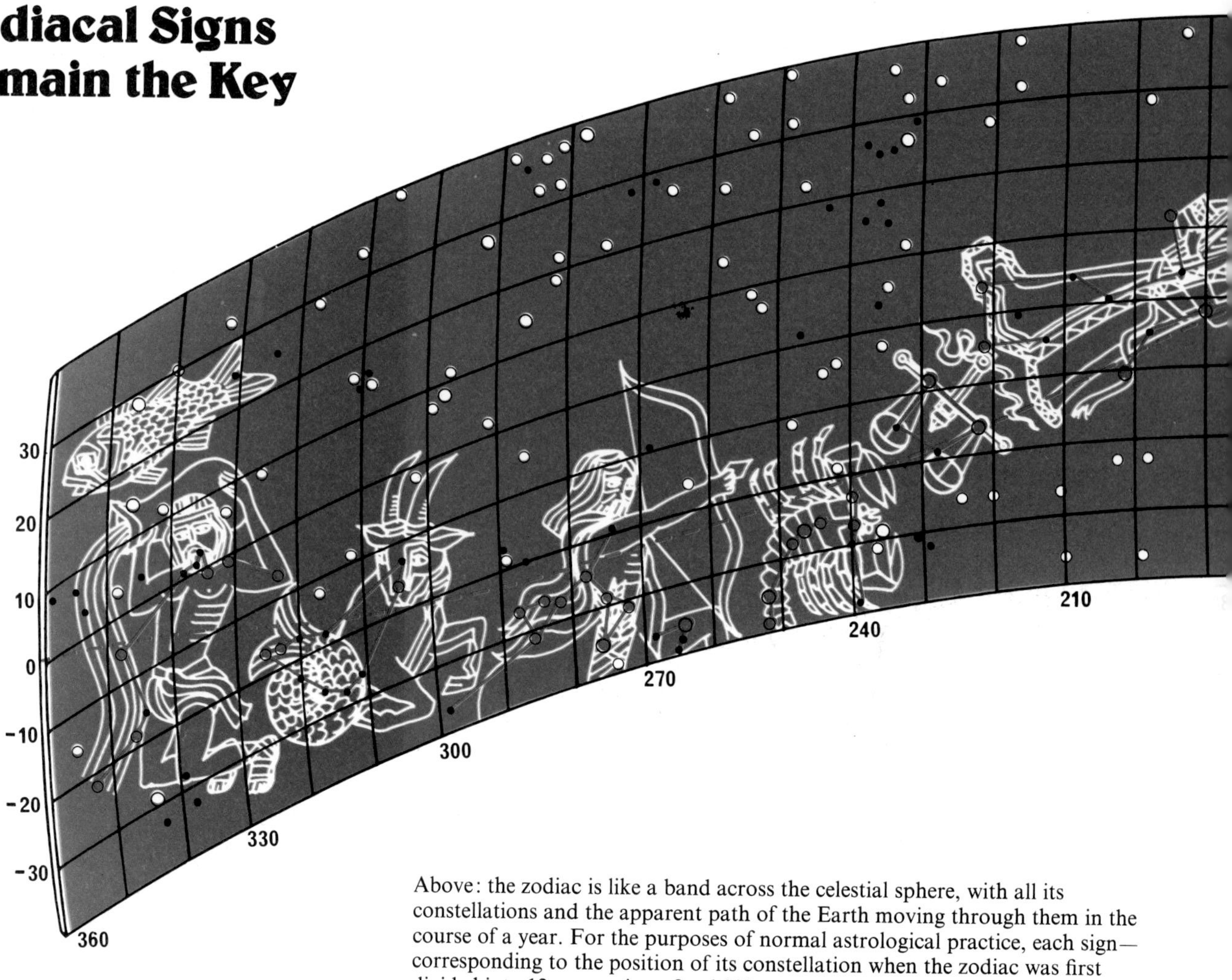

Above: the zodiac is like a band across the celestial sphere, with all its constellations and the apparent path of the Earth moving through them in the course of a year. For the purposes of normal astrological practice, each sign—corresponding to the position of its constellation when the zodiac was first divided into 12—occupies a fixed 30° segment of the complete zodiac. Modern astrologers work only with the signs, not the constellations.

Below: the zodiac is a symbolic concept rather than an astronomical entity, but if it did appear in the heavens, it would circle the Earth like this, lying inside the huge sphere of the heavens, imagined as enclosing our world.

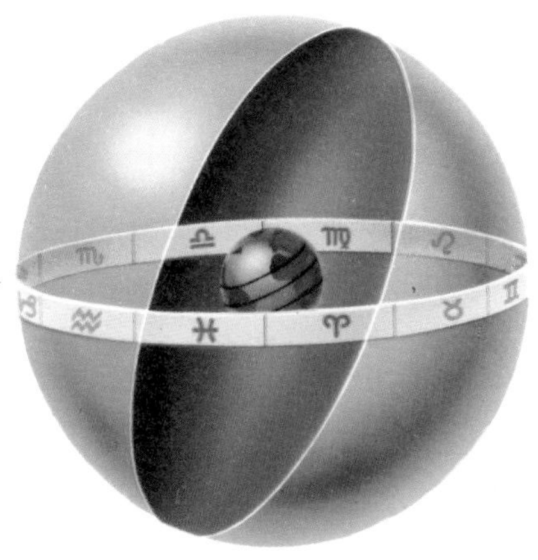

360° into 12 equal and precisely defined zones of 30°, each represented by a sign. The signs are therefore fixed. The Sun is always in Libra for the period September 24 to October 23, just as it is always in Scorpio for the period October 24 to November 22, and so on.

Almost all of us know our Sun Sign, and we have probably read at least one account of the characteristics attached to it. These portraits of character and abilities can be remarkably accurate if we happen to be a pure zodiacal type—a person whose horoscope is heavily influenced by one particular sign. If your Sun Sign is Capricorn, for example, and you happen to have been born at sunrise, Capricorn would also be your *ascendant*—the sign that was rising above the eastern horizon at the time of your birth. This would reinforce the effect of your Sun Sign. If Saturn, Capricorn's ruling planet, were present in the sign at the moment when you were born, this would also enhance your Capricornian characteristics. Again, your horoscope might contain several planets at significant angles in the sign of Capricorn. These would also help to make you a "typical Capricornian."

However, few of us possess such a straightforward astrological makeup. We are not one in 12, but one in a million! Even though

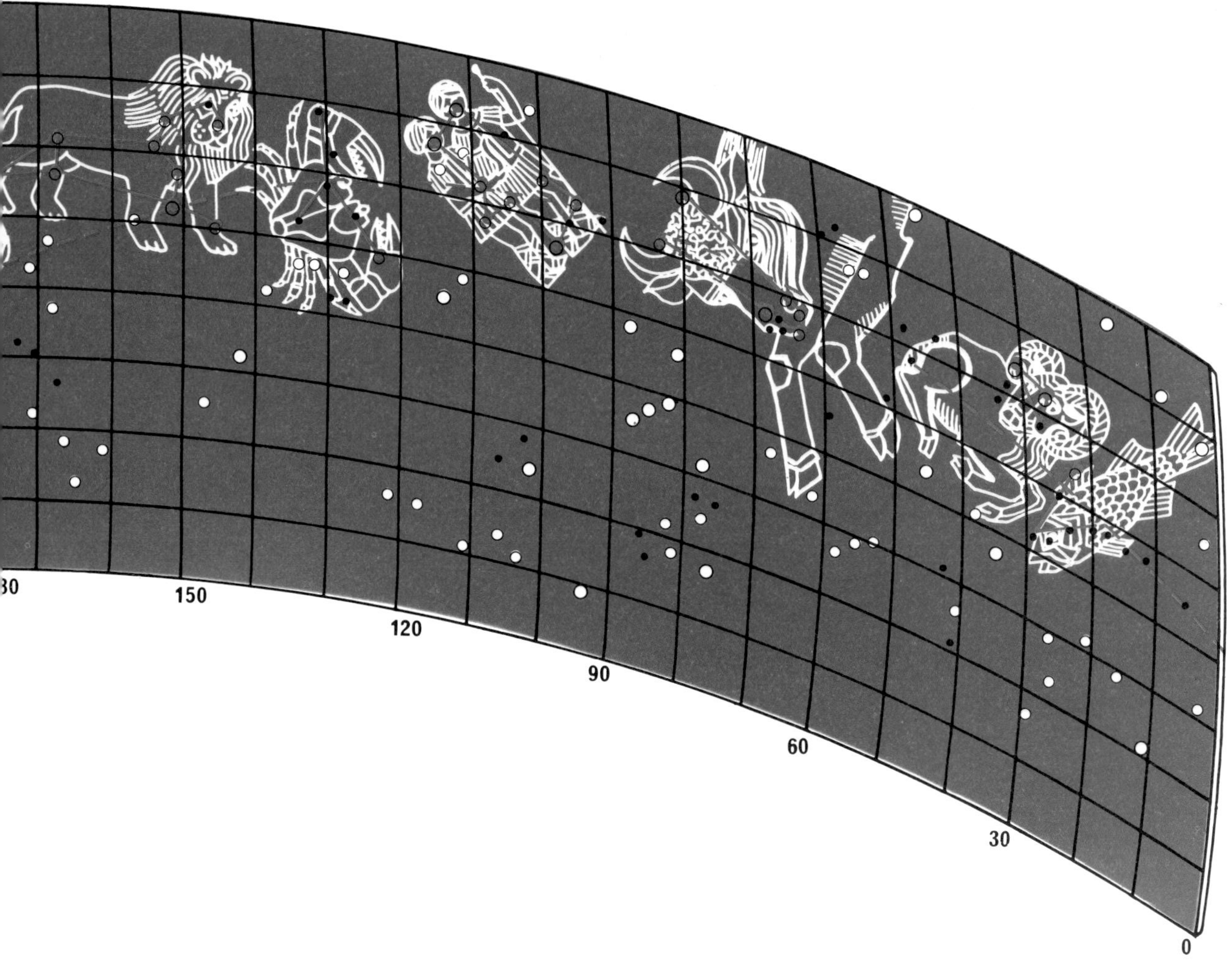

you were born when the Sun was in Capricorn, for instance, you might have had another sign in the ascendant at birth. Similarly you might have several planets in Leo or Pisces or Aquarius, and these will greatly modify the typically Capricornian characteristics in your nature. In certain circumstances in fact, you may be far more like another Sun Sign character than a Capricornian.

Nevertheless the Sun Signs are important, and you will probably recognize some aspects of your character in the description of your own Sun Sign. But you need not reject astrology because these portraits do not fit your personality completely if you bear in mind how other signs may have been present and influential in your horoscope. You are in any case likely to find that some of the statements concerning your Sun Sign are generally accurate, and a few may pinpoint your personality to perfection. Some will doubtlessly be inaccurate.

One other point must be made about the following material on Sun Signs. Because pure zodiacal types are so rare, the people listed as examples have been chosen as being *of the character* of each Sun Sign. They may in some cases have been born under a different Sun Sign, of which they are less typical.

ARIES the Ram (March 21 to April 20)

Early in the last century the astrologer Raphael described the typical Aries person as "commanding, choleric, and violent." Modern astrologers use politer language, but in essence their opinion is basically the same. Aries people are seen as adventurous, pioneering types, respected but not always loved for their independence, their reliance on facts rather than feelings or theories, and their happy concentration upon themselves. This self-absorption is, strangely enough, usually free from any taint of vainity.

Aries is traditionally the most masculine of the signs, and the Aries man tends to have all the characteristics of the "male chauvinist." He takes his own virility for granted—although he sometimes has difficulty in recognizing this quality in other men. Where sex is concerned, he sees himself as a conqueror. The Aries woman also has many qualities still sometimes regarded as typically masculine. She tends to be boisterous and to take the lead in a relationship if she can do so. Ideally, she needs a partner as strong as herself.

The Aries desire for competition and independence makes success at work important to people born under this sign. They want to get to the top of their chosen field. And they may choose careers like gardening, sculpture, public relations, and sport—anything that combines plenty of energetic activity with some, but not too much, theory.

Some examples of people with strong Aries characteristics are show business personalities Louis Armstrong, Marlon Brando, Bette Davis, and Charlie Chaplin; political leader Nikita Krushchev; painter Vincent Van Gogh; novelists George Sand and Emile Zola; and conductors Leopold Stokowski and Arturo Toscanini.

Thomas Jefferson

Below: a man of wide and deep intellectual interests, Jefferson had an enterprising and practical turn of mind which is often a characteristic of the Aries sign.

Above: astrologers in the past considered that Arians might even look like the Ram of their sign. The pictures of Jefferson (opposite) and Van Gogh (below left) do bear a certain resemblance to this Arian type.

Vincent van Gogh

Left: the pushy independence of Aries shows itself in the work of the painter Van Gogh, whose paintings were so far in advance of current artistic taste that it has taken critics decades to appreciate his original genius. His impetuosity is recorded in his reckless gesture of remorse in which he cut off his own ear.

TAURUS the Bull (April 21 to May 21)

Taurus is an earthy sign, and pure Taureans tend to be slow but sure, like the measured tread of the bull that gives the sign its name. Some astrologers of the past even went so far as to suggest that Taureans look like bulls—thick-necked, thickset, and wide of nostrils. Taurus people have a taste for the good things of life, enjoying both work and leisure to the full and taking pleasure in food, drink, material possessions, and affection.

The Taurus man combines self-centeredness with generosity, and is capable of becoming an ideal husband and father. He generally has a friendly attitude toward other men and is slow to respond to provocation. When he does become angry, however, others must beware. Like the bull, his reactions are slow—but he is terrible in his rage. The Taurus woman is strong-minded but does not impose her views on others. She makes a true friend, a perfect wife, and an ideal mother, never trying to dominate her husband or her children.

Where work is concerned, Taureans tend to be competent in most fields, but they are particularly good at jobs pertaining to money and to the earth that marks their sign. They shine as bankers, cashiers, geologists, or potters, and they usually like a job with plenty of security. Famous Taureans and Taurean types include George Washington, Karl Marx, Sigmund Freud, William Shakespeare, Johannes Brahms, Margot Fonteyn, Fred Astaire, Bing Crosby, Gary Cooper, Orson Welles, Honoré de Balzac, and Arnold Bennett.

Right: Taurus, from a 10th-century Indian horoscope. Notice that this Taurean bull is the humped bull, still the bull of India today.

Left: astrological physiognomists thought the typical Taurean would look like a bull—thickset, thick-necked, with a broad forehead.

Honoré de Balzac

Above: the earthy character of Taurus as exemplified not only in Balzac's personality, but even in his solid, bull-like appearance.

Ulysses S. Grant

Left: Grant's relentlessness, so typical of the Taurean, led him to conceive tactics that crushed Confederate resistance, but also meant that in his stubbornness he refused to give up his corrupt presidential advisors and refused to—or was unable to— recognize their callous misuse of his trust.

GEMINI the Twins (May 22 to June 21)

Queen Victoria

Below: her ascendant was Gemini, and although in many ways she was untypical, her letters show the Geminian flair for lively writing.

The pure Gemini is born under a double sign and is a dual personality, forever shifting his or her outlook on life. Geminis is the patron sign of intellectuals, egocentrics, and the mentally unstable. Gemini people tend to be fickle and to change their opinions constantly to suit themselves. They also enjoy arguing, and their conversation is full of twists and turns.

The duality of the sign is typified by the Gemini man. He can talk himself into love with great speed—and out again just as quickly. He has an easy charm and a captivating manner, but tends to be unreliable and even downright disloyal. The Gemini woman has similar characteristics, although her restlessness and changeability are often muted by the pressures exerted upon her by society.

Gemini people hate monotonous work. They need jobs that will give full scope to their agility and urge for change. The factory production line is not for them, but they excel at any kind of work that involves movement and variety—lecturing, publishing, and almost any kind of craftsmanship.

Some well-known Geminis and Gemini personalities are political leader John F. Kennedy; the Duke of Edinburgh; the composer Richard Wagner; the painter Paul Gauguin; Conan Doyle, author of the Sherlock Holmes stories, and Ian Fleming, the creator of James Bond; playwright George Bernard Shaw; movie stars Marilyn Monroe, Judy Garland, and Errol Flynn; and song writer Bob Dylan.

Paul Gauguin

Right top: one of Gauguin's paintings. The restless Gemini urge for change and travel led Gauguin to abandon his family and cross the world to Tahiti, where he painted his savagely splendid masterpieces.

Marilyn Monroe

Right: the sensitive and highly strung Gemini is typified in the troubled, restless life of the famous blonde sex symbol, who died of an overdose of drugs.

CANCER the Crab (June 22 to July 22)

Marcel Proust

Above: typically Cancerian in his attachment to his mother, Proust retreated to his famous cork-lined study when she died and buried himself in his writing, producing his intricately woven masterpiece.

Despite the tough-looking crab that gives this sign its name, Cancerians are motherly gentle people. Like the crab, however, pure Cancerians tend to appear all hardness on the outside, while inside their shells they are soft, vulnerable, and easily hurt. Beneath the mask of a tough and ultralogical personality, they are extremely moody and emotional. They are, like the crab, deeply attached to their homes. This is unquestionably the sign of the man or woman whose home life is the keynote of his or her existence. A Cancerian can be a social asset, and knows a great deal about good food and wine.

The Cancer man is likely to have had an especially close relationship with his mother, and the effects of this usually last into adult life. He tends to keep his emotional distance from other human beings, and may try to cast his partner in a mother role, at least some of the time.

Cancer women tend to be gentle home-loving wives who find the raising of children their most rewarding occupation. They are attracted to two types of men: the weak, well-intentioned male who appeals to their motherly feelings, and the hard, almost brutal type who dominates them and exploits their gentleness. The best partner for a Cancer woman is usually an equally home-centered man.

Cancerians are good at any job in which they do not have to dominate. They are made for occupations connected with the home or children, and for handling people who are going through a difficult time. They therefore make splendid physicians, nurses, and social workers.

Among Cancerians and Cancer types are the painters Rembrandt, Salvador Dali, and Marc Chagall; the philosopher Jean-Jacques Rousseau; the composer Franz Schubert; the poet Lord Byron; writers Jean Cocteau and Marcel Proust; movie director Ingmar Bergman; and actress Gina Lollobrigida.

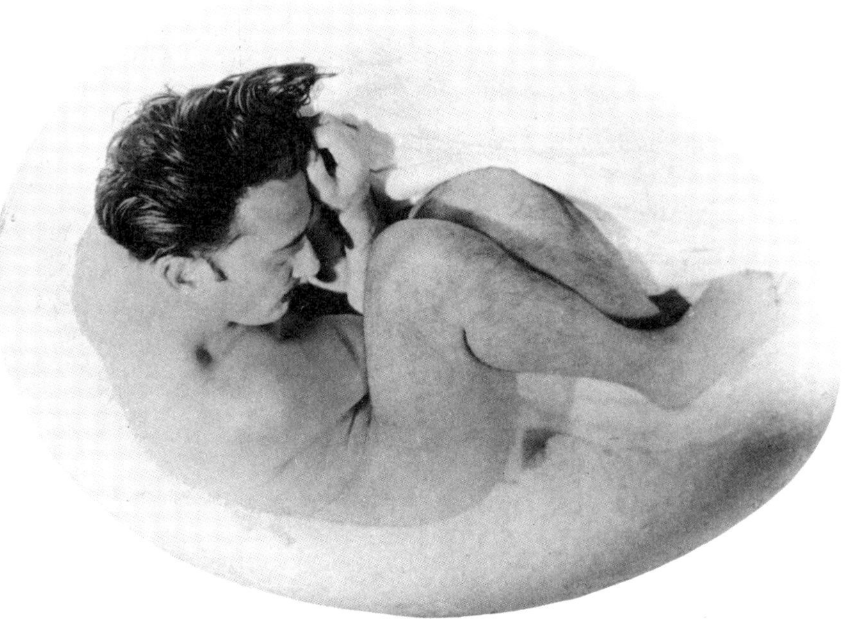

Salvador Dali

Left: this representation of Dali as a fetus in an egg ties up with the Cancerian link with birth and fertility. Dali is a clear example of Cancerian sensitivity, Cancer being his ascendant.

Below: a symbolic representation of the United States, whose sign is Cancer from its "birthday" of July 4, 1776. A strong paternal instinct has shaped recent world history. Detractors might also call it Cancerian in its over-sensitivity to criticism.

John Glenn

Above: the first astronaut to circle the world, Glenn is a Cancer type in his tenacity of purpose that sustained him through the rigors of the space training program. His excellent memory is another typical characteristic of Cancer.

LEO the Lion (July 23 to August 23)

Otto, Prince von Bismarck

Above: a Leo type, the militaristic Bismarck had a vision of a grand design, but impatience with the details. Typically, h[illegible] clung too long to power, and was at last dismissed to bitter retirement.

Leos are extroverts—men and women with a strong presence, a vital magnetism, and an urge to dominate. They like to be in the spotlight, not hovering at the back of the stage.

Leo men are confident of their abilities and their sex appeal, and women tend either to love or loathe a Leo man. At his best the Leo man is a splendid leader; at his worst he is a vain bullying bore.

Leo women are also self-assured, and often want to dominate their partners. They love to be pampered and to lead a life of luxury. They tend to be impractical, preferring a mink coat to a dishwasher, a diamond ring to a typewriter.

Leos do well in any occupation that enables them to dominate others or to be the center of attention. Thus careers in politics, theatre, organizing, or lecturing attract them most strongly, and suit them best.

Notable Leos and Leo types include the political leaders Benito Mussolini, Fidel Castro, and Bismarck; the rulers Louis XIV (the Sun King) of France and the Emperor Napoleon; the painters Rubens and Picasso; the psychologist Carl Jung; the poet Robert Burns; writers Aldous Huxley and John Galsworthy; the movie director Alfred Hitchcock; and the public figure Jacqueline Kennedy Onassis.

Benito Mussolini

Right: the Italian dictator was a Leo from the beginning in his unusually pugnacious and self-assertive qualities when in his first school year. He had the Leonine gift for breadth of vision, but with it a flamboyant braggadocio. This picture of him with his chin thrust forward shows one of his favorite public stances.

Napoleon Bonaparte

Left: a typical Leo, Napoleon had unquestioning assurance that he was the person who knew best how the world should be organized, and mobilized his own considerable talents—and those of France—to make sure he was in a position to arrange matters to his satisfaction. He could be magnanimous, but he was ruthless to those who tried to challenge his Leonine command.

Orville Wright

Below: for him the creativity of a Leo type was expressed in the long struggle to design a craft that would actually fly. This picture shows him at the controls, lifting into the first flight.

VIRGO the Virgin

Virgos combine intelligence and common sense. They are neat, tidy, conscious of the need for order, likely to hoard things, and sometimes almost obsessed with the need for cleanliness.

Their belief in order and doing it right sometimes makes Virgo men seem like human calculating machines. Their precision and neatness does not fit into the conventional image of masculinity. They are rarely capable of really letting go, and even their sex lives may be distinguished for technique rather than enthusiasm.

Virgo women cannot be satisfied with merely exploiting their feminine charms. They want to perform a task in life, and to perform it well. They infinitely prefer honest recognition of their material achievements to idle flattery. They want a partner who lives up to their own high standards. Once they get him they will give him all the supportive love he needs.

Virgos dislike unskilled work, but enjoy any kind of job that requires them to impose order on chaos. They are outstanding in fields that give their neatness and desire for perfection full play. Scientific research, accountancy, record maintenance, or secretarial work are made for Virgos.

Virgo people and types include the statesman Cardinal Richelieu, Prince Albert, the husband of Queen Victoria, the late President Lyndon Johnson, the writers Leo Tolstoy, Goethe, and D. H. Lawrence, and movie stars Greta Garbo, Lauren Bacall, Sophia Loren, and Peter Sellers.

Leo Tolstoy

Right: Tolstoy possessed fully the Virgoan zest for work, and his ruthless analytical powers are a vivid example of the Virgo type. In his quest for perfection, he typically lost sight of the forest for the trees, and the sad end of his marriage and family life are a bleak testimonial to his unrelenting struggle to find a morally good pattern of life.

Louis XIV

Far right: though the planets' positions in his horoscope would tend to make the Sun King a Leo type, his passion for perfection shows that he was indeed born under Virgo.

Below: Virgo the maiden, from an 18th-century celestial atlas. Traditionally Virgo is represented with a sheaf of corn in her hand. This ties in with the time of harvest when the sign occurs.

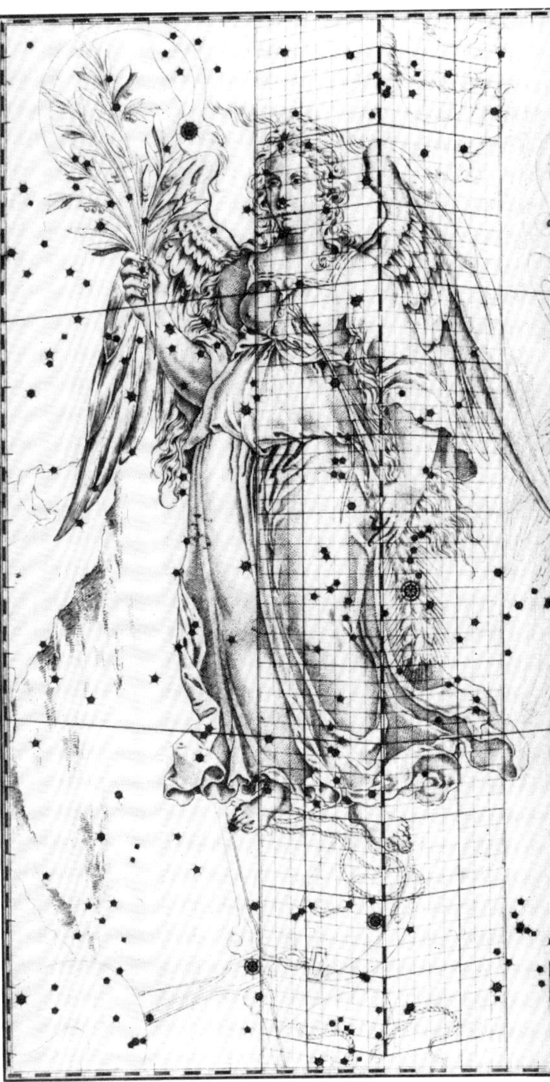

Johann Wolfgang von Goethe

Left: the Virgoan gift for natural philosophy shows brilliantly in Goethe's masterpieces of poetry and drama, and his genius for intellectual discrimination was another typical Virgoan trait.

LIBRA the Scales

(September 24 to October 23)

Above: Botticelli's enduring *The Birth of Venus*. Venus is the ruling planet of Libra, the most feminine of the zodiacal signs, and it is the rulership of Venus that makes those born under Libra typically charming, artistic, and refined. The influence of Venus in Libra is strongly toward goodness and happiness, and the typical Libran is likeable and even-tempered, if a little lazy.

Pure Librans are the salt of the earth. They want to be liked and to like others. Their gentle, tolerant, and diplomatic natures make it perfectly easy for others to get along with them. The scales are their sign, and they tend to be balanced individuals with moderate views who are repelled by extremism of any kind. The Libran's chief failing is being too easily influenced.

The Libra man is in no way effeminate, but to other men he sometimes appears so. This need not worry the Libran—there is nothing to be ashamed of in being sociable, courteous, and cultured. A Libra man is usually attractive to women, although they may dislike his tendency to be so moderate that he never puts forward an independent point of view.

Libra is the most feminine of the signs, and Libra women are exceptionally feminine. In love they display charm and gentleness—as they do to some extent in all their personal relationships—but they know how to use these qualities for their own ends. They get a great deal of happiness from a satisfactory home life and enjoy the company of their children.

Librans tend to be lazy rather than industrious, and jobs that involve strenuous physical effort have little appeal for them. They do well in almost any occupation connected with art, legal matters, diplomacy, and dealing with other people.

Characteristic Libra personalities and Librans include Erasmus, the great 16th-century scholar and humanist; Mahatma Gandhi, the political and religious leader and apostle of nonviolence; the painter Watteau; the composer Franz Liszt; occultist Aleister Crowley; the poet T. S. Eliot; writers Oscar Wilde, Graham Greene, William Faulkner, and Katherine Mansfield, and actresses Sarah Bernhardt and Brigitte Bardot.

Brigitte Bardot

Left: easy-going, charming, and liking harmony, BB is a typical Libran in her relaxed attitude toward life—but must guard against the equally typical Libran indecision.

Oscar Wilde

Above: Libran sociability, culture, and wit were well exemplified in Wilde's career. Perhaps in the tragic end it also showed the Libran danger of recklessness.

SCORPIO the Scorpion

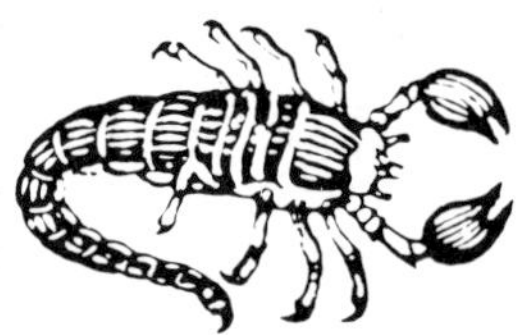

(October 24 to November 22)

Marie Curie

Above: the strong determination that is associated with this sign was clearly obvious in the life of Madame Curie, pictured with her husband Pierre, with whom she discovered radium. She fully demonstrates the Scorpian passion for hard work. In fact, the type excels in careers requiring close and detailed research work.

In the past this sign had a sinister reputation, being associated with death, decay, and deceit. Scorpio people have even been said to have the look of scorpions and snakes.

Since the 17th century, however, such dark views of Scorpio have become less and less fashionable, and present-day astrologers concentrate on the positive aspects of the sign. Only a minority of Scorpio people, they say, reflect the more sinister side of the sign. Most Scorpios are reasonable, life-loving, and honest people. They are often difficult to get along with, however, because of their secretiveness, their fierce will power, and their strong likes and dislikes.

The Scorpio man is intensely conscious of his self-integrity, and displays a keen sense of personal pride. His outstanding characteristics are his aggressiveness and his eroticism. He takes a long time to make up his mind about whether he loves someone, but once he has committed himself he rarely changes course. However, on the rare occasions when he does change his mind about his love life, his beliefs, or his choice of career, he does so abruptly and violently. The Scorpio man doesn't set out to please, but is usually good company.

The Scorpio woman has all the characteristics of her male counterpart although she usually displays them less aggressively. She has a strong and mysterious sex appeal even when she is not physically attractive. She is tenacious in love, and is driven by an urge for power, sexual and otherwise.

Scorpio people like hard work as much as Librans loathe it. They have a serious attitude toward most aspects of life, and have even been said to "make work of their play." Their extreme competitiveness combined with their authoritarianism often brings them success in a military career or other occupation in which they can give the orders. Any tough and demanding job—mining, electronics, working on an oil rig—will attract Scorpio people, and they excel as police detectives, security guards, attorneys, and surgeons.

Famous Scorpios and those like Scorpios include the Indian politician Indira Gandhi; military leader and dictator General Franco; general and statesman Charles de Gaulle; Kemal Ataturk, the brilliant soldier who created modern Turkey; Horatio Nelson, the British admiral who won the Battle of Trafalgar; Mata Hari, the World War I spy and *femme fatale*; Marie Curie, the co-discoverer of radium; writers Victor Hugo, Dostoyevsky, Goethe, and Edgar Allan Poe; singer Edith Piaf; and, illustrating the darker side of the sign, Hitler's lieutenants Herman Göring and Joseph Goebbels.

Theodore Roosevelt

Left: the forceful personality and varied interests of Roosevelt (left) are typical of the positive side of Scorpio. Ted Roosevelt was also Scorpian in his ambition and decisiveness, which made him a natural leader and a popular president. Sickly as a child, in his adult life he welcomed all opportunities to test his strength.

Pablo Picasso

Above: perhaps the most characteristic trait of the true Scorpian is intensity, as can be seen in Picasso's *Weeping Woman*. In his life, he showed other typical Scorpian tendencies of jealousy, ruthlessness, and—most obviously—wholly original creativity.

Mata Hari

Left: one of the definite Scorpian traits is eroticism. Since the sign rules hidden things, it is perhaps not unexpected that the Dutch girl with Scorpio as her Sun Sign became a German spy, built on a career of amorous and political intrigue which ended at last with her execution.

SAGITTARIUS the Archer

(November 23 to December 21)

Sagittarius is a sign particularly associated with success, and fate usually gives the Sagittarian more than one opportunity to achieve it. However, Sagittarians tend to be so happy-go-lucky that they often fail to seize the chances that are offered to them. At best, Sagittarians are highly talented individuals who are interested in almost everything. At worst, they waste their talents in too many fields and become pathetic braggarts.

The Sagittarian man has an outspoken and generous approach to life, and yet somehow other men tend to pick quarrels with him. He is lovable, but often resists the love that is offered for fear of losing his freedom. He loves animals, yet cannot resist the pleasure of hunting.

The Sagittarian woman shares these paradoxical qualities. She prefers activities outside the home to what she sees as the dull round of the housewife. Nevertheless, she makes a good mother, and never a possessive one.

Sagittarians have a genius for communication, and they will succeed at any skilled task in the fields of journalism, television, advertising, publishing, or consultancy work. Where less skilled jobs are concerned, they are prepared to tackle anything that leaves them a certain amount of freedom.

Sagittarian types and Sagittarians include Abraham Lincoln, Winston Churchill, Beethoven, the poet John Milton, writers Mark Twain, Noel Coward, and John Osborne, humorist James Thurber, singers Maria Callas, Frank Sinatra, and Sammy Davies, and moviemaker Walt Disney.

Sir Winston Churchill

Above: blunt, dogged, resolved to meet problems head on, Churchill was a true Sagittarian. Also like others of his Sun Sign, Churchill had a great gift of communication.

Ludwig von Beethoven

Right: Sagittarian expansiveness and magnificence is typified by the music of Beethoven—grand, full, echoing down the centuries with overwhelming vitality. Equally typical determination is shown in his life and his dogged persistence in composing after he became deaf.

William Blake

Left: Blake's painting of Isaac Newton. In his passion for meeting the challenge of a problem— often technical difficulties he found in painting or engraving—Blake was typical of less-often recognized but strongly Sagittarian traits.

Walt Disney

Below: in his creation of Mickey Mouse and many other cartoon characters that seem to have life and personality, Disney expressed the Sagittarian love of animals.

Left: the star map of Sagittarius, half man and half animal—the centaur with his bow drawn. Many Sagittarians are keen horsemen.

James Thurber

Opposite: the Sagittarian love of animals expresses itself in the dogs that Thurber drew so often—and the real ones which he and his wife raised as dog breeders.

CAPRICORN the Goat

(December 22 to January 20)

Sir Isaac Newton

Above: a portrait of Newton. He was Capricornian in his accuracy, determination, and self-reliance. This led him to revolutionize the course of scientific thought.

"One does not invite to dinner the same evening Leo and Capricorn," wrote astrologer Rupert Gleadow. This was probably good advice, for the characteristics of the two signs are almost directly opposite. As the Leo is outgoing, dominating, and attention seeking, the Capricorn is introverted, submissive, and self-effacing. Yet Capricorn people are extremely ambitious, and burn with a desire to succeed. They do not usually seek success in a dramatic way, however. The Capricorn person goes in for long, painstaking struggles whose real nature others ignore, but which eventually take him or her to the top.

Capricorn men tend to have a traditional and unbending approach toward women—a rigidity that both attracts and repels. They are intensely competitive in their attitudes toward other men, and usually command respect rather than affection.

The Capricorn woman likes to be in a position of power, whether within her own family or in the outside world. She is loyal and astute, and often possesses a rather hard veneer of glamour. She is affectionate to her husband and children, but is never really happy if her life is confined to the home, for at heart she always remains a career woman.

Capricorn people are good at most occupations that do not require a high degree of imagination. They excel at monotonous tasks, whether clerical or physical. Their passion for detail and exactness makes them good teachers of subjects like mathematics or science, where there is a definite answer to most questions. In the arts they are usually imitators rather than originators. They can rise to the top of any profession in which effort, accuracy, and determination are the key qualities for success.

Famous Capricornians and those much like them include Woodrow Wilson, Stalin, the philosopher Kant, scientists Johannes Kepler, Isaac Newton, and Louis Pasteur, the missionary Albert Schweitzer, cellist Pablo Casals, beauty expert Helena Rubinstein, and millionaire Howard Hughes.

Henri Matisse

Left: the deep love of beauty of Capricorns showed itself in the prolific work of this artist, also typical in his independent approach.

Josef Stalin

Above: Capricornians are often drawn to politics, and Stalin showed the dark side of the sign in his ruthless use of power.

Benjamin Franklin

Left: Franklin demonstrates the dry subtle Capricornian sense of humor in his writings and talk.

AQUARIUS the Water Carrier

(January 21 to February 19)

Charles Lindbergh

Above: Aquarian originality and genius for inventiveness, often expressed in scientific work, is clear in Lindbergh's character—as was his love of adventure.

The highest aim of the typical Aquarian is personal freedom. Unlike the Capricornian, the Aquarian has little respect for convention or tradition if it obstructs the liberty of the individual. Aquarians are humanitarians, and the freedom of others is almost as important to them as their own. They tend to take an intellectual approach to life, but this never makes them cold or unemotional, and they are often active in groups formed for a social cause—political reform, or the protection of the environment, for example. They are open-minded, and willing to listen to the other person's point of view, although they also have a reputation for being tactless and sometimes obstinate.

The Aquarian man is free of vanity, yet intensely conscious of his dignity as a human being. He despises traditionally masculine values and is the very opposite of a "male chauvinist," treating women as fellow human beings and not mere sexual objects.

Aquarian women are also strong believers in sexual equality, and today are often active members of Women's Liberation. They have an adventurous approach to life. They hate to be dominated sexually or financially, and are at their best with partners who share their belief in the importance of the individual.

For Aquarians work is not primarily a way of making money but a vocation in which their love of freedom can find expression. They are at their best when self-employed or engaged in work that involves helping others, such as medicine, psychology, social work, or politics.

Aquarians and Aquarian personalities include political leader Franklin D. Roosevelt; the 16th-century astronomer Galileo; the naturalist Charles Darwin who formulated the theory of evolution; the aviator Charles Lindbergh; the essayist and philosopher Francis Bacon; writers Charles Dickens, Lewis Carroll, and Somerset Maugham; actresses Vanessa Redgrave and Jeanne Moreau; and actor Paul Newman.

Wolfgang Amadeus Mozart

Left: Aquarians are often clever children, and Mozart's career as a child prodigy is well known. As an adult, however, he was untypical in his use of conventional musical forms, apparently feeling little need to try experiments.

James Dean

Below: his sensitive good looks were typically Aquarian—as was the youthful spirit of rebellion against convention, which he came to typify during his career.

PISCES the Fishes

(February 20 to March 20)

Vaslav Nijinsky

Above: Piscean instability and hyper-sensitivity are obvious in the tragic life of the legendary dancer. Only 10 years after his meteoric success, he left ballet to spend the last 30 years of his life in a mental hospital.

At their best Pisceans are idealists. At their worst they are dropouts and hoboes. They are amiable, vague, and sometimes devious. They have an easy attitude to life, and are liable to be too easily influenced by others. They are the very opposite of egotistical—some of them seem hardly conscious that they have an ego—and they tend to oppose material values with what they consider to be spiritual ones. Pisceans are lovable people because they themselves are very loving.

The Pisces man is rarely effeminate, but he tends to display unashamedly the feminine components of the personality that most men are anxious to conceal. To some women he appears too soft and gentle, but to others his easy-going ways are attractive. He is little suited to the harsh rough and tumble of a purely masculine environment, but he feels thoroughly at home in artistic circles.

The Pisces woman is many men's idea of the perfect partner—loving, tender, submissive, and anxious to please. At the same time, no Piscean wants to be bullied, and she will avoid this by guile rather than outright opposition.

Pisceans are not naturally hard workers, for they lack the motivations of ambition or love of money. Some Pisceans, however, have a passionate desire to serve their fellow human beings, and they can work hard for a cause in spite of their lack of dynamism. On the whole Pisceans do best in jobs connected, however vaguely, with the arts—from doorman at a gallery or concert hall to painter or musician.

Outstanding Piscean types and Pisceans include the ballet dancers Vaslav Nijinsky and Rudolf Nureyev; the poet Hölderlin and the poetess Elizabeth Browning; the composers Handel, Chopin, and Rimsky Korsakov; the opera singer Enrico Caruso; artists Michelangelo and Auguste Renoir; playwright Edward Albee; novelist John Steinbeck; and actress Elizabeth Taylor.

Pisces joins with Aries to complete the zodiac circle. Whether the portrait of your Sun Sign fits you well or not, it is a good idea to take a look at all the signs. That way you may gain an inkling of the other sign, or signs, that might play an important role in your horoscope. For even two people born on the same day, and perhaps only a few minutes apart, can have very different horoscopes. The way to find out the signs that count in your life is to draw up your own personal star chart—and that is not as hard as it sounds.

Buonarotti Michelangelo

Right: David, a superb sculpture by Michelangelo, who was another Piscean, and like others under his sign, did not take kindly to outside attempts at regimentation.

Elizabeth Taylor

Below: some astrologers say that Pisces is such a receptive sign that it picks up infection quickly, and certainly this star's career has been marked by spectacular illnesses of a serious nature.

Frédéric Chopin

Below right: some of the greatest artists—those who have been able to use their emotions through their work—have been Piscean, and in Chopin's case, the melancholy sensitivity was turned into his exquisite and subtle music.

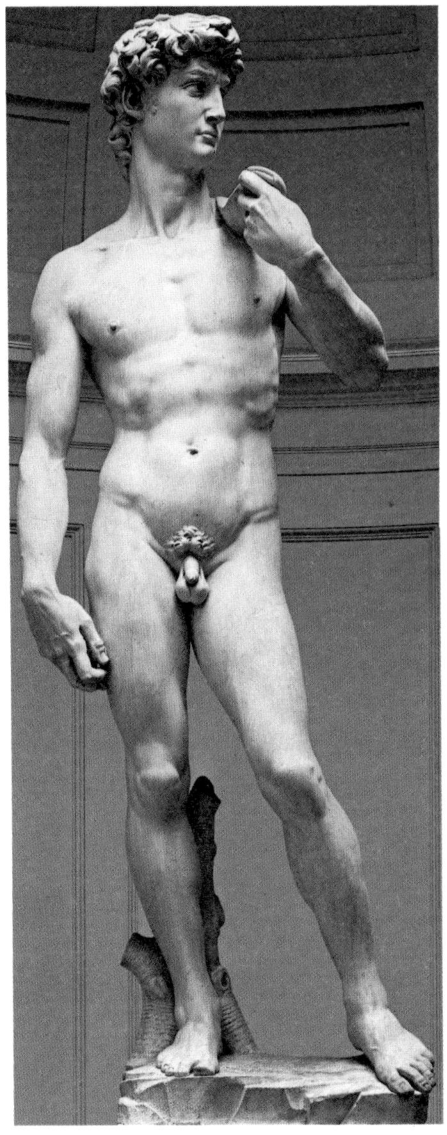

Chapter 13
Your Personal Star Chart

How can an amateur build up more astrological information about himself than the simple Sun Sign description? How can you go about assembling the facts needed for a personal horoscope—and how can that tell you more about yourself than the Sun Sign description? This chapter will lead you, step-by-step, through the process of compiling your own star chart, based on the exact time and place of your birth. The computations are simple—the fascination of producing a completely individual star chart is compelling. What will the stars have to say about your character and destiny?

Astrologers are the first to emphasize that judgments based purely on a person's Sun Sign can be wildly inaccurate and misleading. Yet few of us have any other basis on which to form an opinion of astrology's validity. We may not be willing, or able, to pay a highly qualified astrologer for a detailed horoscope. Nor may we want to spend many hours poring over books several times the length of this one to learn the basic techniques of constructing and interpreting a horoscope.

It is possible, however, to draw up and interpret your own personal map of the zodiac in a few simple stages. This chart is not a detailed horoscope, but it will tell you a great deal more about astrology—and about yourself— than a simple Sun Sign description. Its interpretation will not, of course, be as full or as satisfactory as the one derived from a complete horoscope. But it should prove interesting and self-revealing, and it will probably help you to decide whether to go still further with the study of astrology.

The star chart is your personal map of the zodiac—a picture of the heavens as they appeared at the time and place of your birth. The first step in making the chart is to calculate your time of birth in Star Time. Star Time—usually known as *sidereal time*—is measured by the stars and not, like clock time, by the Sun. To every 24 hours of clock time there are 24 hours 2 minutes and $56\frac{1}{2}$ seconds of Star Time.

Anyone who can add or subtract can calculate the time of their

Opposite: this circular horoscope is the type used in modern astrology.

STAR Formula

birth in Star Time, and there is a simple formula to help you make this calculation with ease.

The formula is S + T + A + or − R.

S stands for Star Time at midnight on the day of birth. A list of the Star Times to the nearest minute at midnight on every day of the year from 1900 to 1975 is given in Tables 1 and 2 opposite.

Supposing you were born on January 10, 1934. You will see from the list of years printed at the foot of Table 1 that for 1934 you have to add one minute to the figure found opposite the date January 10 in the table. The time given for January 10 is 7:14. To this you add one minute, which gives you 7:15. This is the figure for the S in your formula, which now reads:

7 hrs. 15 mins. + T + A + or − R

T stands for the local time of your birth. That means the ordinary clock time used where you were born—Eastern Standard Time in New York, for example, or Greenwich Mean Time in Britain. If you were born in the summer and the place of your birth was on daylight savings time in the year when you were born, you will have to deduct one hour from the clock time of your birth. You can usually get information on daylight savings time at your local library. If you were one of the small minority born in Britain during the recent period of Double British Summer Time the deduction will be two hours.

Let us take an example, saying that you were born in New York at 6 a.m. Eastern Standard Time. Because we have taken your date of birth to be January 10—right in the middle of winter—there is no need to make any adjustment for daylight or summer time, and your T figure is simply 6 hours 0 minutes. If your time of birth had been six in the *evening*, the T figure would have been 18 hours 0 minutes because astrology uses a 24-hour clock.

Your personal formula now reads:

7 hrs. 15 mins. + 6 hrs. 0 mins. + A + or − R

The A of our formula stands for "acceleration"—the adjustment for the difference in length between the clock day and the star day. That is roughly 10 seconds for each hour between midnight and time of birth. We assumed your time of birth was 6 a.m.—six hours after midnight—so the appropriate figure is 1 minute (6 × 10 seconds). This is the A of your formula, which now reads:

7 hrs. 15 mins. + 6 hrs. 0 mins. + 0 hrs. 1 min. + or − R

R in the formula stands for "rectification"—the adjustment for the Zone Time of your birth because your birthplace lies east or west of the exact degree of longitude for which Zone Time is completely accurate.

In Table 3 on page 222 you will find a list of rectifications for most of the world's capital cities and the major North American and British population centers. If your birthplace, or a place close to it, does not appear in the table, you can easily work out the rectification for yourself using a good atlas in any reference library.

If you are making the calculation yourself, first find out from your atlas or local library the degrees of longitude at which the Zone Time for your birthplace is *exactly* correct. Then, from your atlas, count the number of degrees you were born east or west of that longitude. Convert these degrees into time simply by multi-

Table 1

Left: this table gives, in simplified form, Star Time for each day of every year that is not a leap year. Star Time is measured by the stars rather than the Sun.

	Jan.	Feb.	Mar.	April	May	June	July	Aug.	Sept.	Oct.	Nov.	Dec.
1	6 39	8 41	10 31	12 34	14 32	16 34	18 32	20 35	22 37	0 35	2 37	4 36
2	6 43	8 45	10 35	12 37	14 36	16 38	18 36	20 38	22 41	0 39	2 41	4 39
3	6 47	8 49	10 39	12 41	14 40	16 42	18 40	20 42	22 45	0 43	2 45	4 43
4	6 51	8 53	10 43	12 45	14 44	16 46	18 44	20 46	22 79	0 44	2 49	4 47
5	6 54	8 57	10 47	12 49	14 48	16 50	18 48	20 50	22 53	0 51	2 53	4 51
6	6 58	9 1	10 51	12 53	14 52	16 54	18 52	20 54	22 56	0 55	2 57	4 55
7	7 2	9 5	10 55	12 57	14 55	16 58	18 56	20 58	23 0	0 59	3 1	4 59
8	7 6	9 9	10 59	13 1	14 59	17 2	19 0	21 2	23 4	1 3	3 5	5 3
9	7 10	9 12	11 3	13 5	15 3	17 6	19 4	21 6	23 8	1 7	3 9	5 7
10	7 14	9 16	11 7	13 9	15 7	17 10	19 8	21 10	23 12	1 11	3 13	5 11
11	7 18	9 20	11 11	13 13	15 11	17 13	19 12	21 14	23 16	1 14	3 17	5 15
12	7 22	9 24	11 15	13 17	15 15	17 17	19 16	21 18	23 20	1 18	3 21	5 19
13	7 26	9 28	11 19	13 21	15 19	17 21	19 20	21 22	23 24	1 22	3 25	5 23
14	7 30	9 32	11 23	13 25	15 23	17 25	19 24	21 26	23 28	1 26	3 29	5 27
15	7 34	9 36	11 27	13 29	15 27	17 29	19 28	21 30	23 32	1 30	3 32	5 31
16	7 38	9 40	11 30	13 33	15 31	17 33	19 31	21 34	23 36	1 34	3 36	5 35
17	7 42	9 44	11 34	13 37	15 35	17 37	19 35	21 38	23 40	1 38	3 40	5 39
18	7 46	9 48	11 38	13 41	15 39	17 41	19 39	21 42	23 44	1 42	3 44	5 43
19	7 50	9 52	11 42	13 45	15 43	17 45	19 43	21 46	23 48	1 46	3 48	5 47
20	7 54	9 56	11 46	13 48	15 47	17 49	19 47	21 49	23 52	1 50	3 52	5 50
21	7 58	10 0	11 50	13 52	15 51	17 53	19 51	21 53	23 56	1 54	3 56	5 54
22	8 2	10 4	11 54	13 56	15 55	17 57	19 55	21 57	24 0	1 58	4 0	5 58
23	8 5	10 8	11 58	14 0	15 59	18 1	19 59	22 1	0 4	2 2	4 4	6 2
24	8 9	10 12	12 2	14 4	16 3	18 5	20 3	22 5	0 7	2 6	4 8	6 6
25	8 13	10 16	12 6	14 8	16 6	18 9	20 7	22 9	0 11	2 10	4 12	6 10
26	8 17	10 20	12 10	14 12	16 10	18 13	20 11	22 13	0 15	2 14	4 16	6 14
27	8 21	10 23	12 14	14 16	16 14	18 17	20 15	22 17	0 19	2 18	4 20	6 18
28	8 25	10 27	12 18	14 20	16 18	18 21	20 19	22 21	0 23	2 21	4 24	6 22
29	8 29		12 22	14 24	16 22	18 24	20 23	22 25	0 27	2 25	4 28	6 26
30	8 33		12 26	14 28	16 26	18 28	20 27	22 29	0 31	2 29	4 32	6 30
31	8 37		12 30		16 30		20 31	22 33		2 33		6 34

Note: Use this table as it stands for years 1902, 1906, 1910, 1914, 1918, 1922, 1927, 1931, 1935, 1939, 1943, 1947, 1951, 1955.

Deduct one minute from the time given for the years 1903, 1907, 1911, 1915, 1919, 1923.

Add one minute to the time given for the years 1901, 1905, 1909, 1913, 1917, 1921, 1925, 1926, 1930, 1934, 1938, 1942, 1946, 1950, 1954, 1959, 1963, 1967, 1971, 1975.

Add two minutes to the time given for the years 1900, 1929, 1933, 1937, 1941, 1945, 1949, 1953, 1957, 1958, 1962, 1966, 1970, 1974.

Add three minutes to the time given for the years 1961, 1965, 1969, 1973.

Table 2

Left: this table gives Star Time as applicable to leap years.

	Jan.	Feb.	Mar.	April	May	June	July	Aug.	Sept.	Oct.	Nov.	Dec.
1	6 38	8 40	10 34	12 37	14 35	16 37	18 35	20 38	22 40	0 38	2 40	4 39
2	6 42	8 44	10 38	12 40	14 39	16 41	18 39	20 41	22 44	0 42	2 44	4 42
3	6 46	8 48	10 42	12 44	14 43	16 45	18 43	20 45	22 48	0 46	2 48	4 46
4	6 50	8 52	10 46	12 48	14 47	16 49	18 47	20 49	22 52	0 50	2 52	4 50
5	6 54	8 56	10 50	12 52	14 51	16 53	18 51	20 53	22 56	0 54	2 56	4 54
6	6 57	9 0	10 54	12 56	14 55	16 57	18 55	20 57	22 59	0 58	3 0	4 58
7	7 1	9 4	10 58	13 0	14 56	17 1	18 59	21 1	23 3	1 2	3 4	5 2
8	7 5	9 8	11 2	13 4	15 2	17 5	19 3	21 5	23 7	1 6	3 8	5 6
9	7 9	9 12	11 6	13 8	15 6	17 9	19 7	21 9	23 11	1 10	3 12	5 10
10	7 13	9 15	11 10	13 12	15 10	17 13	19 11	21 13	23 15	1 14	3 16	5 14
11	7 17	9 19	11 14	13 16	15 14	17 16	19 15	21 17	23 19	1 17	3 20	5 18
12	7 21	9 23	11 18	13 20	15 18	17 20	19 19	21 21	23 23	1 21	3 24	5 22
13	7 25	9 27	11 22	13 24	15 22	17 24	19 23	21 25	23 27	1 25	3 28	5 26
14	7 29	9 31	11 26	13 28	15 26	17 28	19 27	21 29	23 31	1 29	3 32	5 30
15	7 33	9 35	11 30	13 32	15 30	17 32	19 31	21 33	23 35	1 33	3 35	5 34
16	7 37	9 39	11 33	13 36	15 34	17 36	19 34	21 37	23 39	1 37	3 39	5 38
17	7 41	9 43	11 37	13 40	15 38	17 40	19 38	21 41	23 43	1 41	3 43	5 42
18	7 45	9 47	11 41	13 44	15 42	17 44	19 42	21 45	23 47	1 45	3 47	5 46
19	7 49	9 51	11 45	13 48	15 46	17 48	19 46	21 49	23 51	1 49	3 51	5 50
20	7 53	9 55	11 49	13 51	15 50	17 52	19 50	21 52	23 55	1 53	3 55	5 53
21	7 57	9 59	11 53	13 55	15 54	17 56	19 54	21 56	23 59	1 57	3 59	5 57
22	8 1	10 3	11 57	13 59	15 58	18 0	19 58	22 0	0 3	2 1	4 3	6 1
23	8 5	10 7	12 1	14 3	16 2	18 4	20 2	22 4	0 7	2 5	4 7	6 5
24	8 8	10 11	12 5	14 7	16 6	18 8	20 6	22 8	0 10	2 9	4 11	6 9
25	8 12	10 15	12 9	14 11	16 9	18 12	20 10	22 12	0 14	2 13	4 15	6 13
26	8 16	10 19	12 13	14 15	16 13	18 16	20 14	22 16	0 18	2 17	4 19	6 17
27	8 20	10 22	12 17	14 19	16 17	18 20	20 18	22 20	0 22	2 21	4 23	6 21
28	8 24	10 26	12 21	14 23	16 21	18 23	20 22	22 24	0 26	2 24	4 27	6 25
29	8 28	10 30	12 25	14 27	16 25	18 27	20 26	22 28	0 30	2 28	4 31	6 29
30	8 32		12 29	14 31	16 29	18 31	20 30	22 32	0 34	2 32	4 35	6 33
31	8 36		12 33		16 33		20 34	22 36		2 36		6 37

Note: Use this table as it stands for the years 1924, 1928, 1932, 1936, 1940, 1944, 1948, 1952.

Deduct one minute from the time given for the years 1904, 1908, 1912, 1916, 1920.

Add one minute to the time given for the years 1956, 1960, 1964, 1968, 1972.

Table 3

Look at this table for time rectification—the R of the S+T+A+ or −R formula for calculating your time of birth in Star Time. It lists most of the world's capitals and some of the major population centers of western Europe.

City	R
Albany, New York	+ 5
Algiers	+12
Amarillo, Texas	−47
Amsterdam	−40
Athens	−25
Atlanta, Georgia	+22
Atlantic City, New Jersey	+ 2
Baghdad	− 2
Baker, Oregon	+ 9
Baltimore, Maryland	− 7
Bangor, Maine	+25
Bedford, England	− 2
Belgrade	+22
Berlin	− 6
Berne	−30
Birmingham, Alabama	+13
Birmingham, England	− 8
Bismarck, North Dakota	−43
Bogota	+ 3
Boise, Idaho	−45
Bonn	−32
Boston, England	0
Boston, Massachusetts	+16
Brussels	+17
Bucharest	−16
Budapest	+16
Buenos Aires	+ 7
Buffalo, New York	−16
Bury St. Edmunds, England	+ 3
Cairo	+ 5
Calgary, Alberta	−36
Cambridge, England	0
Canberra	− 3
Cape Town	−47
Caracas	+ 2
Cardiff, Wales	−13
Carlsbad, New Mexico	+ 3
Carlisle, England	−12
Charleston, South Carolina	−20
Charleston, West Virginia	−27
Charlotte, North Carolina	−23
Chelmsford, England	+ 2
Chester, England	−12
Cheyenne, Wyoming	+ 1
Chicago, Illinois	+ 9
Chichester, England	− 3
Cincinatti, Ohio	−38
Cleveland, Ohio	−27
Columbia, South Carolina	−24
Columbus, Ohio	−32
Copenhagen	−10
Dallas, Texas	−27
Delhi	−21
Denver, Colorado	0
Derby, England	− 6
Des Moines, Iowa	−15
Detroit, Michigan	−32
Dublin	−25
Dubuque, Iowa	− 3
Duluth, Minnesota	− 8
Durham, England	− 7
El Centro, California	+18
El Paso, Texas	− 6
Eugene, Oregon	−12
Fargo, North Dakota	−27
Fresno, California	+ 1
Glasgow, Scotland	−17
Gloucester, England	− 9
Grand Junction, Colorado	−14
Grand Rapids, Michigan	+17
Halifax, Nova Scotia	−14
Helena, Montana	−28
Helsinki	−24
Hereford, England	−11
Honolulu, Hawaii	−31
Huntingdon, England	− 1
Idaho Falls, Idaho	−28
Indianapolis, Indiana	+15
Ipswich, England	+ 5
Jackson, Mississippi	− 1
Jacksonville, Florida	−27
Jerusalem	+21
Kendal, England	−11
Key West, Florida	−27
Knoxville, Tennessee	+24
La Paz	−32
Las Vegas, Nevada	+19
Leeds, England	− 6
Leicester, England	− 5
Lima	− 8
Lincoln, England	− 2
Lincoln, Nebraska	−27
Lisbon	−37
Little Rock, Arkansas	− 8
London	0
Los Angeles, California	+ 7
Louisville, Kentucky	+17
Madrid	−15
Manchester, England	− 9
Manchester, New Hampshire	+14
Memphis, Tennessee	0
Mexico City	−36
Miami, Florida	−21
Milwaukee, Wisconsin	+ 8
Minneapolis, Minnesota	−13
Mobile, Alabama	+ 8
Montevideo	−15
Montgomery, Alabama	+15
Montpelier, Vermont	+10
Montreal, Quebec	+ 6
Moscow	+30
Nashville, Tennessee	+13
Newcastle, England	− 6
New Haven, Connecticut	+ 8
New Orleans, Louisiana	0
New York, New York	+ 4
Nome, Alaska	− 2
North Platte, Nebraska	−43
Oklahoma City, Oklahoma	−30
Oslo	−17
Ottawa, Ontario	− 3
Oxford, England	− 5
Paris	+ 9
Peking	−14
Philadelphia, Pennsylvania	− 1
Phoenix, Arizona	−28
Pierre, South Dakota	−41
Pittsburgh, Pennsylvania	−20
Port Arthur, Ontario	−57
Portland, Maine	+19
Portland, Oregon	−11
Prague	− 2
Providence, Rhode Island	+14
Quebec, Quebec	+15
Quito	−14
Raleigh, North Carolina	−15
Reading, England	− 4
Regina, Saskatchewan	+ 2
Reno, Nevada	+ 1
Richmond, Virginia	−10
Riga	−24
Rio de Janeiro	+ 7
Roanoke, Virginia	−20
Rome	−11
Sacramento, California	− 6
St. John, New Brunswick	−25
St. Louis, Missouri	− 1
Salt Lake City, Utah	−28
San Antonio, Texas	−34
San Diego, California	+11
San Francisco, California	−10
Santa Fe, New Mexico	− 4
Santiago	−43
Savannah, Georgia	−24
Scranton, Pennsylvania	− 3
Seattle, Washington	− 9
Shreveport, Louisiana	−15
Sioux Falls, South Dakota	−27
Singapore	−34
Sofia	−27
Spokane, Washington	+10
Springfield, Illinois	+ 1
Springfield, Massachusetts	+10
Springfield, Missouri	−13
Stockholm	+12
Syracuse, New York	− 5
Tampa, Florida	−30
Taunton, England	−13
Teheran	+27
Tokyo	+19
Toronto, Ontario	−18
Vancouver, British Columbia	−12
Victoria, British Columbia	−13
Vienna	+ 5
Wakefield, England	− 6
Warsaw	+24
Warwick, England	− 7
Washington, D.C.	− 8
Watertown, New York	− 4
Wellington	−21
Wichita, Kansas	−29
Wilmington, Delaware	− 2
Winnipeg, Manitoba	−29
Worcester, England	− 9
Yakima, Washington	− 2

Calculating the Houses of Heaven

plying by four. If, for example, your birthplace was 5 degrees away from your Zone Time longitude, it would convert into time as 20 minutes. This 20 minutes would be your R figure in the formula. If you were born *west* of your Zone Time longitude this figure will be subtracted and is preceded by a minus sign. If your birthplace was *east*, R will be added and is therefore preceded by a plus sign.

To return to our example, we do not need to make any calculations for the person born in New York at 6 a.m. on January 10, 1934, since New York is one of the cities listed in Table 3. There we find that the R adjustment for New York is +4 minutes. So our formula now reads:

7 hrs. 15 mins. + 6 hrs. 0 mins. + 0 hrs. 1 min. + 0 hrs. 4 mins.

We now write the whole formula down as a simple addition:

S	7 hrs.	15 mins.
T	6 hrs.	0 mins.
A	0 hrs.	1 min.
R	0 hrs.	4 mins.
Star Time	13 hrs.	20 mins.

If the R figure happened to be a minus one it would, of course, be subtracted from the total of S + T + A.

Sometimes the calculation of Star Time results in a figure of more than 24 hours. When this happens, simply deduct 24 hours from the total to get the correct Star Time. If, for example, our final figure were not 13 hours 20 minutes but 33 hours 20 minutes, we would subtract 24 hours to give us a Star Time of 9 hours 20 minutes.

Following this process for your own time, date, and place of birth you will have arrived at the correct Star Time for your birth. The next step is to calculate the "Houses of Heaven"—the 12 divisions of the zodiac. Although there are 12 Houses just as there are 12 signs, the Houses are different from the signs and should not be confused with them.

Before calculating these Houses as they appear in your personal chart, it is important to note that there are many different methods of making this twelvefold division of the zodiac. All these methods have their supporters and their opponents; all have their advantages and disadvantages. The system of House division that we will be using was devised by the great 17th-century French astrologer Morin de Villefranche, often known as Morinus. His monumental work *Astrologia Gallica*, published in 1661, continues to exert a major influence on astrology.

To calculate the Houses of Heaven, turn to Table 4 on pages 225–228. The first column is a list of Star Times, and the other columns give the corresponding zodiac signs and degrees of the *cusps*—the dividing lines between each of the Houses. Before using the table you will need to know the conventional symbols astrologers use for the zodiac signs, which are the symbols that appear in Table 4. There is no need to memorize the symbols. A list of them, together with their corresponding zodiac signs, appears on pages 226–227. You can simply refer to this list as you consult the table.

Opposite each Star Time in the table is a list of the cusps, or divisions, between each of the first six of the twelve Houses. Re-

Working out the Cusps

turning to our example, we arrived at a Star Time of 13 hours 20 minutes. (This is underlined in red in the table). You will see from column one of the table that the first cusp corresponding to 13 hours 20 minutes is 21° 38′—that is, 21 degrees and 38 minutes. (Each degree is divided into 60 minutes.) This first cusp is 21° 38′ of Capricorn since the symbol for Capricorn appears above it at the top of column one. The second cusp is 22° 25′ of Aquarius. The third cusp is 20° 49′ of Pisces. The fourth is 18° 27′ of Aries. The fifth cusp is 17° 33′ of Taurus, and the sixth is 19° 7′ of Gemini. (Always be careful to move up the table from the line you are using to find the zodiac symbol you need—the one immediately above your line, not necessarily the one at the top of the column.)

We now write down the figures we have found for our first six cusps. For the purposes of our map it is sufficiently accurate to work to the nearest degree, so our list of cusps appears as follows:

Cusp 1 22° Capricorn
Cusp 2 22° Aquarius
Cusp 3 21° Pisces
Cusp 4 18° Aries
Cusp 5 18° Taurus
Cusp 6 19° Gemini

In our example, the exact Star Time of 13 hours 20 minutes is listed in the table. This will not always be the case. For instance, your Star Time might be 14 hours 22 minutes—a time which does not appear in the table. In this case you simply take the two listed Star Times nearest to your own and work out your cusp positions from these. The two listed times nearest to 14 hours 22 minutes are 14 hours 20 minutes and 14 hours 24 minutes. At 14 hours 20 minutes the first cusp is 7° 21′ Aquarius, and at 14 hours 24 minutes it is 8° 23′ Aquarius. The cusp position at 14 hours 22 minutes would clearly be halfway between these two positions, so your first cusp will be Aquarius 7° 21′. (There are 60 minutes to a degree. The difference between 7° 21′ and 8° 23′ is 1° 2′; half of 1° 2′ is 31′; 7° 21′+31′ is 7° 52′.) You can obtain the other five cusp positions by the same process.

Now the time has come to insert your six cusp positions on a map of the zodiac. Draw your map like the diagram on page 229 with the 12 cusps, or dividing lines between the houses, marked on it. On page 230 you will see the map with the first six cusp positions for our example inserted on it. Mark your cusp positions in the same way.

Now you need to find and insert the zodiacal signs and degrees for the other six cusps. This is easily done, for each of these cusps has the same degrees but the opposite sign of the zodiac to the

Table 4

S.T.	1	2	3	4	5	6
0 0	0 ♋ 0	2 ♌ 11	2 ♍ 5	0 ♎ 0	27 ♎ 55	27 ♏ 49
0 4	1 5	3 13	3 3	0 55	28 53	28 52
0 8	2 11	4 16	4 0	1 50	29 49	29 54
0 12	3 16	5 18	4 57	2 45	0 ♏ 47	0 ♐ 57
0 16	4 22	6 20	5 54	3 40	1 45	2 0
0 20	5 27	7 21	6 50	4 35	2 43	3 3
0 24	6 32	8 23	7 47	5 31	3 41	4 7
0 28	7 37	9 24	8 43	6 26	4 39	5 10
0 32	8 43	10 25	9 40	7 21	5 38	6 14
0 36	9 48	11 26	10 36	8 16	6 36	7 18
0 40	10 53	12 27	11 33	9 11	7 35	8 22
0 44	11 58	13 27	12 28	10 7	8 34	9 26
0 48	13 3	14 28	13 24	11 2	9 33	10 30
0 52	14 7	15 28	14 20	11 57	10 33	11 34
0 56	15 12	16 28	15 16	12 53	11 32	12 39
1 0	16 17	17 28	16 11	13 49	12 32	13 43
1 4	17 21	18 28	17 7	14 44	13 32	14 48
1 8	18 26	19 27	18 3	15 40	14 32	15 52
1 12	19 30	20 27	18 58	16 36	15 32	16 57
1 16	20 34	21 26	19 53	17 32	16 33	18 2
1 20	21 38	22 25	20 49	18 27	17 33	19 7
1 24	22 42	23 24	21 43	19 24	18 34	20 12
1 28	23 46	24 22	22 39	20 20	19 35	21 17
1 32	24 50	25 21	23 34	21 17	20 36	22 23
1 36	25 53	26 19	24 29	22 13	21 37	23 20
1 40	26 57	27 17	25 25	23 10	22 39	24 33
1 44	28 0	28 15	26 20	24 6	23 40	25 38
1 48	29 3	29 13	27 15	25 3	24 42	26 44
1 52	0 ♌ 6	0 ♍ 11	28 10	26 0	25 44	27 49
1 56	1 8	1 7	29 5	26 57	26 47	28 55
2 0	2 ♌ 11	2 ♍ 5	0 ♎ 0	27 ♎ 55	27 ♏ 49	0 ♑ 0
2 4	3 13	3 3	0 55	28 53	28 52	1 5
2 8	4 16	4 0	1 50	29 49	29 54	2 11
2 12	5 18	4 57	2 45	0 ♏ 47	0 ♐ 57	3 16
2 16	6 20	5 54	3 40	1 45	2 0	4 22
2 20	7 21	6 50	4 35	2 43	3 3	5 27
2 24	8 23	7 47	5 31	3 41	4 7	6 32
2 28	9 24	8 43	6 26	4 39	5 10	7 37
2 32	10 25	9 40	7 21	5 38	6 14	8 43
2 36	11 26	10 36	8 16	6 36	7 18	9 48
2 40	12 27	11 33	9 11	7 35	8 22	10 53
2 44	13 27	12 28	10 7	8 34	9 26	11 58
2 48	14 28	13 24	11 2	9 33	10 30	13 3
2 52	15 28	14 20	11 57	10 33	11 34	14 7
2 56	16 28	15 16	12 53	11 32	12 39	15 12
3 0	17 28	16 11	13 49	12 32	13 43	16 17
3 4	18 28	17 7	14 44	13 32	14 48	17 21
3 8	19 27	18 3	15 40	14 32	15 52	18 26
3 12	20 27	18 58	16 36	15 32	16 57	19 30
3 16	21 26	19 53	17 32	16 33	18 2	20 34
3 20	22 25	20 49	18 27	17 33	19 7	21 38
3 24	23 24	21 43	19 24	18 34	20 12	22 42
3 28	24 22	22 39	20 20	19 35	21 17	23 46
3 32	25 21	23 34	21 17	20 36	22 23	24 50
3 36	26 19	24 29	22 13	21 37	23 28	25 53
3 40	27 17	25 25	23 10	22 39	24 33	26 57
3 44	28 15	26 20	24 6	23 40	25 38	28 0
3 48	29 13	27 15	25 3	24 42	26 44	29 3
3 52	0 ♍ 11	28 10	26 0	25 44	27 49	0 ♒ 6
3 56	1 7	29 5	26 57	26 47	28 55	1 8
4 0	2 ♍ 5	0 ♎ 0	27 ♎ 55	27 ♏ 49	0 ♑ 0	2 ♒ 11
4 4	3 3	0 55	28 53	28 52	1 5	3 13
4 8	4 0	1 50	29 49	29 54	2 11	4 16
4 12	4 57	2 45	0 ♏ 47	0 ♐ 57	3 16	5 18
4 16	5 54	3 40	1 45	2 0	4 22	6 20
4 20	6 50	4 35	2 43	3 3	5 27	7 21
4 24	7 47	5 31	3 41	4 7	6 32	8 23
4 28	8 43	6 26	4 39	5 10	7 37	9 24
4 32	9 40	7 21	5 38	6 14	8 43	10 25
4 36	10 36	8 16	6 36	7 18	9 48	11 26
4 40	11 33	9 11	7 35	8 22	10 53	12 27
4 44	12 28	10 7	8 34	9 26	11 58	13 27
4 48	13 24	11 2	9 33	10 30	13 3	14 28
4 52	14 20	11 57	10 33	11 34	14 7	15 28
4 56	15 16	12 53	11 32	12 39	15 12	16 28
5 0	16 11	13 49	12 32	13 43	16 17	17 28
5 4	17 7	14 44	13 32	14 48	17 21	18 28
5 8	18 3	15 40	14 32	15 52	18 26	19 27
5 12	18 58	16 36	15 32	16 57	19 30	20 27
5 16	19 53	17 32	16 33	18 2	20 34	21 26
5 20	20 49	18 27	17 33	19 7	21 38	22 25
5 24	21 43	19 24	18 34	20 12	22 42	23 24
5 28	22 39	20 20	19 35	21 17	23 46	24 22
5 32	23 34	21 17	20 36	22 23	24 50	25 21
5 36	24 29	22 13	21 37	23 28	25 53	26 19
5 40	25 25	23 10	22 39	24 33	26 57	27 17
5 44	26 20	24 6	23 40	25 38	28 0	28 15
5 48	27 15	25 3	24 42	26 44	29 3	29 13
5 52	28 10	26 0	25 44	27 49	0 ♒ 6	0 ♓ 11
5 56	29 5	26 57	26 47	28 55	1 8	1 7

This table gives the degrees on the cusps for each four-minute interval of Star Time for use on a Morinus chart. Such a chart divides the Houses according to the system of the 17th-century astrologer known as Morinus.

Aries

Taurus

Gemini

Cancer

Leo

Virgo

S.T.	1	2	3	4	5	6
6 0	0 ♎ 0	27 ♎ 55	27 ♏ 49	0 ♑ 0	2 ♒ 11	2 ♓ 5
6 4	0 55	28 53	28 52	1 5	3 13	3 3
6 8	1 50	29 49	29 54	2 11	4 16	4 0
6 12	2 45	0 ♏ 47	0 ♐ 57	3 16	5 18	4 57
6 16	3 40	1 45	2 0	4 22	6 20	5 54
6 20	4 35	2 43	3 3	5 27	7 21	6 50
6 24	5 31	3 41	4 7	6 32	8 23	7 47
6 28	6 26	4 39	5 10	7 37	9 24	8 43
6 32	7 21	5 38	6 14	8 43	10 25	9 40
6 36	8 16	6 36	7 18	9 48	11 26	10 36
6 40	9 11	7 35	8 22	10 53	12 27	11 33
6 44	10 7	8 34	9 26	11 58	13 27	12 28
6 48	11 2	9 33	10 30	13 3	14 28	13 24
6 52	11 57	10 33	11 34	14 7	15 28	14 20
6 56	12 53	11 32	12 39	15 12	16 28	15 16
7 0	13 49	12 32	13 43	16 17	17 28	16 11
7 4	14 44	13 32	14 48	17 21	18 28	17 7
7 8	15 40	14 32	15 52	18 26	19 27	18 3
7 12	16 36	15 32	16 57	19 30	20 27	18 58
7 16	17 32	16 33	18 2	20 34	21 26	19 53
7 20	18 27	17 33	19 7	21 38	22 25	20 49
7 24	19 24	18 34	20 12	22 42	23 24	21 43
7 28	20 20	19 35	21 17	23 46	24 22	22 39
7 32	21 17	20 36	22 23	24 50	25 21	23 34
7 36	22 13	21 37	23 28	25 53	26 19	24 29
7 40	23 10	22 39	24 33	26 57	27 17	25 25
7 44	24 6	23 40	25 38	28 0	28 15	26 20
7 48	25 3	24 42	26 44	29 3	29 13	27 15
7 52	26 0	25 44	27 49	0 ♒ 6	0 ♓ 11	28 10
7 56	26 57	26 47	28 55	1 8	1 7	29 5
8 0	27 ♎ 55	27 ♏ 49	0 ♑ 0	2 ♒ 11	2 ♓ 5	0 ♈ 0
8 4	28 53	28 52	1 5	3 13	3 3	0 55
8 8	29 49	29 54	2 11	4 16	4 0	1 50
8 12	0 ♏ 47	0 ♐ 57	3 16	5 18	4 57	2 45
8 16	1 45	2 0	4 22	6 20	5 54	3 40
8 20	2 43	3 3	5 27	7 21	6 50	4 35
8 24	3 41	4 7	6 32	8 23	7 47	5 31
8 28	4 39	5 10	7 37	9 24	8 43	6 26
8 32	5 38	6 14	8 43	10 25	9 40	7 21
8 36	6 36	7 18	9 48	11 26	10 36	8 16
8 40	7 35	8 22	10 53	12 27	11 33	9 11
8 44	8 34	9 26	11 58	13 27	12 28	10 7
8 48	9 33	10 30	13 3	14 28	13 24	11 2
8 52	10 33	11 34	14 7	15 28	14 20	11 57
8 56	11 32	12 39	15 12	16 28	15 16	12 53
9 0	12 32	13 43	16 17	17 28	16 11	13 49
9 4	13 32	14 48	17 21	18 28	17 7	14 44
9 8	14 32	15 52	18 26	19 27	18 3	15 40
9 12	15 32	16 57	19 30	20 27	18 58	16 36
9 16	16 33	18 2	20 34	21 26	19 53	17 32
9 20	17 33	19 7	21 38	22 25	20 49	18 27
9 24	18 34	20 12	22 42	23 24	21 43	19 24
9 28	19 35	21 17	23 46	24 22	22 39	20 20
9 32	20 36	22 23	24 50	25 21	23 34	21 17
9 36	21 37	23 28	25 53	26 19	24 29	22 13
9 40	22 39	24 33	26 57	27 17	25 25	23 10
9 44	23 40	25 38	28 0	28 15	26 20	24 6
9 48	24 42	26 44	29 3	29 13	27 15	25 3
9 52	25 44	27 49	0 ♒ 6	0 ♓ 11	28 10	26 0
9 56	26 47	28 55	1 8	1 7	29 5	26 57
10 0	27 ♏ 49	0 ♑ 0	2 ♒ 11	2 ♓ 5	0 ♈ 0	27 ♈ 55
10 4	28 52	1 5	3 13	3 3	0 55	28 53
10 8	29 54	2 11	4 16	4 0	1 50	29 49
10 12	0 ♐ 57	3 16	5 18	4 57	2 45	0 ♉ 47
10 16	2 0	4 22	6 20	5 54	3 40	1 45
10 20	3 3	5 27	7 21	6 50	4 35	2 43
10 24	4 7	6 32	8 23	7 47	5 31	3 41
10 28	5 10	7 37	9 24	8 43	6 26	4 39
10 32	6 14	8 43	10 25	9 40	7 21	5 38
10 36	7 18	9 48	11 26	10 36	8 16	6 36
10 40	8 22	10 53	12 27	11 33	9 11	7 35
10 44	9 26	11 58	13 27	12 28	10 7	8 34
10 48	10 30	13 3	14 28	13 24	11 2	9 33
10 52	11 34	14 7	15 28	14 20	11 57	10 33
10 56	12 39	15 12	16 28	15 16	12 53	11 32
11 0	13 43	16 17	17 29	16 11	13 49	12 32
11 4	14 46	17 21	18 28	17 7	14 44	13 32
11 8	15 52	18 26	19 27	18 3	15 40	14 32
11 12	16 57	19 30	20 27	18 58	16 36	15 32
11 16	18 2	20 34	21 26	19 53	17 32	16 33
11 20	19 7	21 38	22 25	20 49	18 27	17 33
11 24	20 12	22 42	23 24	21 43	19 24	18 34
11 28	21 17	23 46	24 22	22 39	20 20	19 35
11 32	22 23	24 50	25 21	23 34	21 17	20 36
11 36	23 23	25 53	26 19	24 29	22 13	21 37
11 40	24 33	26 57	27 17	25 25	23 10	22 39
11 44	25 38	28 0	28 15	26 20	24 6	23 40
11 48	26 44	29 3	29 13	27 15	25 3	24 42
11 52	27 49	0 ♒ 6	0 ♓ 11	28 10	26 0	25 44
11 56	28 55	1 8	1 7	29 5	26 57	26 47

S.T.	1	2	3	4	5	6
12 0	0 ♑ 0	2 ♒ 11	2 ♓ 5	0 ♈ 0	27 ♈ 55	27 ♉ 49
12 4	1 5	3 13	3 3	0 55	28 53	28 52
12 8	2 11	4 16	4 0	1 50	29 49	29 54
12 12	3 16	5 18	4 57	2 45	0 ♉ 47	0 ♊ 57
12 16	4 22	6 20	5 54	3 40	1 45	2 0
12 20	5 27	7 21	6 50	4 35	2 43	3 3
12 24	6 32	8 23	7 47	5 31	3 41	4 7
12 28	7 37	9 24	8 43	6 26	4 39	5 10
12 32	8 43	10 25	9 40	7 21	5 38	6 14
12 36	9 48	11 26	10 36	8 16	6 36	7 18
12 40	10 53	12 27	11 33	9 11	7 35	8 22
12 44	11 58	13 27	12 28	10 7	8 34	9 26
12 48	13 3	14 28	13 24	11 2	9 33	10 30
12 52	14 7	15 28	14 20	11 57	10 33	11 34
12 56	15 12	16 28	15 16	12 53	11 32	12 39
13 0	16 17	17 28	16 11	13 49	12 32	13 43
13 4	17 21	18 28	17 7	14 44	13 32	14 48
13 8	18 26	19 27	18 3	15 40	14 32	15 52
13 12	19 30	20 27	18 58	16 36	15 32	16 57
13 16	20 34	21 26	19 53	17 32	16 33	18 2
13 20	21 38	22 25	20 49	18 27	17 33	19 7
13 24	22 42	23 24	21 43	19 24	18 34	20 12
13 28	23 46	24 22	22 39	20 20	19 35	21 17
13 32	24 50	25 21	23 34	21 17	20 36	22 23
13 36	25 53	26 19	24 29	22 13	21 37	23 28
13 40	26 57	27 17	25 25	23 10	22 39	24 33
13 44	28 0	28 15	26 20	24 6	23 40	25 38
13 48	29 3	29 13	27 15	25 3	24 42	26 44
13 52	0 ♒ 6	0 ♓ 11	28 10	26 0	25 44	27 49
13 56	1 8	1 7	29 5	26 57	26 47	28 55
14 0	2 ♒ 11	2 ♓ 5	0 ♈ 0	27 ♈ 55	27 ♉ 49	0 ♋ 0
14 4	3 13	3 3	0 55	28 53	28 52	1 5
14 8	4 16	4 0	1 50	29 49	29 54	2 11
14 12	5 18	4 57	2 45	0 ♉ 47	0 ♊ 57	3 16
14 16	6 20	5 54	3 40	1 45	2 0	4 22
14 20	7 21	6 50	4 35	2 43	3 3	5 27
14 24	8 23	7 47	5 31	3 41	4 7	6 32
14 28	9 24	8 43	6 26	4 39	5 10	7 37
14 32	10 25	9 40	7 21	5 38	6 14	8 43
14 36	11 26	10 36	8 16	6 36	7 18	9 49
14 40	12 27	11 33	9 11	7 35	8 22	10 53
14 44	13 27	12 28	10 7	8 34	9 26	11 58
14 48	14 28	13 24	11 2	9 33	10 30	13 3
14 52	15 28	14 20	11 57	10 33	11 34	14 7
14 56	16 28	15 16	12 53	11 32	12 39	15 12
15 0	17 28	16 11	13 49	12 32	13 43	16 17
15 4	18 28	17 7	14 44	13 32	14 48	17 21
15 8	19 27	18 3	15 40	14 32	15 52	18 26
15 12	20 27	18 58	16 36	15 32	16 57	19 30
15 16	21 26	19 53	17 32	16 33	18 2	20 34
15 20	22 25	20 49	18 27	17 33	19 7	21 38
15 24	23 24	21 43	19 24	18 34	20 12	22 42
15 28	24 22	22 39	20 20	19 35	21 17	23 46
15 32	25 21	23 34	21 17	20 36	22 23	24 50
15 36	26 19	24 29	22 13	21 37	23 28	25 53
15 40	27 17	25 25	23 10	22 39	24 33	26 57
15 44	28 15	26 20	24 6	23 40	25 38	28 0
15 48	29 13	27 15	25 3	24 42	26 44	29 3
15 52	0 ♓ 11	28 10	26 0	25 44	27 49	0 ♌ 6
15 56	1 7	29 5	26 57	26 47	28 55	1 8
16 0	2 ♓ 5	0 ♈ 0	27 ♈ 55	27 ♉ 49	0 ♋ 0	2 ♌ 11
16 4	3 3	0 55	28 53	28 52	1 5	3 13
16 8	4 0	1 50	29 49	29 54	2 11	4 16
16 12	4 57	2 45	0 ♉ 47	0 ♊ 57	3 16	5 19
16 16	5 54	3 40	1 45	2 0	4 22	6 20
16 20	6 50	4 35	2 43	3 3	5 27	7 21
16 24	7 47	5 31	3 41	4 7	6 32	8 23
16 28	8 43	6 26	4 39	5 10	7 37	9 24
16 32	9 40	7 21	5 38	6 14	8 43	10 25
16 36	10 36	8 16	6 36	7 18	9 48	11 26
16 40	11 33	9 11	7 35	8 22	10 53	12 27
16 44	12 28	10 7	8 34	9 26	11 58	13 27
16 48	13 24	11 2	9 33	10 30	13 3	14 28
16 52	14 20	11 57	10 33	11 34	14 7	15 28
16 56	15 16	12 52	11 32	12 39	15 12	16 28
17 0	16 11	13 49	12 32	13 43	16 17	17 28
17 4	17 7	14 44	13 32	14 48	17 21	18 28
17 8	18 3	15 40	14 32	15 52	18 26	19 27
17 12	18 58	16 36	15 32	16 57	19 30	20 27
17 16	19 53	17 32	16 33	18 2	20 34	21 26
17 20	20 49	18 27	17 33	19 7	21 38	22 23
17 24	21 43	19 24	18 34	20 12	22 42	23 24
17 28	22 39	20 20	19 35	21 17	23 46	24 22
17 32	23 34	21 17	20 36	22 23	24 50	25 21
17 36	24 29	22 13	21 37	25 28	25 53	26 19
17 40	25 25	23 10	22 39	24 33	26 57	27 17
17 44	26 20	24 6	23 40	25 33	28 0	28 15
17 48	27 15	25 3	24 42	26 44	29 3	29 13
17 52	28 10	26 0	25 44	27 49	0 ♌ 6	0 ♍ 11
17 56	29 5	26 57	26 47	28 55	1 8	1 7

Libra

Scorpio

Sagittarius

Capricorn

Aquarius

Pisces

Table 4 (continued)

S.T.	1	2	3	4	5	6
18 0	0 ♈ 0	27 ♈ 55	27 ♉ 49	0 ♋ 0	2 ♌ 11	2 ♍ 5
18 4	0 55	28 53	28 52	1 5	3 13	3 3
18 8	1 50	29 49	29 54	2 11	4 16	4 0
18 12	2 45	0 ♉ 47	0 ♊ 57	3 16	5 18	4 57
18 16	3 40	1 45	2 0	4 22	6 20	5 54
18 20	4 35	2 43	3 3	5 27	7 21	6 50
18 24	5 31	3 41	4 7	6 32	8 23	7 47
18 28	6 26	4 39	5 10	7 37	9 24	8 43
18 32	7 21	5 38	6 14	8 43	10 25	9 40
18 36	8 16	6 36	7 18	9 48	11 26	10 36
18 40	9 11	7 35	8 22	10 53	12 27	11 33
18 44	10 7	8 34	9 26	11 58	13 27	12 28
18 48	11 2	9 33	10 30	13 3	14 28	13 24
18 52	11 57	10 33	11 34	14 7	15 28	14 20
18 56	12 53	11 32	12 39	15 12	16 28	15 16
19 0	13 49	12 32	13 43	16 17	17 28	16 11
19 4	14 44	13 32	14 48	17 21	18 28	17 7
19 8	15 40	14 32	15 52	18 26	19 27	18 3
19 12	16 36	15 32	16 57	19 30	20 27	18 58
19 16	17 32	16 33	18 2	20 34	21 26	19 53
19 20	18 27	17 33	19 7	21 38	22 25	20 49
19 24	19 24	18 34	20 12	22 42	23 24	21 43
19 28	20 20	19 35	21 17	23 46	24 22	22 39
19 32	21 17	20 36	22 23	24 50	25 21	23 34
19 36	22 13	21 37	23 28	25 53	26 19	24 29
19 40	23 10	22 39	24 33	26 57	27 17	25 25
19 44	24 6	23 40	25 38	28 0	28 15	26 20
19 48	25 3	24 42	26 44	29 3	29 13	27 15
19 52	26 0	25 44	27 49	0 ♌ 6	0 ♍ 11	28 10
19 56	26 57	26 47	28 55	1 8	1 7	29 5
20 0	27 ♈ 55	27 ♉ 49	0 ♋ 0	2 ♌ 11	2 ♍ 5	0 ♎ 0
20 4	28 53	28 52	1 5	3 13	3 3	0 55
20 8	29 49	29 54	2 11	4 16	4 0	1 50
20 12	0 ♉ 47	0 ♊ 57	3 16	5 18	4 57	2 45
20 16	1 45	2 0	4 22	6 20	5 54	3 40
20 20	2 43	3 3	5 27	7 21	6 50	4 35
20 24	3 41	4 7	6 32	8 23	7 47	5 31
20 28	4 39	5 10	7 37	9 24	8 43	6 26
20 32	5 38	6 14	8 43	10 25	9 40	7 21
20 36	6 36	7 18	9 48	11 26	10 36	8 16
20 40	7 35	8 22	10 53	12 27	11 33	9 11
20 44	8 34	9 26	11 58	13 27	12 28	10 7
20 48	9 33	10 30	13 3	14 28	13 24	11 2
20 52	10 33	11 34	14 7	15 28	14 20	11 57
20 56	11 32	12 39	15 12	16 28	15 16	12 52
21 0	12 32	13 43	16 17	17 28	16 11	13 49
21 4	13 32	14 48	17 21	18 28	17 7	14 44
21 8	14 32	15 52	18 26	19 27	18 3	15 40
21 12	15 32	16 57	19 30	20 27	18 58	16 36
21 16	16 33	18 2	20 34	21 26	19 53	17 32
21 20	17 33	19 7	21 38	22 25	20 49	18 27
21 24	18 34	20 12	22 42	23 24	21 43	19 24
21 28	19 35	21 17	23 46	24 22	22 39	20 20
21 32	20 36	22 23	24 50	25 21	23 34	21 17
21 36	21 37	23 28	25 53	26 19	24 29	22 13
21 40	22 39	24 33	26 57	27 17	25 25	23 10
21 44	23 40	25 38	28 0	28 15	26 20	24 6
21 48	24 42	26 44	29 3	29 13	27 15	25 3
21 52	25 44	27 49	0 ♌ 6	0 ♍ 11	28 10	26 0
21 56	26 47	28 55	1 8	1 7	29 5	26 57
22 0	27 ♉ 49	0 ♋ 0	2 ♌ 11	2 ♍ 5	0 ♎ 0	27 ♎ 55
22 4	28 52	1 5	3 13	3 3	0 55	28 53
22 8	29 54	2 11	4 16	4 0	1 50	29 49
22 12	0 ♊ 57	3 16	5 18	4 57	2 45	0 ♏ 47
22 16	2 0	4 22	6 20	5 54	3 40	1 45
22 20	3 3	5 27	7 21	6 50	4 35	2 43
22 24	4 7	6 32	8 23	7 47	5 31	3 41
22 28	5 10	7 37	9 24	8 43	6 26	4 39
22 32	6 14	8 43	10 25	9 40	7 21	5 38
22 36	7 18	9 48	11 26	10 36	8 16	6 36
22 40	8 22	10 53	12 27	11 33	9 11	7 35
22 44	9 26	11 58	13 27	12 28	10 7	8 34
22 48	10 30	13 3	14 28	13 24	11 2	9 33
22 52	11 34	14 7	15 28	14 20	11 57	10 33
22 56	12 39	15 12	16 28	15 16	12 53	11 32
23 0	13 43	16 17	17 28	16 11	13 49	12 32
23 4	14 48	17 21	18 28	17 7	14 44	13 32
23 8	15 52	18 26	19 27	18 3	15 40	14 32
23 12	16 57	19 30	20 27	18 58	16 36	15 32
23 16	18 2	20 34	21 25	19 53	17 32	16 33
23 20	19 7	21 38	22 25	20 49	18 27	17 33
23 24	20 12	22 42	23 24	21 43	19 24	18 34
23 28	21 17	23 46	24 22	22 39	20 20	19 35
23 32	22 23	24 50	25 21	23 34	21 17	20 36
23 36	23 28	25 53	26 19	24 29	22 13	21 37
23 40	24 33	26 57	27 17	25 25	23 10	22 39
23 44	25 30	28 0	28 15	26 20	24 6	25 40
23 48	26 44	29 3	29 13	27 15	25 3	24 42
23 52	27 49	0 ♌ 6	0 ♍ 11	28 10	26 0	25 44
23 56	28 55	1 8	1 7	29 5	26 57	26 47
24 0	0 ♋ 0	2 11	2 5	0 ♎ 0	27 55	27 49

Zodiacal Signs and their Opposites

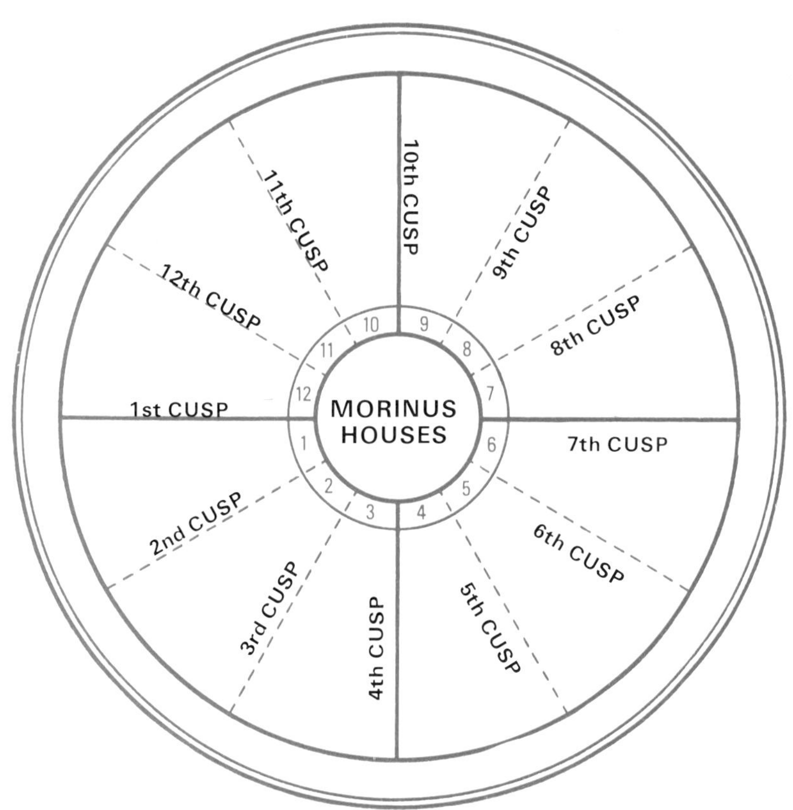

Left: a blank Morinus chart ready to have the zodiacal degrees inserted on the cusps.

cusp immediately opposite it on the map. The opposites for each sign on the zodiac are listed below.

Sign	Opposite Sign
Aries	Libra
Taurus	Scorpio
Gemini	Sagittarius
Cancer	Capricorn
Leo	Aquarius
Virgo	Pisces
Libra	Aries
Scorpio	Taurus
Sagittarius	Gemini
Capricorn	Cancer
Aquarius	Leo
Pisces	Virgo

So for our example we can now make a list of cusps seven to 12—remember the *same degrees* but the *opposite signs*.

Cusp 7	22° Cancer
Cusp 8	22° Leo
Cusp 9	21° Virgo
Cusp 10	18° Libra
Cusp 11	18° Scorpio
Cusp 12	19° Sagittarius

Then mark these positions on our map (see diagram page 231).

You will already have noticed that the 12 cusps go around the chart in counterclockwise order. Therefore the sign and degree

Final Step: Insert the Sun

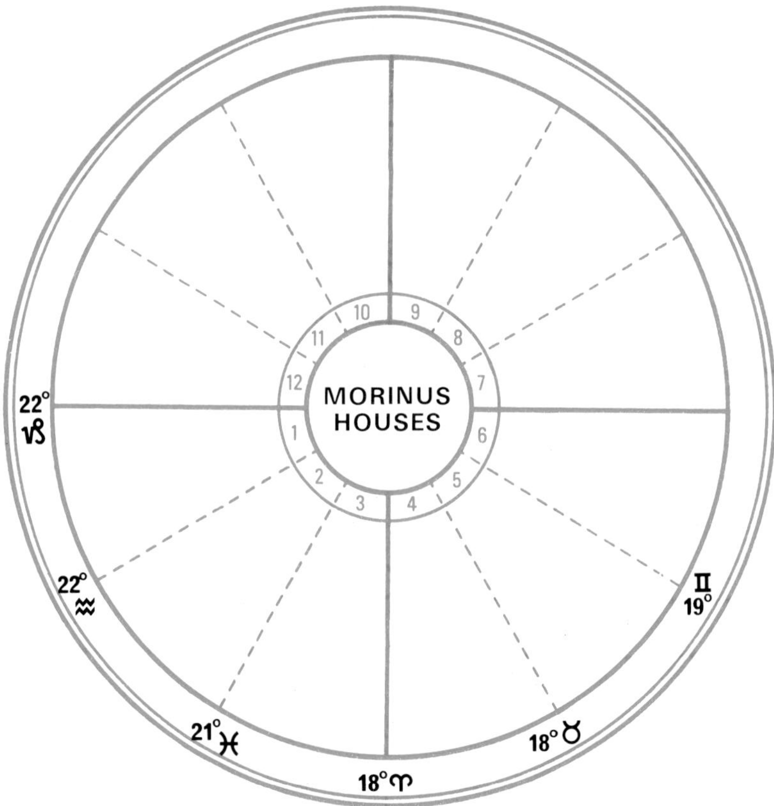

Right: a Morinus chart with the zodiacal degrees inserted on the cusps of the first six Houses.

of the first cusp—22° Capricorn in our example—appears at the position corresponding to nine o'clock on a watch, and the sign and degree of the second cusp—22° Aquarius in our example—comes at the eight o'clock, not the ten o'clock, position. The sign for the third cusp appears at the seven o'clock position, and so on.

The cusps divide off the 12 Houses. The First House therefore covers the section from the first cusp (22° Capricorn) to the second cusp (22° Aquarius), the Second House lies between the second cusp (22° Aquarius) and the third cusp (21° Pisces), and so on counterclockwise around the circle.

The degree on our first cusp is the 22° of Capricorn. But remember that each sign occupies 30° of the zodiac circle. This means that the first 22 degrees of Capricorn are in the *Twelfth House*, and only the remaining eight degrees of that sign are in the First House. Similarly, in our example, 22 degrees of Aquarius are in the First House and only eight in the Second House, and so on round to the last sign, Sagittarius, which has 19 degrees in the Eleventh House and 11 degrees in the Twelfth House.

The final step in constructing your chart is to insert the position of the Sun. Table 5 on page 232 shows the Sun's position to the nearest degree for every day of the year. These positions are for midnight at Greenwich, England—the point from which all degrees of longitude, East or West, are measured. In order to find the Sun's position when you were born, therefore, you will need to translate your local time of birth into Greenwich Mean Time. Your local library should be able to tell you how much your local time is ahead of, or behind, Greenwich Mean Time. If your Greenwich time of birth is *before* noon simply use the Sun posi-

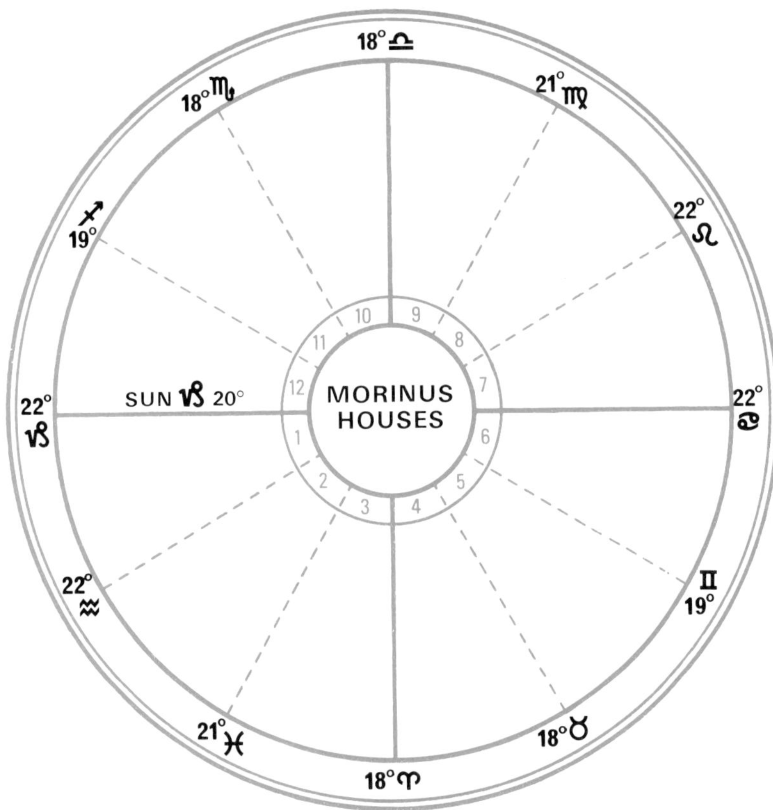

Left: a Morinus chart with the zodiacal degrees inserted on the cusps of all 12 Houses, and the Sun placed in its House position. Notice that the zodiacal degrees on the cusps of Houses 7–12 are exactly six Houses from those on cusps 1–6. Sometimes more than one House is ruled by the same sign. An example of this is provided by the map of General Gordon on page 239, where Aries rules the First and Second Houses and Libra both the Seventh and Eighth Houses. In such cases certain signs do not rule any house, and these are known as "intercepted signs." In General Gordon's map the intercepted signs are Gemini and Sagittarius. If you have intercepted signs on your own map, mark them in the same way as they are on General Gordon's map.

tion shown in Table 5 for your date of birth. If your Greenwich time of birth is *after* 12 noon, use the Sun positions for the day *following* your birth date.

In our example, the person was born in New York on January 10, 1934 at 6 a.m. New York uses Eastern Standard Time which is five hours behind Greenwich. So, according to Greenwich Mean Time, the person was born at 11 a.m., or eleven o'clock in the morning on January 10. We can therefore use the Sun position on the date of bith as shown in Table 5. If the person had been born at 6 *p.m.* rather than 6 a.m., the Greenwich time of birth would have been eleven o'clock in the evening, so we would have used the Sun position for the following day, January 11.

The Sun position for January 10 (see Table 5 on next page) is 20° Capricorn. We therefore insert this on our map of the zodiac as shown in the map above. Your own Sun position should be marked in the same way in the relevant House on your chart.

In our example the Sun (positioned at 20° Capricorn) is inserted in the Twelfth House. This is because the degree and sign on the cusp between the Twelfth and First Houses is the 22° of Capricorn and the first 22 degrees of Capricorn therefore lie in the Twelfth House.

To insert your Sun in the correct House, first find the cusp sign that corresponds to the sign given for your Sun position. Then, if the number of degrees given for your Sun are *lower* than those of the particular cusp sign, the Sun goes in the House *before* that cusp; if they are *higher*, the sun goes in the House *after* that cusp.

Table 5

These simplified charts show the Sun's position in the zodiac for each day in the ordinary year (top) and in leap year (bottom).

Ordinary Years

	Jan.	Feb.	Mar.	April	May	June	July	Aug.	Sept.	Oct.	Nov.	Dec.
1	10♑	12♒	10♓	11♈	10♉	11♊	9♋	8♌	8♍	7♎	8♏	9♐
2	11	13	11	12	11	11	10	9	9	8	9	10
3	12	14	12	13	12	12	11	10	10	9	10	11
4	13	15	13	14	13	13	12	11	11	10	11	12
5	14	16	14	15	14	14	13	12	12	11	12	13
6	15	17	15	16	15	15	14	13	13	12	13	14
7	16	18	16	17	16	16	14	14	14	13	14	15
8	17	19	17	18	17	17	15	15	15	14	15	16
9	18	20	18	19	18	18	16	16	16	15	16	17
10	20	21	19	20	19	19	17	17	17	16	17	18
11	21	22	20	21	20	20	18	18	18	17	18	19
12	22	23	21	22	21	21	19	19	19	18	19	20
13	23	24	22	23	22	22	20	20	20	19	20	21
14	24	25	23	24	23	23	21	21	21	20	21	22
15	25	26	24	25	24	23	22	22	22	21	22	23
16	26	27	25	26	25	24	23	23	23	22	23	24
17	27	28	26	27	26	25	24	24	24	23	24	25
18	28	29	27	28	27	26	25	25	25	24	25	26
19	29	0♓	28	29	28	27	26	26	26	25	26	27
20	0♒	1	29	0♉	29	28	27	27	27	26	27	28
21	1	2	0♈	1	0♊	29	28	28	28	27	28	29
22	2	3	1	2	1	0♋	29	29	29	28	29	0♑
23	3	4	2	2	1	1	0♌	29	0♎	29	0♐	1
24	4	5	3	3	2	2	1	0♍	1	0♏	1	2
25	5	6	4	4	3	3	2	1	2	1	2	3
26	6	7	5	5	4	4	3	2	3	2	3	4
27	7	8	6	6	5	5	4	3	4	3	4	5
28	8	9	7	7	6	6	5	4	5	4	5	6
29	9		8	8	7	7	5	5	6	5	7	7
30	10		9	9	8	8	6	6	6	6	8	8
31	11		10		9		7	7		7		9

Leap Years

	Jan.	Feb.	Mar.	April	May	June	July	Aug.	Sept.	Oct.	Nov.	Dec.
1	10♑	11♒	11♓	11♈	11♉	11♊	9♋	9♌	9♍	8♎	9♏	9♐
2	11	12	12	12	12	12	10	10	10	9	10	10
3	12	13	13	13	13	12	11	11	11	10	11	11
4	13	14	14	14	14	13	12	12	12	11	12	12
5	14	15	15	15	15	14	13	13	13	12	13	13
6	15	16	16	16	16	15	14	14	14	13	14	14
7	16	17	17	17	17	16	15	15	14	14	15	15
8	17	18	18	18	18	17	16	16	15	15	16	16
9	18	19	19	19	18	18	17	16	16	16	17	17
10	19	20	20	20	19	19	18	17	17	17	18	18
11	20	21	21	21	20	20	19	18	18	18	19	19
12	21	22	22	22	21	21	20	19	19	19	20	20
13	22	24	23	23	22	22	21	20	20	20	21	21
14	23	25	24	24	23	23	22	21	21	21	22	22
15	24	26	25	25	24	24	23	22	22	22	23	23
16	25	27	26	26	25	25	24	23	23	23	24	24
17	26	28	27	27	26	26	24	24	24	24	25	25
18	27	29	28	28	27	27	25	25	25	25	26	26
19	28	0♓	29	29	28	28	26	26	26	26	27	27
20	29	1	0♈	0♉	29	29	27	27	27	27	28	28
21	0♒	2	1	1	0♊	0♋	28	28	28	28	29	29
22	1	3	2	2	1	1	29	29	29	29	0♐	0♑
23	2	4	3	3	2	2	0♌	0♍	0♎	0♏	1	1
24	3	5	4	4	3	3	1	1	1	1	2	2
25	4	6	5	5	4	4	2	2	2	2	3	3
26	5	7	6	6	5	4	3	3	3	3	4	4
27	6	8	6	7	6	5	4	4	4	4	5	5
28	7	9	7	8	7	6	5	5	5	5	6	7
29	8	10	8	9	8	7	6	6	6	6	7	8
30	9		9	10	9	8	7	7	7	7	8	9
31	10		10		10		8	8		8		10

You may find that your Sun falls directly on a cusp. If so, the Sun should be placed in the House *after* that cusp. Thus, in our example, had the Sun's position been precisely on the cusp at 22° Capricorn, we would have placed it in the First House.

To give you a complete picture, and to help you further in compiling your own birth chart, we have repeated the entire procedure to follow, shown below in a shortened version. Use this step-by-step guide for quick and easy reference, and refer to the chapter for fuller details on making each calculation.

When you have applied this process to your own birth data, you will have your own personal chart of the heavens. Now comes the exciting business of learning what your chart means and how to interpret it.

A Step-by-Step Guide to Making Your Horoscope

1 Write down your date, time, and place of birth.

2 Calculate your time of birth in Star Time as follows:
(a) Find Star Time at midnight on your day of birth by looking up your birth date in Tables 1 or 2, page 221.
(b) Find the local time of your birth.
(c) Adjust the clock time of your birth to Star Time by counting 10 seconds for each hour between midnight and the clock time of your birth.
(d) Find the Zone Time of your birth by looking up your birthplace (or the nearest large town) in Table 3, page 222.
(e) Add together the four figures you have found to give the Star Time of your birth. (If the result is higher than 24, subtract 24 from your total.)

3 Draw a map of the zodiac as a circle divided into 12 segments, representing the Houses.

4 Look up your Star Time in Table 4, pages 225–228, to find the zodiac signs and degrees to mark on your first six *cusps* or dividing lines between the Houses.

5 Insert the cusp positions you have found on your map of the zodiac, beginning at the nine o'clock position and working counterclockwise around the circle.

6 Find the zodiac signs to mark on the other six cusps by referring to the list of "opposite signs" on page 229. Remember that each of these cusps should have the opposite sign of the zodiac to the cusp immediately opposite it on your own map, but it should have the same degrees.

7 Insert the positions for cusps 7 to 12 on your map.

8 Find the position of the sun in your chart as follows:
(a) Convert your local time of birth into Greenwich Mean Time.
(b) Turn to Table 5 on opposite page. If your Greenwich time of birth is *before* noon, find the sun position shown in the table for your date of birth. If your Greenwich time of birth is *after* noon, find the sun position for the day following your birth date.

9 Insert your sun position in the appropriate House on your chart, using the following method:
(a) Find the cusp sign that corresponds to the sign given for your sun position.
(b) If the number of degrees given for your sun are *lower* than those of the relevant cusp sign, put the sun in the House *before* that cusp; if they are *higher*, put the sun in the House *after* that cusp.

RII BORE
ET TERRÆ
CASCENO
PHIA.
Cassiopeia
Cepheus
Draco
Cygnus
Ursa Major
Ursa Minor
Aquila
Engonasi
Antinous
Corona
Coma Berenices
Serpens
Bootes
VIRGO
Æquinoctialis
LIBRA
Serpentarius
SCORPIO
Nova Hollandia
Crater
Corvus
Centaurus
Fera
Argo

Chapter 14
Interpreting Your Chart

Casting a horoscope is far more than simply preparing the star chart, and it is in the skills of interpretation that astrology becomes an art. But as with the preparation of the chart, the guidelines are relatively straightforward, and this chapter guides you through your own star chart, showing how the positions of the signs may provide insights into your personality and the patterns of your future. Most of us are intrigued by the idea of understanding ourselves a little better—will your horoscope be the mirror that presents a new view of yourself, or a confirmation of traits you had always half suspected?

Your personal chart of the zodiac is divided into 12 Houses. Each House has its own significance, and its particular meaning for each individual is indicated by the sign that "rules" it. The position of the Sun in your chart also has its own special importance. In order to interpret your chart, therefore, we need to look at each of the Houses in turn as to what they mean, how you should read them according to their ruling signs, and what the significance of the Sun's position in each House is. By putting all these elements together, you will be able to build up a complete picture from your own star chart—a unique portrait of yourself and of your potential for self-fulfillment, and self expression.

The general characteristics of the 12 Houses have been fairly well established since ancient times. Astrologers may today disagree about the system of House division, but almost all of them accept the traditional view of what the Houses mean. Astrologers of the Middle Ages used a simple Latin couplet to help them remember these meanings:

Vita, lucrum, fratres, genitor, nati, valetudo,
Uxor, mors, pietas, regnum, benefactaque, carcer

Which is translated into English as:

Life, money, brothers, father, children, health,
Wife, death, duty, career, benefits, prison.

These headings merely summarize the spheres of influence of

Opposite: a celestial map of about 1600, showing the magnificently intricate constellations circling around the sky in endlessly changing but eternal patterns.

Alexander Graham Bell

Right: Bell is most famous for his invention of the telephone in 1876. Less well known is the fact that Bell's research and discoveries arose out of his own altruistic desire to teach the deaf to speak. Idealism of this kind is often characteristic of those who, like him, are born with the Sun in Pisces. Pisceans are often easy-going, which Bell certainly appears to have been.

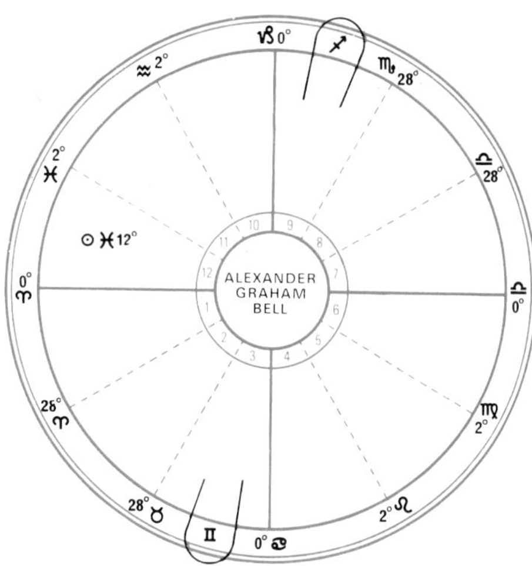

Above: in this and all following horoscopes the Sun Sign is indicated in its House by the Symbol ☉.

the 12 Houses, and they must often be interpreted symbolically. Thus the Twelfth House can mean a real prison so that one would expect this House to be emphasized in the horoscope of a long-term convict. But the Twelfth House also stands for anything that delays and restricts a person's free will—from secret enemies to a spell of army service.

The following details will tell you more about the areas of life covered by the 12 Houses, but even these are bound to be incomplete. You will need to use your own intuitive powers to extend these attributes into every aspect of life.

First House

The personality and temperament of the *native*—the person for whom the chart is drawn. His or her physical condition, appearance, and general outlook on life. Everything about the individual that is inborn and not the product of environment.

Second House

The possessions of the native. This includes the native's ambition to succeed, as distinct from the capacity to do so. It concerns financial resources—but not money or goods obtained by inheritance.

Third House

The intellectual qualities of the native and every other faculty through which he or she expresses personality to fellow human beings. All means of communication with the world at large, and the intellectual rather than emotional relationships that the native has with close relatives, neighbors, and friends. The House also rules short casual journeys.

Fourth House

The original environment of the native—the birth place and the parental home. This includes the individual's parents and inheritance generally, but particularly from the father. It covers

The Twelve Houses of the Zodiac

houses, land, and any property closely connected with the earth (for example, stock in a mining company). This House is also concerned with the conclusion of any matter, including the latter years of the native's life.

Fifth House

This House is associated with the native's sexual life and with all activities from which he or she derives particular pleasure or amusement. It therefore refers to inmost desires and to children. Gambling and speculation, as distinct from long-term investment, are also attributed to this House as long as they are undertaken in a pleasure seeking spirit.

Sixth House

The health and physical resources of the native. Everything closely connected with the individual's body, particularly food and clothing. It also refers to services that the person receives from others, to his or her employees and to any domestic pet. The House also covers any speculations undertaken purely for gain and not amusement.

Seventh House

The partners of the native, particularly the husband or wife and/or any partner in a long-lasting sexual relationship, but also including business partners. This House is also associated with

Empress Charlotte of Mexico

Left: the Empress Charlotte, also known as Carlotta, and her husband Maximilian who was the first—and last—Emperor of Mexico. In 1864 she accompanied Maximilian on his ill-fated attempt to try to establish an imperial dynasty in Mexico. Mexican and United States resistance to the plan made his position untenable, and he was executed in 1867. She suffered a mental collapse, but later made a recovery and lived in Belgium until her death in 1927. Carlotta's horoscope shows that she was born with her Sun in Gemini. What is known of her life and character demonstrates some of the best and worst aspects of the Sun-Geminians—that is, she had great personal charm combined with a perpetual restlessness and dread of boredom.

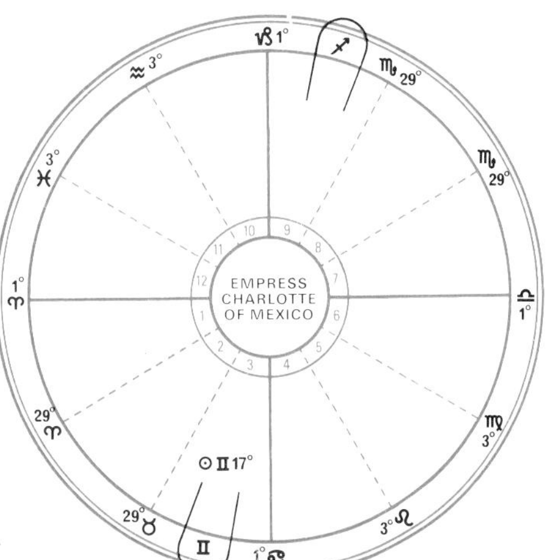

Annie Besant

Above: Annie Besant, the early social reformer, birth control pioneer, and occultist, was born with her Sun in Libra. However, she was far from being the typical Libran, and almost totally lacked the Libran quality of moderation. Far more influential in her make-up seems to have been Aries in the First House. Like many Arian types, her temperament was "commanding, choleric, and violent."

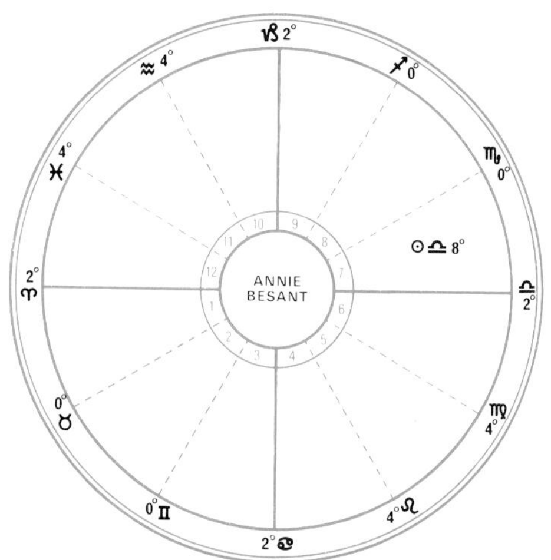

legal disputes and with what astrologers used to call "open enemies"—people who frankly oppose the native's aims in life.

Eighth House

The astrologers of ancient times called this "The House of Death." They saw it as indicating the probable length of the native's life, and the way in which he or she would die. Modern astrologers tend to regard it rather as "The House of Regeneration," concerned with anything that might give new life to the individual—mentally, spiritually, or physically. All astrologers agree that legacies, wills, and other forms of inheritance come under this House.

Ninth House

The ideology of the native, his or her views on science, mysticism, and philosophy. This House describes the individual's spiritual longing and capacity to realize them. Long journeys, or travel with a serious end in view, are also attributed to this House.

Tenth House

The native's occupation and career, his or her professional status and the responsibilities and privileges it involves. The individual's relationship with superiors, whether employers or the government. This House also denotes the person's mother.

Eleventh House

This is traditionally known as "The House of Friendship." It describes the people to whom the native is naturally attracted, and the kind of relationships he or she has with them. The native's social life and general attitudes toward humanity are the concern of this House.

Twelfth House

This "House of Prison" denotes anything that interferes with the native's exercise of free will. It is the House of limitation and restraint. Such restraints may be self-imposed or may come from any number of outside factors—from interference by superiors to hostile intrigues. Secret matters generally are ruled by this House. Therefore it also denotes any secret associations—Freemasonry for example—with which the native is connected. Finally, this House denotes any sphere, from prison to the army, in which discipline is the prime consideration.

The Ruling Signs in Your Chart

Each of the 12 Houses is ruled by the sign of the zodiac on its cusp—the dividing line between it and the preceding House—irrespective of any other sign which may be included in the House. In the zodiac map on page 231, for instance, the First House covers the section from the degree and sign on the first cusp (22° Capricorn) to the degree and sign on the cusp of the Second House (22° Aquarius). The First House therefore contains 22° of Aquarius. But in interpreting our map we disregard this and take the First House as being ruled by Capricorn, the Second by Aquarius, and so on.

Using the indications that follow, go through your own chart, House by House, noting down the sign that rules each one and details of the interpretations that apply in each case.

If the **First House** is ruled by

Aries: Courage, enterprise, and the ability to work hard are the

General Gordon

Left: the murder of General Gordon in Khartoum, the Sudan, in 1885. An outstanding British soldier, Gordon has a horoscope that shows Aries 0° on the cusp of the First House of his chart, a placing which is traditionally associated with military success. Gordon was killed at the siege of Khartoum, having managed to get himself into a tactically hopeless position mainly by continually and obstinately defying his orders to withdraw. Such foolish obstinacy, often found in combination with tactlessness, is often found in Sun-Pisceans.

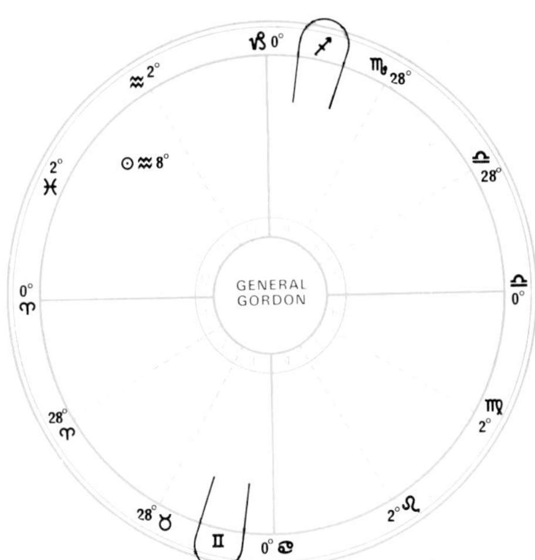

main attributes of the personality. There is a notable capacity for administration, and a strong possibility that success will be achieved early in life. There is an inherent tendency to rash action which must be resisted strongly.

Taurus: The personality is friendly and cheerful. There is a love of pleasure and social life that helps to bring popularity. A tendency to be too easy-going can lead to difficulties unless it is kept firmly under control.

Gemini: The personality is quick-witted and mentally able, seeking knowledge wherever it may be found. Literature and science will be equally attractive. There is an ability to adapt to circumstance—good or bad—which will persist throughout life.

Cancer: A restless personality which may be tempered by an easy-going and comfort-loving disposition. Love of travel and change will be characteristic from youth to old age.

Leo: An ambitious and power-seeking personality which will

Isadora Duncan

Above: "Beloved Isadora," the unconventional American dancer who took Europe by storm in the years before World War I. She was born with her Sun in Gemini in the Second House. She earned big money and spent it with abandon, so it is interesting to see that this Sun's House position is supposed to indicate a tendency to extravagance, which is often balanced by good earning ability.

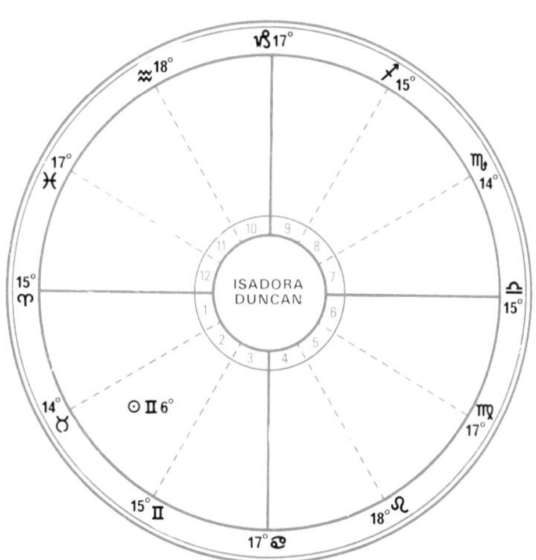

burn for success. Generally good health and a vitality of spirit that could almost be too intense.

Virgo: The personality is a studious one, devoted to books and reading. Quick-wittedness and adaptability are the outstanding characteristics.

Libra: An amiable personality, delighting in the company of both friends and casual acquaintances. There is sometimes a tendency to be overfriendly and to place too much trust in others which can lead to trouble if not restrained.

Scorpio: At its worst, a criminal personality, seeking fulfillment of personal aims without regard for the feelings of others. However, if these tendencies are resisted, honest success can be achieved by means of a thrusting, purposeful nature and a capacity for hard work.

Sagittarius: A generous, honorable character that inspires respect. Its only drawback is a tendency to be self-righteous and priggish. Pleasurable activities often exert a great attraction, particularly those involving travel or outdoor life.

Capricorn: A persistent, self-controlled personality capable of achieving success through hard work. Practical abilities are usually combined with a shrewd mind and inner stability.

Aquarius: Independence, originality, and even eccentricity are the outstanding characteristics. There is a love of freedom and a hatred of interference which may extend to a headstrong disregard for the feelings of others. Such personalities usually have some intellectual interests and are particularly attracted by new and unusual theories.

Pisces: A strongly artistic personality often with an interest in the psychic, the mystical, and the occult. There is a tendency to be impractical and to concentrate on visions of the future rather than on the present.

If the **Second House** is ruled by:

Aries: Throughout life hard work and individual effort will be the biggest factors in earning money and acquiring wealth.

Taurus: There is some ability in handling money but also a tendency toward extravagance. In material matters much will be achieved through the goodwill of others.

Gemini: Material gain is most likely to arise from an occupation connected with communications—for example, television or journalism—or where the native acts as a go-between for other people. Some skill in the handling of money is a frequently found tendency.

Cancer: While financial affairs tend on the whole to be satisfactory, there is considerable fluctuation in fortune. This is sometimes combined with extravagance and a love of rich living.

Leo: There is an ability to acquire money easily. Unfortunately this is often accompanied by gross extravagance.

Virgo: Occupations involved with communication are most likely to prove profitable. Good at handling money and conducting financial affairs in general.

Libra: Extravagance and financial skill fight for supremacy. The help of friends is often financially advantageous.

Scorpio: Financial success can be achieved through a combination of industriousness and adventurousness.

Sagittarius: A talent for financial matters and the accumulation of personal wealth are frequent tendencies.
Capricorn: Financial ability combined with carefulness result in a slow but steady accumulation of material possessions.
Aquarius: Extravagance is likely to imperil financial stability. There is a risk of unexpected losses, possibly arising from the native's own restlessness.
Pisces: A love of luxury and imprudence with money endanger happiness, as does the possibility of losing money through fraud.

If the **Third House** is ruled by:
Aries: Alertness and drive can lead to early success, but the native must learn to control his or her argumentativeness.
Taurus: There is a marked interest in literature and the arts and a notably happy disposition.
Gemini: Intellectual faculties are good, and a full use of these combined with adaptability and practicality are likely to lead to a successful life.
Cancer: The individual will do well and be thoroughly happy as long as life involves a certain amount of travel and change.

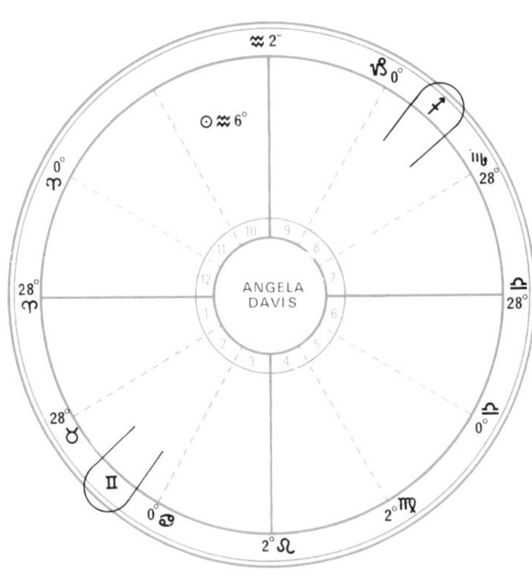

Angela Davis

Left: with her undoubtedly sincere concern for those whom she believes to be oppressed, Angela Davis demonstrates the characteristics of a certain type of Sun-Aquarian. Such Aquarians are often, like Angela Davis, deeply involved in political or humanitarian causes. For her, as for all strongly Aquarian personalities, a career is a vocation rather than just a means of making money. Her belief in a total equality between the sexes is also typical of the Aquarian type of woman.

Greta Garbo

Right: Greta Garbo, the world-famous film star, was born with her Sun in the sign of Virgo, and is in fact a typical Virgoan. Despite her undoubted charm and sex appeal she, like all strongly Virgoan women, has found that mere femininity is not enough for her. She has not wanted to confine herself to the exploitation of her womanhood, but rather to perform a task in life—and to do it well, Also typically Virgoan is Greta Garbo's lifelong preference for genuine criticism of her artistic achievement rather than journalistic flattery that concentrates on her beauty as a woman—a preference she now expresses by her shunning of all publicity during her extended and intensely private retirement.

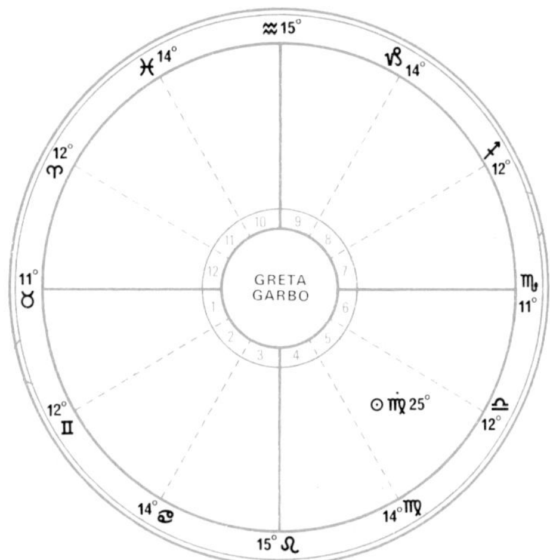

Leo: A keen mind leads to an expansive and pleasant existence.
Virgo: The native is happiest if life involves travel and/or the handling of money.
Libra: Life will be particularly happy if it involves travel or the arts.
Scorpio: Energy and hard work bring a happy and successful life.
Sagittarius: An optimistic and good-tempered individual who will prove popular with others.
Capricorn: A serious mind, not always good at communicating, but capable of concentration and getting to the heart of matters.
Aquarius: This individual has good mental and intuitive abilities combined with a tendency to eccentricity. A lover of travel and all things new.
Pisces: A person who thoroughly enjoys traveling and communicating with others. A tendency to gloom is sometimes present and needs to be controlled.

If the **Fourth House** is ruled by:
Aries: The rewards or personal effort may be supplemented by gains from inheritance or marriage. Throughout life there will be the temptation and the opportunity to engage in domestic

quarrels.

Taurus: The native will care intensely for attractive home surroundings. Home life can, and probably will, contribute much to personal happiness.

Gemini: The home and home conditions are likely to dominate the native's mind to an unhealthy degree.

Cancer: Family life, whether with parents or marriage partner, is always of great importance. Frequent moving may occur. There is some possibility of gain from trading in houses or land.

Leo: Family ties are strong and there is a possibility of inheritance from the father.

Virgo: Too much concentration on domestic matters can lead to neurosis.

Libra: Home life is of major importance and does much to enrich the personality.

Scorpio: A tendency to quarrel can disrupt home life unless strictly controlled. There may be gains by inheritance.

Sagittarius: Home life is of great importance. There is a possibility of gain from trading in land, houses, or other possessions connected with the earth.

Capricorn: Home life tends to give rise to cares and difficulties.

Aquarius: Frequent changes of home are likely, and there may be a tendency to adopt an unconventional way of life.

Pisces: Home life tends to be harmonious and family links strong.

If the **Fifth House** is ruled by:

Aries: The native will have a strong interest in the opposite sex—an interest mingled with a desire for domination.

Taurus: Sexuality and all pleasurable activities will be a strong center of interest.

Gemini: A rather refined attitude to sex—technique not passion being noticeable in close personal relationships.

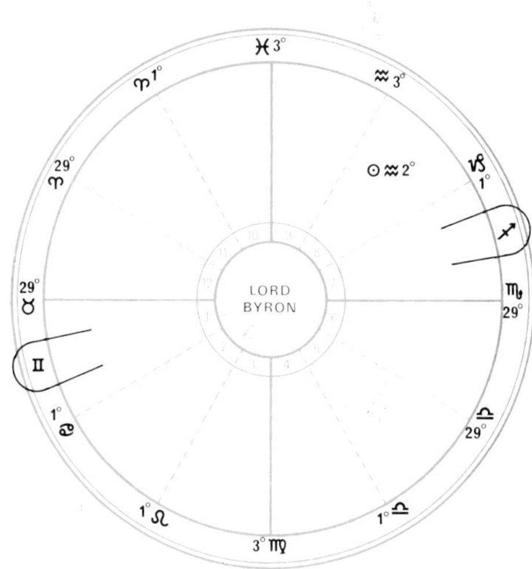

Lord Byron

Left: "Mad, bad Lord Byron," the club-footed Romantic poet whose amorous exploits scandalized English society until his death in 1824, when he gave his life for the cause of Greek independence. Byron was born with the Sun in Aquarius. His life and character show in many ways the marks of that unconventional sign. Personal freedom and the determination to overcome everything that opposes it is the highest aim of the strongly Aquarian personality. Hardly any Aquarian ever displayed these characteristics more blatantly than Byron, whose defiance of convention even ran to his having an affair with his own half-sister.

J. P. Morgan

Above: in Morgan's horoscope, shown below, the rulership by Leo of the First House suggested that this swashbuckling 19th-century multimillionaire would prove ambitious, power-seeking, eager for success. Moreover, the Virgo rulership of the Second House suggests that he would be "good at handling money and financial affairs conducting in general." In fact, he was the master of Wall Street of his period. Morgan's Sun was in Aries, which indicates that he was a pioneering, adventuring type who always took the lead.

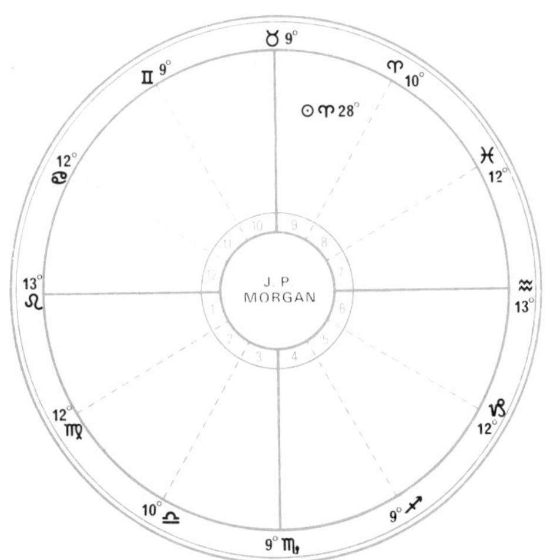

Cancer: Sexual attachments tend to be short lived. A somewhat fickle attitude toward the opposite sex is sometimes displayed.
Leo: Sexual drives are strong but not all-powerful. Charm of personality is often a strong element in attracting members of the opposite sex to the native.
Virgo: A tendency to act, rather than to feel, genuine emotion in sexual relationships.
Libra: Pleasure, including sexual pleasure, is often of great importance for the native's happiness in life.
Scorpio: A powerful sexual drive is allied with a desire to be the dominant partner in all relationships, whatever their nature.
Sagittarius: Sexual and social success is likely throughout life. This success may not only bring pleasure but also result in material gain.
Capricorn: The sexual drive is not usually strong. Gambling or other kind of speculation will often be successful if it is for pleasure alone.
Aquarius: Attitudes toward sexual relationships will tend to be unconventional.
Pisces: Love of luxury is likely to be allied with great indulgence in sexual and other pleasurable activities.

If the **Sixth House** is ruled by:
Aries: Health is likely to be good. The native will prosper as the member of a large organization.
Taurus: Health will probably be good. The native will be able to achieve success through his or her harmonious relationships with others.
Gemini: There is a tendency to overtax both physical and mental resources, and this should be controlled.
Cancer: Service to others will lead to success in life.
Leo: There is a marked ability to take responsibility and a tendency to change occupation frequently.
Virgo: Worry, excessive mental activity, and a tendency to overtax the body are the main dangers to health.
Libra: Health, both physical and mental, is likely to be good.
Scorpio: Health is generally good. There are great reserves of physical and mental energy.
Sagittarius: Health is usually excellent. The general psychological makeup of the native inspires respect and calls forth cooperation from others.
Capricorn: Health is sound and there is a probability of long life. Emotions are controlled and disciplined.
Aquarius: A highly strung temperament. A tendency to excessive irritability must be controlled if psychological ill health is to be avoided.
Pisces: There is a strong tendency to introversion and a love of solitude.

If the **Seventh House** is ruled by:
Aries: There is a tendency to marry early in life. The chosen partner is often a person of strong, even dominating, character.
Taurus: Marriage or other romantic partnerships tend to play an important part in life.
Gemini: Marriage and partnership generally are likely to play

an important part in the native's occupation.
Cancer: Marriage and partnerships are both likely to prove financially advantageous.
Leo: Marriage and partnership play a major role in life and may well bring a rise in social status.
Virgo: Marriage or romantic partnership may well be with a younger person.
Libra: Marriage and romance play an exceptionally important part in life.
Scorpio: A certain quality of impetuousness may well lead to unusual domestic circumstances.
Sagittarius: Marriage and partnerships are likely to bring great material benefits.
Capricorn: Marriage may well be delayed until late in life. When it comes it should bring great happiness.
Aquarius: A quality of inconstancy can, if not mastered, lead to difficulties in marriage and partnerships.
Pisces: Fickleness is a threat to relationships. If this is guarded against, marriage and partnerships should prove happy.

If the **Eighth House** is ruled by:
Aries: Some financial gain is likely to come from legacies or partnerships.
Taurus: Marriage and partnership will probably be of major importance materially, producing either great gains or losses.
Gemini: Financial gain is likely through partnerships.
Cancer: There is a possibility that money will be acquired from the native's marriage partner or mother.
Leo: There is a possibility of financial benefit through marriage.
Virgo: A partnership involving literature or science is the most likely source of gain.
Libra: Partnership, marriage, and legacies will have a major financial impact—sometimes good, and sometimes bad.
Scorpio: Financial gain is probable from marriage or inheritance.
Sagittarius: Financial gains from marriage and inheritance are likely.
Capricorn: Major financial gains are likely to come from hard work rather than marriage or inheritance. The span of life should be long.
Aquarius: Sudden and unexpected gains are a possibility.
Pisces: Financial affairs are always liable to fluctuation.

If the **Ninth House** is ruled by:
Aries: A marked love of change and a certain argumentativeness are strong characteristics.
Taurus: A charming personality with a strong artistic bent.
Gemini: Travel is likely to be an important source of pleasure.
Cancer: An imaginative personality whose opinions are liable to sudden change.
Leo: An ambitious and idealistic personality inclined to intellectual pursuits.
Virgo: Occupation may be linked with travel which will, in any case, be an important factor in life.
Libra: An idealistic, sensitive, artistic, and generous personality.
Scorpio: A mentally alert personality with a love of change and a

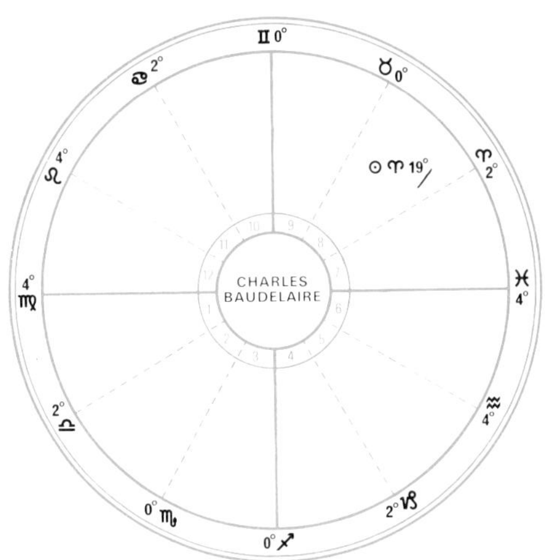

Charles Baudelaire

Below: Baudelaire—drug taker, Satanist, close to madness yet one of France's greatest 19th-century poets—ended his life in a mental asylum. Several features in his astrological make-up made such an end a likely one. The rulership of the Sixth House by Aquarius is taken by many to show a highly strung temperament that must at all costs avoid a way of life that could lead to psychological ill health. With his drug taking, his hectic love life, and his other extravagances, Baudelaire courted his tragic fate.

John Lennon

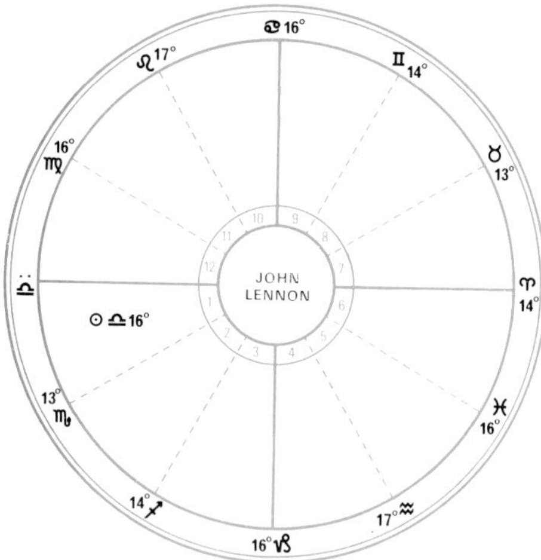

Below: John Lennon, perhaps the most famous of all the Beatles and one who continues a noteworthy career in his own right, was born with the Sun in the First House of his chart, a position traditionally associated with a personality that is ambitious and eager for fame and power. The Libra rulership of the First House and the Sun's position in the same sign also suggest an amiable and pleasant character.

tendency to quarrelsomeness.
Sagittarius: A tolerant, kind-hearted, and philosophical personality.
Capricorn: A personality that holds strongly to its opinions.
Aquarius: Unconventional ways of thought can lead to a certain fanaticism.
Pisces: An imaginative, intuitive, and beauty-loving personality.

If the **Tenth House** is ruled by:
Aries: An ambitious and masterful temperament which can lead to great success.
Taurus: Success is most likely to be achieved through the good will of superiors.
Gemini: Business ability and mental alertness can lead to early success in occupations.
Cancer: Occupations connected with the public at large are most likely to lead to popularity and success.
Leo: An ability to hold positions of some prominence should be exploited for the achievement of success.
Virgo: A capacity for self-expression and a marked business ability make success highly probable.
Libra: Popularity, especially with superiors and people of the opposite sex, can lead to success.
Scorpio: Ambition, executive ability, and a certain ruthlessness can bring success.
Sagittarius: The native's occupation is likely to bring prestige and financial prosperity.
Capricorn: Self-reliance, hard work, and ambition can lead to success, though sometimes not until late in life.
Aquarius: Hatred of restrictions and an undue love of change often prevent success from being achieved.
Pisces: The achievement of success in an occupation depends on whether ambition or irresponsibility is most prominent in the makeup of the personality.

If the **Eleventh House** is ruled by:
Aries: The essential energy of the native's social life usually ensures many friends.
Taurus: Friendship is of great importance and friends are many.
Gemini: Friends are plentiful if the native can control a tendency to indulge in too much criticism of others.
Cancer: A wide range of friends, many of whom will be women, whatever the sex of the native.
Leo: Friends can contribute much to success in every sphere of life.
Virgo: Many friends can be acquired through travel and active participation in clubs and societies.
Libra: A great many friends make friendship a major factor in the life of the native.
Scorpio: Energy in social affairs brings friends who must not be alienated by any temptation to exploit their friendship.
Sagittarius: A popular personality whose friends help in the achievement of the native's desires.
Capricorn: Friends are not many in number, but they are extremely loyal.

Mahatma Gandhi

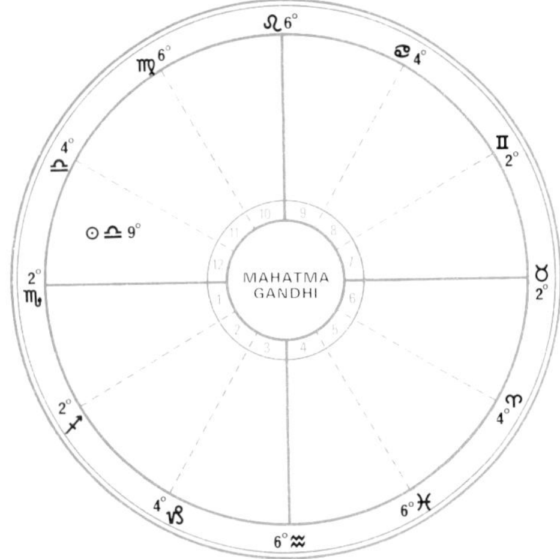

Aquarius: Friends are most likely to be found among people of unconventional views.
Pisces: A wide circle of friends, some of whom may prove inconstant or even false.

If the **Twelfth House** is ruled by:
Aries: Strong administrative ability often brings success in spite of obstacles.
Taurus: The personality will be at its best away from the public eye.
Gemini: Worry can be a major obstacle to success, and must be avoided to achieve success.
Cancer: The native should avoid too much public prominence.
Leo: There is always some possibility of conflict with those in authority.
Virgo: A tendency to be too concerned with petty matters can be an obstacle to success.
Libra: Some element of seclusion in life makes for happiness.
Scorpio: Powerful abilities can overcome obstacles.
Sagittarius: Willingness to help others means that they, in turn, help the native to overcome obstacles.
Capricorn: A certain desire for solitude is likely.

Aquarius: Sudden and unexpected misfortunes sometimes stand in the native's way.
Pisces: A love of seclusion is combined with a taste for clandestine friendships.

By now you should have noted down the interpretations of the 12 zodiac signs that rule the Houses in your map. Next you should make a similar note of the significance of the Sun's position in the zodiac, which you can obtain from the 12 Sun Sign outlines contained in Chapter 12. If, for instance, your Sun is in Libra, look up the description of the Libran personality on page 206.

Finally, you need to check the meaning of the Sun's House position from the following list.
Sun in First House: An ambitious, even power-loving, personality blessed with good physical health.
Sun in Second House: An extravagant personality is balanced by

Above: this remarkable man, the architect of India's independence through his own brand of nonviolent revolution, has his Sun in the Twelfth House. This suggests he would both be a lover of solitude and be likely to suffer family disagreements. In fact, Gandhi spent long hours in quiet meditation, and was estranged from his son.

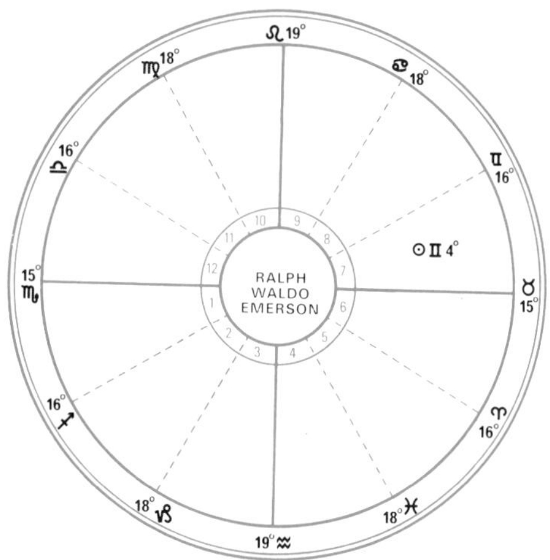

Ralph Waldo Emerson

Below left: Emerson, the American poet, essayist, and philosopher, had his Sun in Gemini, traditionally the patron sign of intellectuals. His Sun was in the Seventh House, which shows that he was capable of enjoying a happy and emotionally satisfying marriage, which he did in fact have. Emerson's Ninth House was ruled by Cancer, suggesting a tendency to change one's opinions—and Emerson frequently reconsidered his judgments. For example, he once believed that all philosophers should do some manual labor, but later said that "intellectuals should not dig."

a capacity to earn money easily.

Sun in Third House: A somewhat intellectual personality with a keen interest in science and literature.

Sun in Fourth House: A family-minded individual with a gift for managing property and land.

Sun in Fifth House: A sociable personality strongly interested in music, drama, and the opposite sex.

Sun in Sixth House: A capacity for administration can lead to an extremely successful life.

Sun in Seventh House: A personality to whom marriage is both important and socially advantageous.

Sun in Eighth House: A financially lucky individual who may obtain wealth through marriage or inheritance.

Sun in Ninth House: An intellectual, ambitious, and travel-loving personality.

Sun in Tenth House: An ability to take responsibility will lead to favors from those in authority.

Sun in Eleventh House: Friends may well help this individual toward the fulfillment of ambitions and desires.

Sun in Twelfth House: A lover of solitude tending to have disagreements with relatives.

You now have 14 pieces of information on which to make your overall judgment of the map—the 12 interpretations of the zodiac signs that rule the Houses, the meaning of the Sun's position in the zodiac, and the significance of the Sun's position in each House. All that remains is to blend these 14 indications into a composite portrait.

Some people find this process easy; for others it is extremely difficult. It is a knack that you have to acquire for yourself, using a combination of intuition and practice. Nevertheless, a few hints can help you learn how to blend the various elements into a successful reading of your map.

Firstly, do not reject your chart out of hand because some of the indications seem to contradict each other, or because some of them do not appear to fit your personality—or that of the person for whom you may have prepared the map. The contradictory factors may well exist in you or the individual concerned, but may either be totally repressed or only apparent in times of stress.

For example, suppose most of the 14 factors indicate an ex-

Louis Pasteur

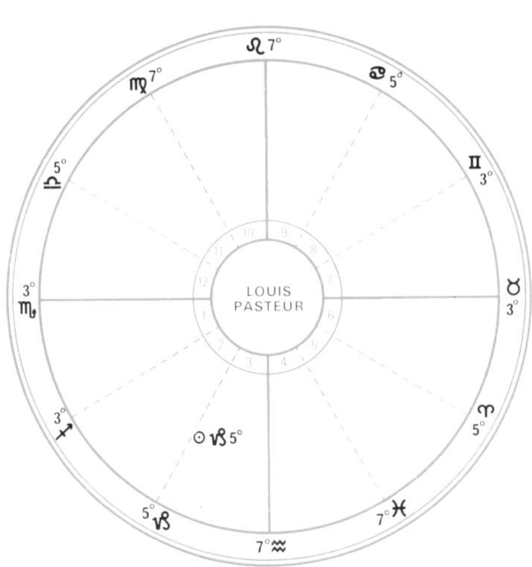

Left: Pasteur, the great 19th-century French chemist and microbiologist who firmly established the germ theory of disease, had his Sun in the Third House. This strongly suggested that he would prove to be an intellectual with a particular interest in science. The Sun was in Capricorn, a position associated with a passion for detail and precision. Pasteur clearly showed this characteristic in his painstaking experiments.

Mary Baker Eddy

Above: the founder of Christian Science was born with her Sun in Cancer, which is above all the sign of motherliness. Certainly this remarkable woman became a mother to the thousands of faithful followers she gained in her lifetime. In fact, many of her close adherents referred to her as "Mother." Her husbands—she had three—were weak-willed, unstable personalities, the type of man, in fact, to which Cancerian women are often attracted.

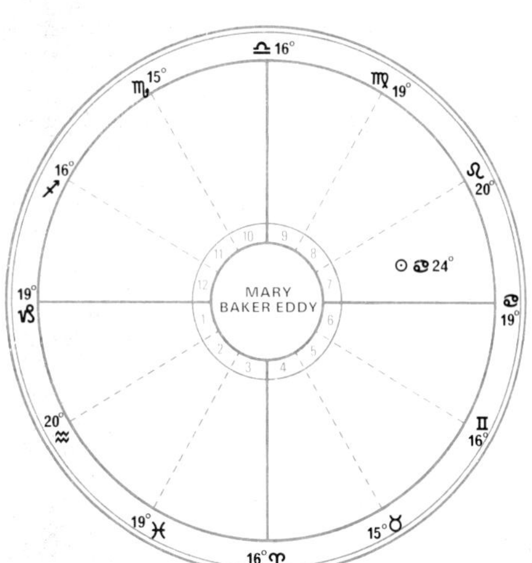

tremely sociable and popular personality. The Sun, however, is in the Twelfth House, which indicates a love of solitude. This would probably be an individual who is normally extremely fond of company, but who wishes to be alone at times.

Again, say that one House showed a capacity to manage money well while another showed a tendency to extravagance. We could expect the behavior pattern of the person concerned to fluctuate, probably cyclically, between the two extremes.

The second thing to remember when blending your interpretations is that you can apply the brief interpretation given for the ruling sign of each House to any of the various aspects of life covered by that House. These are listed earlier in the chapter under the meanings of the Twelve Houses.

On this basis, if the Tenth House is ruled by Aquarius the interpretation given is: "Hatred of restrictions and an undue love of change often prevent success from being achieved." However, as you can see from the list of House meanings, the Tenth House refers among other things to the mother of the native. Therefore two interpretations can be extended to the mother: firstly, the mother may tend to hold unorthodox and changeable opinions; secondly, she may have strained relationships with her children.

The final method to use in making your overall interpretation of the map is to write a short character sketch. Do this even if you have prepared the chart for yourself, in which case it can help to imagine that you are describing someone else. Take all 14 interpretations as representing various facets of this one particular person. Then try to produce a composite portrait of the person in which all the factors, even those that may at first sight appear contradictory, are combined to form a unified whole.

This is a technique that comes more easily with practice—and you may be surprised at some of the insights you gain into your character or that of your friends. If you are tempted to go deeper into astrology by drawing up maps for other people, you will gradually develop your skill at interpreting your findings.

One thing is certain. Your experience in drawing up and interpreting your own star chart will have told you a great deal more about how astrology and astrologers work. Modern astrologers are wary of predicting events. They believe that astrology's greatest practical value lies in the diagnosis of a person's character, and the assessment of his or her potentialities. Whatever the heavens may indicate about a person's destiny, astrologers believe that their particular brand of insight can offer people fuller and happier lives through a deeper understanding of themselves and others, and a greater awareness of mankind's place as an integral part of the Universe.

Bobby Fischer

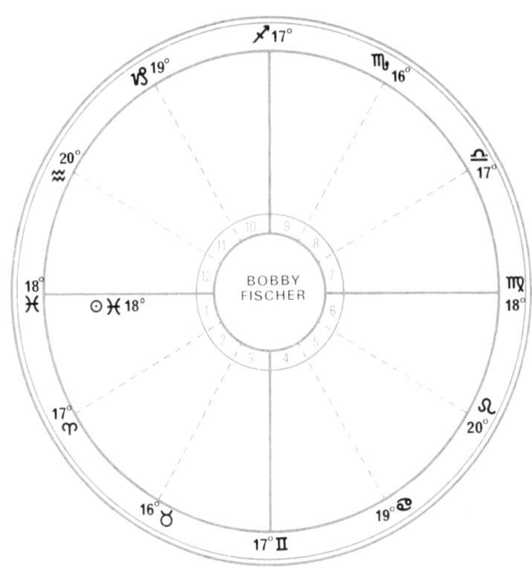

Below: Fischer has his Sun in Pisces, and Sun-Pisceans are often "amiable, vague, and sometimes devious"—an excellent description of this outstanding chess player and his relationship both with his opponents and with some of those who have promoted his matches. Since no exact time of birth is available, this is a solar chart with the Sun on the cusp of the First House, but it is still interesting to notice that his Tenth House is ruled by Sagittarius, which would suggest that Fischer's occupation is likely to bring him both fame and prosperity—as it surely has.

Index

References to illustrations are shown by italics.

Picture Credits

Key to picture positions: (T) top (C) center (B) bottom; and in combinations, e.g. (RT) top right (BL) bottom left.

John M. Addey 166, 167(T); Albright-Knox Art Gallery, Buffalo, New York. The Room of Contemporary Art Fund 213(T); Aldus Archives 26(L), 42–43(B), 60, 63(R), 67, 76(L), 77, 102, 147(R), 148, 152(B), 182(BR), 194(B), 211(B); © Aldus Books (Mike Busselle) 106–107(B), 218, (Gianetto Coppola) 184–185, (Gino d'Achille) 27, 104–105, (Bruno Elettori) 94–95, 134–135, (Christopher Foss) 20–21, 120–121, (Richard Hatswell) 2, 31(B), 56–57, 84, 86(T), 88(T), (David Swann) 18; J. H. Nelson, *Cosmic Patterns*, American Federation of Astrologers Inc., Tempe, Arizona 160, (after) 161; Artist Ann Dunn © Aldus Books, after Frank A. Brown, *Biological Clocks*, Pamphlet No. 2, Biological Sciences Curriculum Study, American Institute of Biological Sciences, 1962 164; Wilhelm Wulff, *Zodiac and Swastika*, Arthur Barker Ltd., London, Coward McCann & Geoghegan Inc., New York, and Agence Hoffman, Munich 175, 177(L); Kim Young Eun/Bavaria-Verlag 41(T); Bayerische Staatsbibliothek, München 186; Courtesy of Bell Laboratories 236(T); The Bettmann Archive 8, 110, 114(B), 209(T); Photo Steve Bicknell 58; Bilderdienst Süddeutscher Verlag 98(T), 138, 237(L); Steve Shapiro/Black Star, New York 37(B); By permission of the British Library Board 140(T), 143(L), 196(B), 197(T), 234; Reproduced by permission of the Trustees of the British Museum 15(R), 38, (Photo Michael Holford) 142, (© Aldus Books) (John Freeman) 100, 195(T), 201(BL), 204(BL), 205(R), (David Swann) 48, 142(B), (Eileen Tweedy) 168; Photo by courtesy of The British Tourist Authority 151; Photo John Wright © Aldus Books, by kind permission of Lord Brooke, Warwick Castle 147(L); Camera Press, London 139(T), 156, 157, 163, 172, 207(L), 210(TL), 246(B), (Rudolfo Bertorelli) 127(T), (Marvin Lichtner) 73(T), (Gianni Roghi) 34(T), (Rominger) 59(B); Photos J.-L. Charmet 61(R), 111; CIBA-GEIGY Limited, Basel 245(B); City of Birmingham Museums and Art Gallery 116; City of Manchester Art Galleries 47; Photo Peter Clayton 31(T); Henri Dauman/Colorific! 127(BR); Color Library International 96; Courtauld Institute Galleries 195(B); Culver Pictures 153; *Daily Telegraph* Colour Library 93; after © Walt Disney Productions Ltd. 211(R); Documentation Photographique des Mus es Nationaux 199(T); The Estate of J. W. Dunne 16(T); Ebertin Verlag, Aalen 190, 191; Radoux et Vaucouleurs, *L'Astronomie*, Editions Flammarion, Paris 49(T); Mary Evans Picture Library 32(B), 33(L), 35(T), 50, 65(R), 74(B), 81(T), 118; FPG 122, (Theodore Donaldson) 37(T); Fondation Saint-Thomas, Strasbourg 146; after Sigmund Freud, *The Interpretation of Dreams* 98–99(B); © Commander Gatti Expeditions 30; Leif Geiges, Staufen 170, 171; Musée du Louvre, Paris/Giraudon 204(BR); © Philippe Halsman 201(T); The Hamlyn Group Picture Library 29(B), 66; Sybil Sassoon/Robert Harding Associates 140(B); Max Beerbohm, *The Poet's Corner*, William Heinemann Ltd., London, and Dodd, Mead & Company, New York 207(B); Photo John Freeman © Aldus Books, with permission of The High Commissioner of India, London 247(R); The John Hillelson Agency 131(B); Michael Holford Library Photo 15(L), 70; Ellic Howe 178, 182(BL); *Illustrated London News* 10, 11, 52–53(B), 132; Imperial War Museum, London 127(BL), 181; Institut Pasteur, Paris 249(B); Courtesy Peter Jackson 62; Cheiro, *You and Your Hand*, Jarrold & Sons, Ltd., London, 1932 53(TL), 54–55, 68(TL), 69; Keystone 72, 73(B), 199(B); Kunsthistorisches Museum, Vienna 203(T); Courtesy of the Library of Congress 197(BL); © *Life* 1976 (Harry Benson) 139(B), 173, (Hugo Jaeger) 155, 177(R); Lowell Observatory photographs 189; The MacQuitty International Collection 46(T); Maison de Balzac, Paris 197(R); The Mansell Collection, London 32(T), 33(R), 35(B), 36, 44, 45(T), 53(TR), 64, 65(L), 101, 107(T), 115, 123, 144, 202(BL), 205(L), 239(L); © Marshall Cavendish Ltd. (after) 192(B), (Photo Malcolm Scoular) 42(T); Biblioteca Nacional, Madrid/Photo Mas © Aldus Books 149; after Mitchell Beazley Ltd. 192–193(T); Josef Muench 28, 29(T) (C); Musée Guimet, Paris 40; The Museum of the American Indian. Heve Foundation 25; Museum of the History of Science, Oxford/Photo Ken Coton © Aldus Books 14(L); NASA photos 129, 162; The National Gallery, London/Photos © Aldus Books (John Freeman) 12–13, (Eileen Tweedy) 136; National Portrait Gallery, London 198(B), 212(B), 212(B), (Photo John Freeman © Aldus Books) 243(L); Biblioteca Estense, Modena/Photo Umberto Orlandini 158; Artist Ann Dunn © Aldus Books, after Michel Gauquelin, *The Cosmic Clocks*, Peter Owen Ltd., London, and Henry Regnery Company, Chicago 169; David Paramor Picture Collection, New Market 240(T); Philadelphia Museum of Art: The Mr. and Mrs. Wharton Sinkler Collection 213 (BL); Pictorial Press, London 182(T); Picturepoint, London 97; Uffizi Gallery, Florence/Photo G. B. Pineider 45(B); Popperfoto 114(T), 154, 167(B), 202(BR), 209(BL), 215(B); Pragopress 165; Private Collection, London 209(R); *Psychic News* 119; *Radio Times* Hulton Picture Library 16(B), 24(T), 34(B), 41(B), 49(B), 61(L), 68(R), 81(B), 103, 179, 183, 200(B), 213(R), 214(B), 238(T), 242(T), 244(T), 248(B), 250(T); Real Cartuja Validemosa, Mallorca 217(BR); Rex Features 131(T), 241(L); Published by Rider & Company, London 76(R), 79(TR); Reproduced by kind permission of Lord Primrose, Earl of Rosebery 117; Witte-Lefeldt, *Rules for Planetary-Pictures, The Astrology of Tomorrow*, Ludwig Rudolf (Witte-Verlag), Hamburg, 1959 188(L); Scala (Accademia, Florence) 217(TR), Salzburg Museum) 215(T), (Uffizi, Florence) 206(B); Science Museum, London/Photos Mike Busselle © Aldus Books 143(R), 203(B); Photo John S. Shelton 133(R); Courtesy J. M. Simon 79(TC); Snark International 59(T), 78, 80, 108; Staatliche Museen, Berlin 46(B); Staatliche Museen für Volkekunde, München 24(B); *The Sunday Times* 90; Fotohronika Tass 128(T); The Tate Gallery, London 112–113, (Photo John Freeman © Aldus Books) 211(TL); By courtesy of The Theosophical Society in England 152(T); © 1938 James Thurber. Renewed 1966 Helen Thurber. From *How to Raise a Dog* by Kinney & Honeycutt. Published by Simon & Schuster, New York 210(BR); *Life* © Time Inc. 124; Transworld Features 217(L), 251(B), (Gene Daniels) 133(L); UPI Photo, New York 126; Reprinted by courtesy of U.S. Games Systems, Inc., New York, and A. G. Müller et Cie 79(TL), 82–83, 85, 86(R), 87, 88–89(B), (Tarot Deck) 74–75(T); One card from the James Bond deck by Fergus Hall reprinted by permission of U.S. Games Systems, Inc., Eon Productions Ltd., and Glidrose Publications Limited 79(BR); Ullstein Bilderdienst 176; United States Information Service, London 128(B), 201(R); Anton Lubke, *Die Uhr*, VDI-Verlag, Düsseldorf, 1958 14(R); Victoria & Albert Museum, London/Photos © Aldus Books (John Freeman) 210(CB), (Eileen Tweedy) 145, 150, 216(B); (Ordinary Card Deck) Waddingtons Playing Card Co. Ltd. 74–75(T); Courtesy Samuel Weiser, Inc., and Llewellyn Publications, Inc. 79(BL); By courtesy of the Wellcome Trustees 208(B); Wiener Library/Photo Eileen Tweedy © Aldus Books 174; Yerkes Observatory photograph 188(R); Taya Zinkin/Photo John Webb © Aldus Books 22.